ENCOUNTERS AND POSITIONS ARCHITECTURE IN JAPAN

SUSANNE KOHTE HUBERTUS ADAM DANIEL HUBERT (EDS.)

ENCOUNTERS AND POSITIONS
ARCHITECTURE IN JAPAN

BIRKHÄUSER
BASEL

Table of Contents

Architecture in Japan: Perceptions, developments and interconnections

Hubertus Adam / Daniel Hubert / Susanne Kohte

> *"Japan is in many respects the country that comes closest to one's dream of paradise."*[1]
> HERMANN MUTHESIUS, 1903

In view of the fact that the Orient—the Near East, Middle East and Far East—offers us a range of contrasting images, perceptions and experiences, many of them projections that in turn reinforce how the West sees itself,[2] it is remarkable that Japan has been viewed almost entirely positively over the ages. Ever since its portrayal in the *Travels of Marco Polo*, Japan has exerted a mixture of mystery and fascination as a country with both a rich tradition and amazing innovative potential. This applies equally and especially to its architecture. From the 19th century onwards, through the periods of modernism and postmodernism to the present day, it has continued to fascinate the West, even as Western perceptions of architecture in Japan have changed over time in accordance with changing areas of interests and the respective focus of architectural discourse.

This has not, however, been a one-way process: Japan's perception of architecture in the West has likewise changed over the years, influencing the production of architecture in Japan just as changing perceptions of what is typically Japanese did in the West. Contemporary architecture in Japan is a product of this interplay of own and different, foreign viewpoints, and of tradition and modernity. And it is more diverse than is commonly presumed, encompassing numerous different positions. This publication documents the multi-dimensional nature of contemporary architecture in Japan, comprising 13 interviews with Japanese architects and six texts exploring the background of and interrelationships within Japanese architecture. The interviewees have been chosen to reflect the views of several generations—from the eldest, Fumihiko Maki, born in 1928, to the youngest, Go Hasegawa, born in 1977. Aside from their age, these 13 architects also represent different standpoints and approaches to architecture in Japan: some are prominent architects, others members of the profession who have pursued specific directions and are less well-publicized outside Japan (and sometimes within the country, too). Six essays discuss different aspects of architecture in Japan, its development, reception and present-day state as well as the reciprocal influences between cultures. This publication therefore offers a broader perspective on architecture in Japan, looking beyond the popular image of Japan portrayed in the architectural press to reveal the variety of different positions beneath the surface.

Ongoing fascination

Hermann Muthesius, quoted at the outset of this essay, lived in Tokyo from 1887 to 1889. While his professional experience of Japan[3] had made him rather more sceptical of the European enthusiasm for Japan at the time, he held Japanese culture in high regard, especially in its traditional form which was coming increasingly under threat following the modernization tendencies of the 19th century after the opening of the country to Western influences. The sense of ideological superiority that characterized much of the West's dealings with other parts of the Orient did not apply in the same way to Japan, almost certainly because the island nation had not been subject to the same process of colonialism.

Ever since the end of two centuries of isolationism in 1853, Japan has continued to exert a special fascination for the West that has remained predominantly positive even as perception has changed over time with the prevailing political or social climate.

A recent example from the field of architecture is the Museum of Modern Art exhibition "A Japanese Constellation" in New York in spring 2016. The exhibition's curator, Pedro Gadanho, had originally intended to put on a solo exhibition of the work of Toyo Ito, but opted later to expand this into a group exhibition on "the network of architects and designers that has developed around Pritzker Prize winners Toyo Ito and SANAA."[4] The exhibition showed projects by architects from three generations with Toyo Ito as the point of historical reference. The second generation was represented by his student Kazuyo Sejima and her office partner Ryue Nishizawa, the third by students of SANAA, Junya Ishigami and Akihisa Hirata as well as by Sou Fujimoto. The main works that Gadanho chose to present were Toyo Ito's Mediatheque in Sendai (2001) and the 21st Century Museum of Contemporary Art in Kanazawa (2004) by SANAA. Exhibitions are inevitably constructions, and in Gadanho's one can see a conscious attempt to trace a line of tradition and to operationalize it for contemporary architectural discourse.[5] The curator highlights a shift towards transparency and lightness, as well as innovative construction as a shared theme in the work of the featured architects. The image that the MoMA exhibition portrays is paradigmatic of the contemporary perception of Japanese architecture. The works on show confirm the qualities of structural elegance, transparency and lightness, purism and minimalism that characterize today's popular perception of the architecture of the island nation. By way of example, one of the many publications that propagate this image is a collection of new architecture and design from Japan with the telling title *Sublime*.[6] Its chapter headings could populate a tag cloud describing the contemporary image of Japanese architecture: transparency, blurred boundaries, inside-outside, new spatial structures, house-in-house, traditional/modern, nature/technology/materials, defying gravity, etc.

Perception and reality

The perception of Japanese architecture in the West and the themes propagated in books and exhibitions that in turn influence architects in Europe should be viewed with a measure of caution. In recent years, Western media has devoted particular attention to small houses in the Japanese metropolitan cities. Shigeru Ban's "Curtain

Shigeru Ban, Curtain Wall House,
Tokyo, 1995

Wall House," the "Small House" by SANAA or "House NA" by Sou Fujimoto have become iconic examples of mini-houses, not only in the architectural press and internet blogs but also in the culture sections of national newspapers. Given the banal building conventions, for instance in much of Germany, these mini-houses have been heralded as models for future living, as prototypical building blocks of the city of tomorrow.[7] The euphoric reception of some of these excellent and striking examples of architecture is therefore understandable. However, this "Pet Architecture," as Atelier Bow-Wow have dubbed these small houses in Japan's cities, most notably Tokyo, can only be properly understood in the context of the specific tradition of dense neighborhoods, the high cost of building and way of life in Japanese conurbations. As fascinating as these buildings are, their one-dimensional presentation in today's Western press is problematic.[8] Many of the highly-publicized icons, when seen against the everyday background of their built environment—a bricolage of home-spun extensions and prefabricated houses—are not nearly as spectacular as they seem in the carefully orchestrated glossy photos. A particularly blatant example in this respect is the "Curtain Wall House" by Shigeru Ban in Tokyo, made famous by the now iconic image of the house corner shrouded by a two-story billowing curtain.[9] On visiting the building, the curtain is nowhere to be seen; rather one sees the metal protuberances of the stairs and washrooms, stacked above one another on the adjacent corners. Without the curtain, the building has none of the ethereal character of the image. Indeed, its somewhat haphazard arrangement of metal-clad forms fits perfectly into its immediate surroundings. Here perception and reality are diverging, not least because perceptions are conditioned largely by the respective focus of attention in each day and age. Perceptions and areas of interest change with the concerns and prevailing ideologies of each era—and in turn influence the development of architecture in Japan and in the West.

Dominant perspectives influencing the view of Japan have existed for a while. Reyner Banham has discussed how the perception of contemporary Japanese architecture in the 1930s and 40s focussed on the same primary visual character-

Junzo Sakakura, Museum of Modern Art, Kamakura, 1951

Takamasa Yoshizaka, Inter-University Seminar House, Tokyo, 1965

istics that it does today.[10] This can be traced back to Bruno Taut's interpretation of the Villa Katsura where clarity and simplicity were posited as the most important criteria of Japanese architecture, whether historical or contemporary. These criteria are embodied in the Japanese Pavilion at the Paris World Expo in 1937 by Junzo Sakakura, who worked in Le Corbusier's office from 1930 to 36. Banham relates that the highly delicate articulation of the pavilion was more purist than the works of Mies van der Rohe. Alfred Roth accorded it canonical status in a publication in 1940 by including it as the only Japanese project among 20 buildings that for him most embodied the programmatic qualities of "The New Architecture."[11] Conditioned by Taut's eulogies of the Villa Katsura, Walter Gropius traveled to Japan for the first time in 1954. To the surprise of his hosts, the Bauhaus founder seemed most interested in the historical architecture of Japan. Gropius' interest lay in the structural logic of Japanese timber construction which for him offered historical parallels to the principles of prefabrication and standardization which had preoccupied him for years, first in Germany, and especially later in the United States. He found it hard to understand why Japan's younger architects were choosing to pursue a different direction: "Nowadays the young Japanese architect is often ready to sacrifice all these advantages because to him they are associated with the feudal past [...]. His new love is the unpenetrable, unmovable concrete wall which seems to embody for him the strength and sturdiness he wants to give to his modern dwellings."[12]
Within the space of a few years, Japanese architecture had changed. While Sakakura's design for the first Japanese Museum of Modern Art in Kamakura maintained a lightness and elegance reminiscent of his Paris pavilion, the general trend was towards massive concrete architecture. The most important proponents of this new approach were Kunio Maekawa, whose large municipal and cultural buildings shaped much of the national rebuilding effort after the World War II, and Takamasa Yoshizaka. Both had worked with Le Corbusier and developed their own respective interpretations of the formal language of Corbusier's late, sculptural work. Yoshizaka's main work is the "Inter-University Seminar House" in Hachioji, a western suburb of Tokyo. The massive concrete volume takes the form of an inverted pyramid

Antonin Raymond, Gunma Music Center, Takasaki, 1961

Antonin Raymond, St. Paul's Chapel, Rikkyo Niiza Junior and Senior High School, Niiza, 1963

wedged into the sloping site, the rough imprint of its formwork highlighting the impression of weighty solidity. The idea of a placing a stereometric volumetric body on end gives it the impression of a postmodern gesture before its time.

The Metabolist decade

1965, the year in which Yoshizaka's "Seminar House" was completed, is mid-way through the decade in which Metabolism brought Japan international recognition.[13] During this period, Kenzo Tange advanced to become both the father figure and reformer of new Japanese architecture after the World War II, at least from an international perspective. But Tange was not, as is often maintained even today, the founding hero of post-war modernism in Japan. He too stood in a line of tradition, having learned his sculptural use of concrete from Kunio Maekawa, where he had worked from 1937 to 1941 prior to his own academic career and before opening his own office. Maekawa too had not only worked with Le Corbusier but also with the Czech-American architect Antonin Raymond, who had come to Japan while working for Frank Lloyd Wright. In the years that followed, Raymond became one of the most important modern architects in Japan. While his early works were primarily adaptations of Wright's approach, his later works echoed the International Style of the 1930s and later still the expressive concrete sculptures of the 1950s and 60s, such as the "Gunma Music Center" (1956–61) or "St. Paul's Chapel" on the Niiza Campus of Rikkyo University in Saitama (1963). Like Maekawa, Raymond and his contribution is little-known outside Japan. The same applies to Togo Murano, who practiced successfully as an architect for over five decades from the 1930s onwards, producing an extremely diverse *oeuvre* of works. In his best works he achieved an exciting fusion of Western ideas and Eastern traditions, most notably in his organic-expressive buildings from the 1960s.
Robin Boyd speaks of the exceptional importance of the World Design Conference in Tokyo in 1960 in his monograph on Tange. After having been "virtually an architec-

Kenzo Tange, St. Mary's Cathedral, Tokyo, 1965

tural colony of Europe,"[14] Japan made what amounted to a declaration of independence at the conference, asserting its position on the global architectural stage and confirming Tange in his position as "the West's favorite Japanese architect."[15]
For Tange, the 1960s were his most productive phase, a period that coincided with the decade of Metabolism, which began with the publishing of the manifesto at the World Design Conference in 1960. The main reason why Tange and the Metabolists came to represent Japanese contemporary architecture was their international connections, which Maekawa, Raymond and Murano lacked. Tange had previously become known outside of Japan for his design for the Hiroshima Peace Memorial in 1949. In 1954, Tange, Isozaki and other Japanese architects took part in a seminar by Konrad Wachsmann in 1954 in Tokyo, which later also took place in other cities. Wachsmann's ideas were to prove formative for the Metabolist idea of extensible mega-structures, as envisaged by the young architects, organized in the background by Tange's partner, the engineer Takashi Asada, from 1959 onwards.
In addition, Tange had the opportunity in 1951, brokered by Maekawa, to take part in the Congrès Internationaux d'Architecture Moderne CIAM VIII "The Heart of the City" in Hoddesdon, England. Prior to the war there had been only individual contacts between Japanese architects and the CIAM—Maekawa himself had taken part in CIAM II in Frankfurt am Main, Germany in 1929 while working for

Junichiro Ishikawa, Insho Domoto Museum, Kyoto, 1966

Le Corbusier—but now a group of Japanese architects took part: Maekawa, Sakakura and Tange.[16] In 1959, Tange also took part in the last CIAM congress in Otterlo in the Netherlands,[17] where he was able to forge new contacts. In the following year, he invited Peter and Alison Smithson, Louis Kahn, Jean Prouvé and Paul Rudolph to the World Design Conference in Tokyo.

While the World Design Conference in 1960 marked the beginning of the decade of the Metabolists, the Expo in 1970 marked its end. Compared with the lofty visions of the 1960s, the buildings of the World Expo were disappointing. Arata Isozaki remarked at the time that the entire Expo was dominated by technocrats. Tange and Kikutake had completed their most convincing works in the years before, and the social and economic upheavals in the years leading up to 1970 had brought about a change in which post-war modernism began to lose ground. The student protests in 1968, the oil crisis and the Report of the Club of Rome on "The Limits of Growth" challenged the very basis of such large-scale urban experiments.

Back in 1968, Robin Boyd noted in his overview of *New Directions in Japanese Architecture* that what the West perceived as new Japanese architecture accounted for only a fraction—albeit a prominent fraction—of the spectrum of contemporary building in Japan.[18] To offer evidence of other stylistic tendencies, Boyd chose to feature the "Insho Domoto Art Museum" (1966) by Junichiro Ishikawa in Kyoto,[19] whose exuberant decorated façades recall the Art Nouveau and were a precursor to the decorative tendencies of the 1980s. Boyd presented the work of a series of architects, tracing an arc from Maekawa and Sakakura to Tange and the Metabolists and on to Togo Murano and Kazuo Shinohara.

Diversity and postmodernism

The 1970s and 80s in Japan were characterized by different contrary tendencies, none of which attained a dominant position. Fumihiko Maki developed an adaptation of the International Style, Tadao Ando fused perfectly executed concrete with

Takamitsu Azuma, Azuma Residence, Tokyo, 1967

Seiichi Shirai, Noa Building, Tokyo, 1974

Togo Murano, Japan Lutheran Seminary, Mitaka, 1969

Japanese traditions, Osamu Ishiyama combined bricolage with high-tech aesthetics, and Shin Takamatsu combined concrete and steel to form sculptural buildings of semi-martial stature. Kazuo Shinohara, who as an extreme individualist and long-time professor at Tokyo Institute of Technology had been a counterpart to Tange at the University of Tokyo, concentrated on building at a small scale. In the process, he developed strategies for dealing with the chaos and apparent irrationality of the city by replicating the chaos of the urban metropolitan realm in his interiors in compressed form. As far back as 1967, Takamitsu Azuma showed how architecture could respond to the skyrocketing land prices in Tokyo by building a six-story concrete tower in Shibuya with 65 m^2 of usable floor area on a footprint of just 20 m^2. In this respect, his project is an early predecessor to the "small houses" in Tokyo featured currently in the architectural press. A series of other architectural positions from this period have, unfortunately, been largely forgotten. One of these was Seiichi Shirai, who had studied philosophy under Karl Jaspers in Berlin before becoming a self-taught architect. His "Noa Building" (1974) stands like a vast totem pole in Tokyo. Another was Team Zoo, founded in 1971 by several students of Takamasa Yoshizaka at Waseda University, who pursued a highly idiosyncratic approach of their own. One of the best overviews of architecture in Japan from the beginning of the 1960s to the mid-80s is still Reyner Banham's and Hiroyuki Suzuki's *Contemporary Architecture of Japan.* The authors present a total of 92 works, taking care not to place undue emphasis on any one direction. The book features the work of architects born between 1891 (Togo Murano) and 1948 (Shin Takamatsu), and demonstrates the diversity of Japanese architecture between late and postmodernism.[20] Michael Franklin Ross examines the 1960s and 70s, choosing to concentrate on the tendencies after Metabolism.[21]

The significance of Japan for postmodernism can be seen in Charles Jencks' seminal work on *The Language of Post-Modern Architecture,*[22] published in 1977, which features a Japanese building on the cover: the Ni-Ban-Kahn in Tokyo by Minoru Takeyama.[23] Although Jencks' published his extensive essay on "The Pluralism of Japanese Architecture" in his later book on late-modern architecture,[24] there are

repeated references to Japan in his book on postmodernism and on *Bizarre Architecture*[25] as well as in his other titles. In these one can find Shirai's "Noa Building", buildings by Toyokazu Watanabe and Monta Mozuna, Kazumasa Yashamita's "Face House" in Kyoto, and later also several projects by Arata Isozaki, whose "Gunma Museum of Modern Art" in Takazaki (1974) he had previously not included due to its technocratic expression.[26] In many respects, postmodernism in Japan exhibited a greater breadth of expression than in Europe or the United States. Kengo Kuma's "M2 Building" is a striking case in point. Among the various exotics was Von Jour Caux, a name that proved to be a pseudonym for the architect Toshiro Tanaka.
The bubble economy of the second half of the 1980s made it possible for several foreign architects to build projects in Japan, among them Zaha Hadid and Aldo Rossi, Nigel Coates and David Chipperfield, Christopher Alexander, Peter Eisenman and Philippe Starck. Several of them were just embarking on their architectural careers and had the opportunity to realize their first buildings in Japan. Today, where very few foreign offices work actively in Japan, that would be all but unthinkable.
In the 1980s and 90s, Arata Isozaki was without doubt the most important representative of architecture in the country, promoting cultural exchange between Japanese architects and the West. In 1988 he was appointed Commissioner of the Kumamoto Artpolis, a position he held for ten years before passing it on to Toyo Ito. Public buildings in Kumamoto Prefecture were subsequently awarded to excellent, and often young architects. Over the years a veritable open-air museum of modern architecture has arisen that is marketed astutely. In 1989, Isozaki developed a master plan for "Nexus World" in Fukuoka, an 8 ha large site on which he invited architects such as Steven Holl, Rem Koolhaas, Mark Mack, Osamu Ishiyama, Christian de Portzamparc and Oscar Tusquets to build projects. Between 1994 and 2001, Isozaki was responsible for the planning of a large residential area in Gifu in which all buildings were designed by women architects: Elizabeth Diller, Catherine Hawley, Kazuyo Sejima and Akiko Takahashi designed the four residential blocks, while Martha Schwartz was responsible for the landscape architecture. In 1990, Isozaki also curated the "Osaka Follies" program for the International Garden and Greenery Exposition in Osaka. Twelve architecture offices including Bolles + Wilson,

Team Zoo – Atelier Zo, Miyashiro Municipal Center, Saitama, 1980

Kazumasa Yamashita, Face House, Kyoto, 1974

Zaha Hadid, Ryoji Suzuki, Coop Himmelb(l)au and Daniel Libeskind built pavilions for the site.[27]

With his designs for the "Tsukuba Center Building" (1978–83) and the "Mito Art Tower" (1986–90), Isozaki himself also contributed two key works of postmodern architecture, but he was most prominent in his role as an architectural theorist. Of special note is his study of Japanese tradition[28] as well as his consideration of the subject of ruins,[29] a topic that has ongoing currency given the war destruction, earthquakes and tsunamis the land has been subjected to and gained increasing recognition in the age of postmodernism. In addition, he made several contributions to the ANY conferences, which were the most important contemporary forums for architectural discourse during the 1990s.[30]

Since 2000

The end of the bubble economy has led once again to a shift in the Japanese architectural landscape. In the year 2000, the Nederlands Architectuur Instituut (NAI) in Rotterdam put on an exhibition called "Towards Totalscape"[31] presenting an extensive overview of building in Japan. The projects on show ranged from designs for mini houses to urban design plans, as well as commercial projects of lesser architectural interest. Since the 1990s, Tokyo has been subject to a process of ongoing transformation that is particularly apparent in its high-rise districts. This largely investor-driven urban redevelopment only rarely brings forth works of remarkable architectural quality. In other quarters, however, such as along the Omotesando and the Ginza where the fashion labels have planted their flagship stores, the works of national and international star architects jostle for attention in a manner reminiscent of the postmodern spirit, albeit with another formal language. Every now and then, renowned architects are commissioned to build extraordinary buildings in other sectors, as evidenced by Toyo Ito's "Gifu Media Cosmos," which opened in 2015. However, many internationally-known Japanese architects—whether SANAA, Toyo Ito or Shigeru Ban—are now building their largest projects abroad, and the upcom-

Arata Isozaki, Gunma Museum of Modern Art, Takazaki, 1974

Kengo Kuma, M2 Building, Tokyo, 1991

Von Jour Caux, Waseda Eldorado, Tokyo, 1983

Terunobu Fujimori, Jinchokan Moriya Historical Museum, Chino, 1991

Terunobu Fujimori, Dandelion House, Tokio, 1995

ing generation of architects, for example Sou Fujimoto or Go Hasegawa, are actively seeking commissions, competitions and teaching positions abroad.
The architectural historian and architect Terunobu Fujimori, whose own works since the early 1990s make unconventional reference to Japanese building traditions and vernacular architecture, has proposed the image of two opposing poles to explain how modern architecture has developed in Japan, which he calls the white school and the red school: abstraction and mathematical thought versus plasticity and a preoccupation with material.[32] The white school draws historical inspiration from the Bauhaus, the red school from Le Corbusier's late work. According to Fujimori, the white school includes Fumihiko Maki, Kazuo Shinohara and Yoshio Taniguchi, the red school Antonin Raymond, Kunio Maekawa, Junzo Sakakura, Takamasa Yoshizaka, Kenzo Tange and Arata Isozaki. Tadao Ando lies somewhere in-between (Fujimori calls him "pink"), while Toyo Ito is in the process of shifting from white to red. The white school is headed currently by SANAA.
Architecture in Japan encompasses many positions. It is shaped by manifold references to Japanese tradition, as well as by the reciprocal influence of architectural production and discourses outside the country where Japanese architecture continues to be a subject of ongoing fascination. What Europe or the United States has held to be typically Japanese has changed over the years: at times it has been seen as solid and massive, then as light and elegant, at times made of concrete, then of glass, at times articulated through clear forms, then through dematerialized elegance. But the reality of Japanese architecture has always been more diverse than our perception of it.
This publication aims to reveal this diversity. The 13 interviews with personalities from different generations offer insight into the self-conception of modern Japanese architects. This insider's perspective is contrasted with views from outside in the form of six texts that examine topics from the interviews and attempt to identify their points of reference and underlying currents.

1 Hermann Muthesius, "Das Japanische Haus", in: *Zentralblatt der Bauverwaltung*, Year 23, Nr. 49 (20/06/1903), p. 306 f., here p. 306.

2 Edward W. Said, *Orientalism* [1978], London 2003, p. 1/2: "In addition, the Orient has helped to define Europe (or the West) as its contrasting image, idea, personality, experience".

3 Cf. Inga Ganzer, *Hermann Muthesius und Japan*, Petersberg 2016, p. 37–58.

4 Press release, MoMA, http://www.moma.org/calendar/exhibitions/1615, last accessed on 15/04/2016.

5 Cf. Pedro Gadanho, "An Influential Lightness of Being: Thoughts on a Constellation of Contemporary Japanese Architects", in: idem., Phoebe Springstubb (ed.), *A Japanese Constellation*, New York 2016, p. 11–18.

6 Robert Klanten et al. (ed.), *Sublime. New Design and Architecture from Japan*, Berlin 2011.

7 Cf. for example Laura Weissmüller, "Leben ohne Zwangsjacke", in: *Süddeutsche Zeitung*, 09/07/2012; idem., "Setzkasten des Lebens", in: *Süddeutsche Zeitung*, 25/04/2013; Niklas Maak, "Der Fluch des Eigenheims", in: *Frankfurter Allgemeine Zeitung*, 04/01/2012; idem., "Wie man das Wohnen neu denken kann", in: *Frankfurter Allgemeine Zeitung*, 20/07/2012. Maak expanded his article into an entire book: *Wohnkomplex. Warum wir andere Häuser brauchen*, Munich 2014.

8 For example Cathelijne Nuijsink, *How to make a Japanese House*, Rotterdam 2012; Philip Jodidio, *The Japanese house reinvented*, London 2015.

9 Cf. for example Matilda Mc Quaid, *Shigeru Ban*, London 2008, p. 193.

10 Cf. Reyner Banham, "The Japonization of World Architecture", in: idem., Hiroyuki Suzuki, *Contemporary Architecture of Japan*, Michigan 1985.

11 Alfred Roth, *La Nouvelle Architecture/Die Neue Architektur/The New Architecture*, Zurich 1940, p. 167–174.

12 Walter Gropius, "Architecture in Japan", in: *Apollo in the democracy: the cultural obligation of the architect*, Michigan 1968, p. 121.

13 On Metabolism: Rem Koolhaas, Hans Ulrich Obrist (ed.), *Project Japan. Metabolism Talks…*, Cologne 2011.

14 Robin Boyd, *Kenzo Tange*, New York, London 1962, p. 23.

15 ibid.

16 On the participation of Japanese architects at the CIAM congresses: Evelien van Es et al., *Atlas of the Functional City. CIAM 4 and Contemporary Analysis*, Bussum, Zurich 2014, p. 431/32.

17 On the CIAM congress in Otterlo: Oscar Newman (ed.), *CIAM '59 in Otterlo* (Dokumente der Modernen Architektur, Jürgen Joedicke (ed.), Vol. 1), Stuttgart 1961.

18 Cf. Robin Boyd, *New Directions in Japanese Architecture*, London, New York 1968, p. 31.

19 ibid., p. 32.

20 Reyner Banham, Hiroyuki Suzuki, *Contemporary Architecture of Japan*, Michigan 1985.

21 Michael Franklin Ross, *Beyond Metabolism*, New York 1979.

22 Charles Jencks, *The Language of Post-Modern Architecture*, London 1977.

23 Charles Jencks, *The Language of Post-Modern Architecture*, 2nd edition, London 1978.

24 Charles Jencks, "The Pluralism of Japanese Architecture", in: idem., *Late-modern architecture and other essays*, Michigan 1980, p. 98–128.

25 Charles Jencks, *Bizarre Architecture*, London 1979.

26 Cf. Charles Jencks, *The Language of Post-Modern Architecture*, 2nd edition, London 1978, p. 22.

27 Architectural Association, Arata Isozaki et al., *Osaka Follies*, London 1991.

28 Arata Isozaki, *Japan-ness in Architecture*, David B. Stewart (ed.), Cambridge/MA, London 2011.

29 Arata Isozaki, *Welten und Gegenwelten*, Yoco Fukuda, Jörg H. Gleiter and Jörg R. Noennig (ed.), Bielefeld 2011.

30 Cf. Arata Isozaki, Akira Asada, *10 Years after ANY—The End of Buildings. The Beginning of Architecture*, Tokyo 2010.

31 Moriko Kira, Mariko Terada (ed.), *Japan. Towards Totalscape*, Rotterdam 2000.

32 Most recently for example in: Terunobu Fujimori, "Magical Spatial Inversion", in: Gadanho, Springstubb (ed.), Op. cit., p. 11–18.

ENCOUNTERS

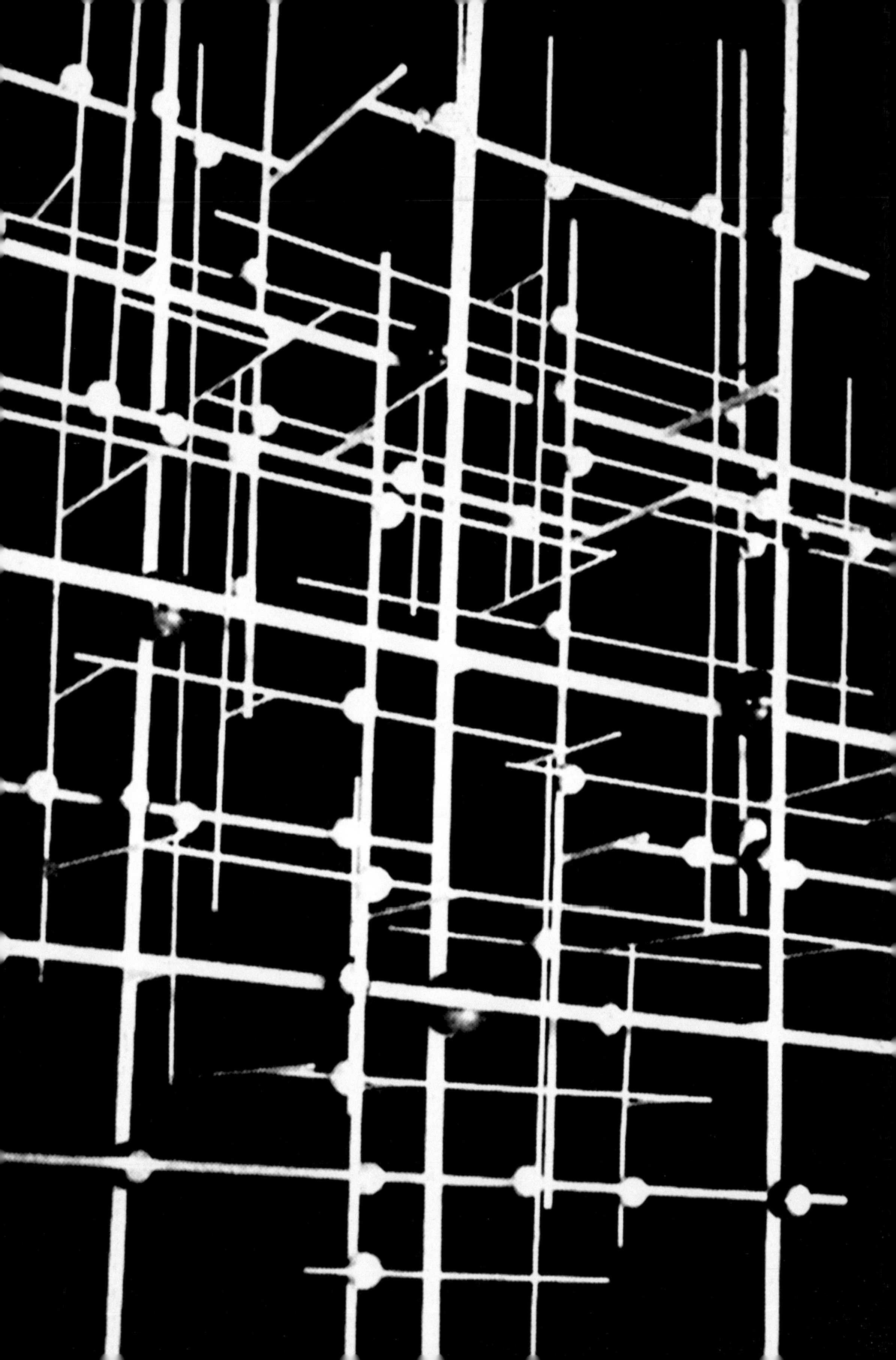

FUMIHIKO MAKI

This kind of ambiguous view

Mr. Maki, as a young man, why did you decide to study architecture? Did you have any relationship to architecture during your childhood?
During World War II, I attended high school in Tokyo and thought I would become an aeronautical engineer because I liked to make model planes. But after the war, it was impossible because that profession was prohibited. I still liked to design, to make and build things for the future, so I decided to become an architect.

You studied at the University of Tokyo. Why did you choose this university and who were your most important teachers?
The University of Tokyo was one of the best architecture schools in Japan at that time, so I went there and studied in the studio of Kenzo Tange. I thought he would be a good mentor as he was interested in the relationship between city and architecture, so it was quite natural for me to be part of his laboratory. I worked briefly in his studio before I left for the United States in the same year I graduated.

Why did you decide to go to the United States to further your studies?
I graduated from the University of Tokyo in the early 1950s, when we were still trying to recover from World War II in Japan. I had some knowledge of the architectural scene in the United States from magazines—for instance, I knew that Walter Gropius was teaching at Harvard. Harvard was therefore attractive and I decided to go there to continue my studies. I applied but it was too late in the year and they asked me to apply again the following year. So I waited a whole year and studied instead at the Cranbrook Acadamy of Arts before going to Harvard. But when I arrived at Harvard, Walter Gropius had already retired and Josep Lluís Sert was the Dean. He was more interested in urban design than Gropius and I was very lucky to have him as one of my teachers.

Later, you worked in Sert's office and you taught together with him in the urban design program. How did that evolve?
I knew Josep Lluís Sert from Harvard and while I was working in other offices, my classmate Dolf Schnebli was working with him. When Dolf decided to go back to Switzerland, he suggested that I replace him at Sert's office.

Can you describe your experiences in the office of Josep Lluís Sert?
The office was very small, maybe four or five people in New York. At that time, Sert had a few projects in Latin America, most of them urban design projects. The American embassy in Baghdad was the only architectural project, so I worked on that. When he decided to move to Cambridge to take up his responsibility as Dean,

he also moved his office to Cambridge and I followed him there. Later, I had the chance to teach with him at Harvard in the urban design program.

When you were in the United States, were you still in contact with architects in Japan and did you sometimes travel back to Japan?
Sure. Travelling became easier between the 1950s and 60s, the period during which I was mostly abroad. In 1958, I became a Graham Foundation fellow, and was given the chance to travel for two years. So I came back to Tokyo every once in a while. At that time I became a member of the Metabolists, because of my connection with Kenzo Tange and my colleagues of the Tange lab at the university.
I also had the chance to design my first project in Japan at that time. Kurokawa and Kikutake had already been quite active and, although I was teaching in the United States, I thought that the time had come to start my own practice in Japan. I had never thought of staying in the United States forever.
Metabolism started and became well known internationally. We published the Metabolism manifesto in 1960 and I participated very actively in the Metabolist movement from the very beginning.

You played a special role in the Metabolist movement as the only member outside Japan, travelling a lot and meeting architects from all over the world?
Yes, at that time few people had the same opportunity to travel abroad and meet architects in Europe or the United States as I did.

You also made contact with members of Team X and participated in Team X meetings in Europe?
In 1960, the World Design Conference took place in Tokyo and we invited well-known architects such as Paul Rudolph, Louis Kahn and Minoru Yamasaki from the United States, and Peter and Alison Smithson from Europe. Peter Smithson invited me to a conference of Team X in Bagnols-sur-Cèze in France.

Did you stay in contact with members of Team X after the conference?
Yes, for instance with Aldo van Eyck. He came to Washington to teach during the time I was there. Later, when I moved to Harvard to teach, I met Aldo, Jacob Bakema and all those people there. I also became acquainted with Giancarlo de Carlo and we had a very good relationship until he passed away. I also got to know some people from Archigram too. It was a very fascinating time for me.

In 1968, the quite important "PREVI" project in Lima began, involving architects from all over the world, including yourself.
Yes, "PREVI" was a housing project in Lima, Peru. It was very interesting. Many architects took part, the Metabolists including myself, Atelier 5, Christopher Alexander, Aldo van Eyck, James Stirling, Charles Correa and others. The project remains interesting to this day because you can see the work of all these architects at once in one place.

You were a member of the Metabolists and also in contact with many architects in Japan and abroad who belonged to international movements, including Team X. You were part of an "international circle" exchanging lots of ideas. So, the

Metabolist movement and your architecture, isn't it something where influences from international movements from Europe, America and Japan were coming together?

Yes, the Metabolist movement was a hybrid of many ideas, some from Japan and others from Europe, as you describe. It is true, it was a product of many mutual influences and also stimulated reciprocal influences.

Your text on group form, written together with Masato Otaka, was part of the Metabolist manifesto in 1960. Could you describe your interest in group form and the mutual influences you worked with?

When I wrote the text "Group Form," I was interested in investigating systems where individual elements like houses can combine to form a meaningful whole. In 1959 and 1960, I had the chance to make an extensive trip to Asia, the Middle East and Europe. It was an encounter with ancient towns. It was there that I developed the idea of group form. When I visited the Greek islands for example, houses with slight variations of form created a sense of wholeness. That was also group form.

Some architects in Europe, as well as in Japan, began to advocate mega-structures and the investigation of collective form became an important subject, along with the question of how structure and connections are made.

During this time, many architects in Europe and America were interested in linkages and structure or vernacular architecture like Aldo van Eyck, Christopher Alexander or Bernard Rudofsky. Were you in contact with them concerning these topics?

I was friends with Aldo van Eyck and we always talked about these subjects. He was a philosopher of architecture, and I am very sympathetic to his thoughts on architectural structure. Likewise, I knew the work of Christopher Alexander and Bernard Rudofsky. Rudofsky's book *Architecture without Architects* in particular

Meeting with Kenzo Tange

Maki at Harvard Graduate School of Design, United States, 1953

drew attention to vernacular architecture. The vernacular architecture he describes is created by people, not just architects. With long processes of trial and error spanning sometimes centuries, they were able to produce particular types of houses, from which classical architecture also developed. Vernacular architecture also exists in Japan, just as it does everywhere.

With regard to vernacular architecture in Japan: In the 1960s, Arata Isozaki and Teiji Ito also conducted a survey on vernacular architecture and traditional towns in Japan.

Yes, Arata Isozaki and Teiji Ito's survey is about traditional urban spaces in Japan. Teiji Ito was an important figure in producing this book, and also taught at the University in Washington. I hope Teiji Ito's writings will be translated to English so that they can reach a wider audience.

When did you start to work on traditional architecture in Japan and especially on traditional concepts of architecture and aesthetics in Japan?

I was too much of a modernist and I was not really concerned about newly created or recreated traditional buildings, but I was interested in the structure, and in principles like *oku* and *ma*. In the 1960s, Günter Nitschke wrote texts about *ma* and later Arata Isozaki did too, so the *ma*-ideas had already been reintroduced before I became interested in *oku*. My text "Oku" was first published in a Japanese magazine in the 1970s.

I was particularly interested in certain aspects of *oku*, for example, that people going up to temples or shrines do not see the destination, but always have the feeling of moving into unknown places. It is a technique the Japanese have used for centuries and still do.

I try to reinterpret those principles into the architecture of today. In our crematorium in Kaze-no-Oka, we used the same technique. You do not see the major space in

Team X meeting, Bagnols-sur-Cèze, France, 1960

Maki at PREVI, low-cost housing project, Lima, Peru, 1972

Shinjuku terminal redevelopment project, 1960

Compositional form (left), Mega form (center), Group form (right)

front of you. Instead, you go through a sequence to discover the next place. Then follow the way again and so on. To some extent, the crematorium also creates these ambiguous spatial experiences. We tried to recreate the essence of *oku* and the spaces reflect this.

So in your buildings, and especially in your crematorium Kaze-no-Oka, you were working with modern architecture as well as the history and interpretations of Japanese principles of space?

Yes. Cremations have a long history over many centuries in Japan. When somebody dies, the body is taken to a crematorium where certain rituals take place. Today a crematorium still offers these rituals and traditions developed within Japanese history.

How did you deal with that? Can you describe important elements of your design for the crematorium?

Since the city owned a large plot of land outside the center, we had the chance to make most of the area a park and placed the crematorium within it like a group of sculptures. You do not see a major building in front of you; instead you follow a path and discover the place in the process. Inside the crematorium, certain places and rituals are very important, as I mentioned. It is fundamental for the visitor to have a sense of the specific place and of time.

When you enter the crematorium you see the open forecourt. The naturally lit space looks very quiet.

From here there is a long corridor that helps people experience the passage of time—not just a door to open and step through. Entering such a building should, I think, be designed as a process, which is quite important in Japanese culture. For this reason, we intentionally created a long path.

In the entry porch, you face a special column illuminated by natural light in order to lend it a sense of lightness. The materials are very primordial: exposed concrete

Chandigarh, India, journey 1959, photo taken by Fumihiko Maki

Jaipur, India, journey 1959, photo taken by Fumihiko Maki

and stone, that's all. Another important element in the room is the screen. It is not a door, it is only a screen offering a hint of the next space. This is very important. In Japan the *shoji* screen is made of paper; it gives a place a different quality of light and affords a vague view of the adjacent space. We always like to have this kind of ambiguous condition instead of a clear "yes" or "no" or "open" or "closed."
In the crematory space, where you bid your final farewells to the deceased, there is an open court filled with water. Only water and sky. That's all. It is very simple, but with a certain differentiation of natural light. When the cremation is over, the ashes and bones are taken in boxes to the enshrinement room where people share the bones and ashes. Here we brought light in from above because this ritual should be celebrated. Consequently the space is lighter and brighter. It is a modern building, but it refers to rituals and architectural principles with Japanese tradition.

When you were designing the crematorium, how did you work?
We always work in a group, not alone. When the idea began to emerge in discussions, we invited the landscape architect to create meaningful relationships between the building, the open courts and the park.

For the crematorium you also worked with principles from Japanese tradition. Is there a different way of designing a building in Japan than, for example, a building in India, the United States or in Lebanon?
We try to produce something specific to each country, and certainly the purpose is to make a good building. The approach may be different, but in the end, the public and society determines how good the quality of the architecture is. We try not to do the same thing everywhere. For instance, for the "Bihar Museum" in Patna, India, there was a competition. A children's museum was part of the program, and I chose to make it a very distinctive children's place. I am always interested in sequences of spaces and experiences, so in my design the children have a museum of their

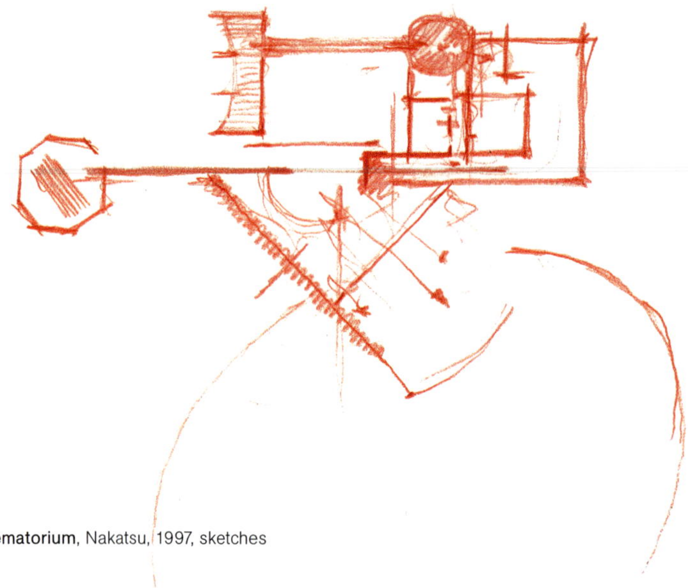

Kaze-no-Oka crematorium, Nakatsu, 1997, sketches

own, with its own ambience, place, character that is distinct from that of the major gallery. I conceived it more as a campus—and I won the competition.
While the way we design is not so different, the differences between designing in Japan, America or India certainly becomes very evident: The design and the early stages of planning are always done in Tokyo, whether we are doing a building in Lebanon or England. In that respect there is no difference. But as a project gets into the detailed stages, different laws and architectural conditions apply. We have designed many buildings abroad and we always learn what we can do. It is a learning process.

Do you think the process of learning from different countries and cultures as well as the exchanges in international architecture are different today than in the 1960s?
I think that until the 1970s, we architects from all over the world had different design approaches and architectural philosophies, but there was still some kind of commonality shared among more or less the same generation of architects, which led to the formation of groups. That does not exist any more.
When I was young, I had more time for travelling. When I was supposed to go to one place, I could stay on a few more days to visit other places or meet someone for longer. Today, that has become almost impossible—we fly somewhere, then fly back the next day to catch another meeting. Lifestyles have changed and it is a different kind of culture now. Some people—young people—might meet at conferences or workshops, but these meetings do not lead to the formation of a group that could produce a kind of a manifesto. Not any more.

Kaze-no-Oka crematorium

Site plan

The Bihar Museum, Patna, Bihar, India, 2015

Maybe it is no longer the time for manifestos. To come back to the Metabolist manifesto, can you still see influences from the Metabolist movement today?
I'm not sure. Metabolism was a phenomenon during a particular period. Today, there is still interest in Metabolism as a historical movement, as a certain architectural period. We are approached quite often by people who would like to write their Ph.D. thesis on Metabolism, but that is all. That said, I am still optimistic: as much as I enjoyed the good old days, there also has to be new days.

FUMIHIKO MAKI

Biography

1928 Born in Tokyo
1952 Bachelor of Architecture, University of Tokyo
1953 Master of Architecture, Cranbrook Academy of Art, Bloomfield Hills, United States
1954 Master of Architecture, Graduate School of Design, Harvard University, United States
1955–58 Employee at Sert, Jackson and Associates, Cambridge, United States
1956–61 Associate Professor, Washington University, United States
1958–60 Graham Foundation fellow, Journeys to Southeast Asia, the Middle East and Europe
1962–65 Associate Professor, Graduate School of Design, Harvard University, United States
1965 Established Maki and Associates, Tokyo
1965–85 Visiting Critic at universities in the United States and Europe
1979–89 Professor, Department of Architecture, University of Tokyo
1993 Awarded Pritzker Prize

Principal Works

1960 Toyota Memorial Hall, Nagoya University, Nagoya
1969–92 Hillside Terrace Complex I–VI, Tokyo
1972 PREVI project, with Kionori Kikutake and Kisho Kurokawa, Lima, Peru
St. Mary's International School, Tokyo
1973 Embassy of Japan, Brazilia, Brazil
1974 Toyota Kuragaike Memorial Hall, Toyota
1985 Keio University Library, Mita Campus, Tokyo
Spiral Building, Tokyo
1990 Tokyo Metropolitan Gymnasium, Tokyo
1995 Tokyo Church of Christ, Tokyo
Isar Büropark, One World, Munich, Germany
1997 Kaze-no-Oka crematorium, Nakatsu
2009 Square 3 Novartis Campus, Basel, Switzerland
2013 4 World Trade Center, New York, United States
2014 Aga Khan Museum, Ontario, Canada
2015 Bihar Museum, Patna, Bihar, India

Publications—Selection

1960 With Masato Otaka: "Towards the Group Form," in: Noboru Kawazoe (ed.), *Metabolism 1960: Proposals for a New Urbanism*, Bijutsu Shuppansha, Tokyo
1964 *Investigations in Collective Form* (as editor), School of Architecture, Washington University, St. Louis
1965 *Movement Systems in the City*, Graduate School of Design, Harvard University, Cambridge
1980 *Miegakure suru toshi* (Morphological analysis of Edo-Tokyo), Kajima Shuppankai, Tokyo
2008 *Nurturing Dreams: Collected Essays on Architecture and the City*, MIT Press, Cambridge

TOYO
ITO

Materiality is coming back

Mr. Ito, did you have any specific connection to architecture during your childhood?
My grandfather was a timber supplier and my father was interested in collecting, researching and looking at antiques and historic artefacts. For example, he collected ceramics from Korea. As a child I had the opportunity to look at all these artefacts. That might have been a bit of an influence, but I wouldn't call it a very drastic architectural influence.

How and when did you develop your interest in architecture?
I gained an interest in architecture when I started university education. In Japan, you start university with no particular specification, and after one and a half years of more general studies you can choose a specific discipline. If I had passed my exams with more flying colors, I would have had more choices, but I was not that good in school. It's the truth (*he laughs*).

Why did you choose to go to the University of Tokyo?
Two thirds of the people at the high school I attended went to the University of Tokyo, so to some extent it followed naturally. It was quite intuitive and I didn't put that much thought in it.

Who were your teachers at the university?
Kenzo Tange was professor at the university as well as Kisho Kurokawa and Arata Isozaki. I was part of the Kenzo Tange Lab and Isozaki was involved in the doctoral course of the Tange Lab while I studied there.

After graduation you decided to work with Kiyonori Kikutake?
Yes, during my fourth year of undergraduate studies, there was an open school over the summer vacation and for one month we had the chance to do an internship in an office, so I worked at Kikutake's office. That one month was the first time I experienced the joy and passion of architecture.

So that was the reason why you started working at Kikutake's office after you graduated from the University of Tokyo in 1965?
Yes, I worked for Kikutake for four years after graduation. At university I always had the feeling that architecture was the product of theoretical approaches. Theory drives architecture—that was my initial perspective of architecture. But after encountering Kikutake's architecture, I realized that the works he produced are not just theory but also about bodily sensations. It was designed with and for all the senses. That was

something I wanted to pursue and that was why I chose to work there. Kikutake was 36 years old at the time and he was really beginning to take off.

You say that architecture at university was more about theory. What kinds of theoretical approaches were that?
In terms of theories, the most obvious one was the Metabolists' approach, which suggests that architecture should be ever growing, something that unfolds and grows. A lot of architects subscribed to that approach and every student studied that in detail.

So, on the one hand there was the Metabolist movement and on the other there was Kazuo Shinohara. Was he also influential to you?
Kazuo Shinohara was more popular after 1965, so he didn't influence me during my time at university in the first half of the 1960s, but he did later. One of the reasons why I went to Kikutake's office in 1965 was to work on the Expo '70 in Osaka. All the Metabolists had big dreams and visions for the future of the city. But at the end of the day, after everything had been built, I was disappointed by the outcome. I felt that it did not really achieve what the Metabolists had set out to do. By comparison, Shinohara's theories seemed more appealing. I found his introverted, small world quite attractive compared to the one that made so many promises but failed to deliver.

Aluminum House, Kanagawa, 1971

Shinohara's approach gained ground when conditions started to change at the end of the 1960s, when there were the student riots and the oil crisis. Shinohara's thinking was anti-Metabolist. I had just opened my own office when I attended one of his lectures and his thoughts really blew my mind.

You established your own office in 1971.
I had wanted to go back to university in 1969 but it was closed due to the student riots, so I started my own office—with no project and no money.

The name of your office was URBOT, which stands for Urban Robot. Why did you choose that name?
It was a cynical response to the Metabolists, a form of sarcasm if you like. By way of example, Kisho Kurokawa saw Metabolism as many units mounted on something tree-like in the sky. My robot was down to earth—like the fruit that fell off the tree. The tree is a vision but my office was more like something that fell out of a dream into reality.

In 1979 you changed your office name to "Toyo Ito & Associates, Architects." Why did you change the name?
Everybody kept on asking me why it's called URBOT. I eventually got tired of explaining and it seemed URBOT didn't bring in any jobs either, so I changed the name.

You mentioned that you started your office without a project. How did you finally get a commission to build your first house?
My first house, the "Aluminum House," was my brother's house and my second building, the "White U" was my sister's house. So I only did projects for my brother, my sister and some friends. Just one or two projects a year.

Good to have family!
Yes, indeed.

Let us talk about your design principles. Which projects would you show someone interested in understanding your way of designing?
My most prominent and strongest project is the "Sendai Mediatheque." After the 1980s I started to get more commissions, but I still feel that the architecture I created before the "Sendai Mediatheque" was very pristine and nice—you might call it beautiful—but people found it hard to identify with. The "Sendai Mediatheque" is used by everyone. As soon as it opened, it was embraced by its users: everybody approved of it, understood it, became a part of it. It is so much more open to society, and that was something new.
The previous projects were more about how to create beautiful spaces and not so much about making spaces open to the public. My earlier buildings were not so well accepted by society, but I put that right with the "Sendai Mediatheque."

If one looks at your work on a timeline, one sees a change in your way of designing, for example in your use of materials and structures. Could you describe the evolution of your designs over the years?

White U, Tokyo, 1976

Since the 1990s I went through a phase where I was always thinking about how to express the structure. Structure is very important—almost like a theme in many of my buildings. At the same time, I was inspired by organic, natural phenomena like forests and water and the question of how things work in nature. So, the projects after the 1990s are more inspired by the question of how to express structure in a way they might occur in nature.

Does your change in design approach also relate to changes in society?
Of course. I am also affected by the era, the time and the social background of the time I live in. For example, since the year 2000, Tokyo has been largely driven by the global economy, so the buildings you see are very monotonous, although very accurately built. To me that is suffocating. I want to create a counterbalance to that monotony, something that allows human beings to be more energetic and to live and to enjoy space without feeling confined or that everything is the same.

In your text "Blurring Architecture" from 1999 you describe the changes in society from the industrial society to the information society. As society is important for your way of designing; what do you think about current developments? Are we still in an information society?
Society has changed. The society driven by production, where everything is mass-produced in a factory and the product is valued most highly, has transformed into

a society that values information more. If you have information, you have power. I think this is still the case in today's society.
I still have this wish to create architecture that allows human bodies to adapt to information-driven societies without losing their human quality, their physicality and energy. So I always imagine what kind of town or city would be appropriate to allow people to evolve with societal changes. Today, I am gradually sensing a slight change in the era again with a shift towards materiality and not just information. Maybe people are beginning to feel more drawn to the materiality of things again.

So materiality is coming back? If we compare the "Sendai Mediatheque" and the "Minna no Mori Gifu Media Cosmos"—leaving aside the differences in size and use—a key aspect seems to be their treatment of materiality. Would you agree?
The concept of the "Sendai Mediatheque" is not really about materiality. It is about light and transparency and I had wanted the structure to be almost transparent. But that changed during construction: when it started to be built on site, I realized that the material is very strong. By that I mean the strength and power of the steel as a material. I became very drawn to it and this affection for materiality continues to the present day.
A good example for an approach to materiality is the recently-finished "Minna no Mori Gifu Media Cosmos" because this building really has undergone a transition from a non-existent, very conceptual, abstract building to a very material one. You can feel and smell the timber, it is really about materiality. So, I think materiality is indeed coming back.

Do you think it is important to make the structure visible?
It really depends on the project. We do not always show the structure. In the case of the "Minna no Mori Gifu Media Cosmos," it is more about the flow of air and environmental issues—how to create microclimates within a larger climate—and less about structure.
It has an undulating roof that became a shell structure made out of timber. Structurally it is efficient, but at the same time it helps to collect air underneath the "globe" and helps to create a comfortable environmental zone. In contrast, the "TOD'S Omotesando Building" really shows its structure. There are lots of very distinctive buildings on Omotesando Avenue, lots of brand stores showing themselves, and because we were facing these buildings, we needed an appropriate response. Since it is also a very small building, we needed something visually strong, and that's why we decided to show the structure on the façade so prominently.

In all these different projects, what methods do you use when you design? Does that change with each project? Or do you have a typical way of designing?
A rule I always hold dear as a principle in my work is that I don't want to create a style, a Toyo-Ito-style. I want to design projects that are basically driven by place, locality, culture, local knowledge and the team involved. Projects change with the people who work on them and in response to the situation rather than adhering to some same style regardless of the task. So, that is one of my principles.
When developing a design, I always have some strong underlying design principle, for example how to get closer to nature, or to open up to society. I discuss this with my staff in the office so that everyone understands the underlying philosophy, has

Minna no Mori Gifu Media Cosmos, Gifu, 2015

an idea of the bigger picture and knows what the office is aiming to do. Teams are formed for each project and the team members come up with a lot of ideas, so the design evolves in a dialog. I am not interested in establishing a strong, uniform design direction, but rather in design that changes through dialog with different people, be they staff, users or experts and engineers. We always engage structural and environmental engineers at a very early stage in the design process and their input also has an impact on the design. So my method is that I don't have one, except that I build teams so that something different can happen every time.

How do you develop the initial ideas to discuss with your team? Do you prefer to use drawings, sketches or models?

I don't really bring material to the team. I make sketches but not of details, more like a cloud—a very vague, very open image that allows room for creativity and stimulates team members to use their own minds and design creativity to bring new ideas to the table.

Based on the vague images I sketch, team members come back with ideas and through these brainstorming sessions one or two good ideas may emerge that are then followed through and made more concrete with drawings, models and sketches before the next meeting. After the next meeting, we may take it further or discard

Minna no Mori Gifu Media Cosmos

Sketches

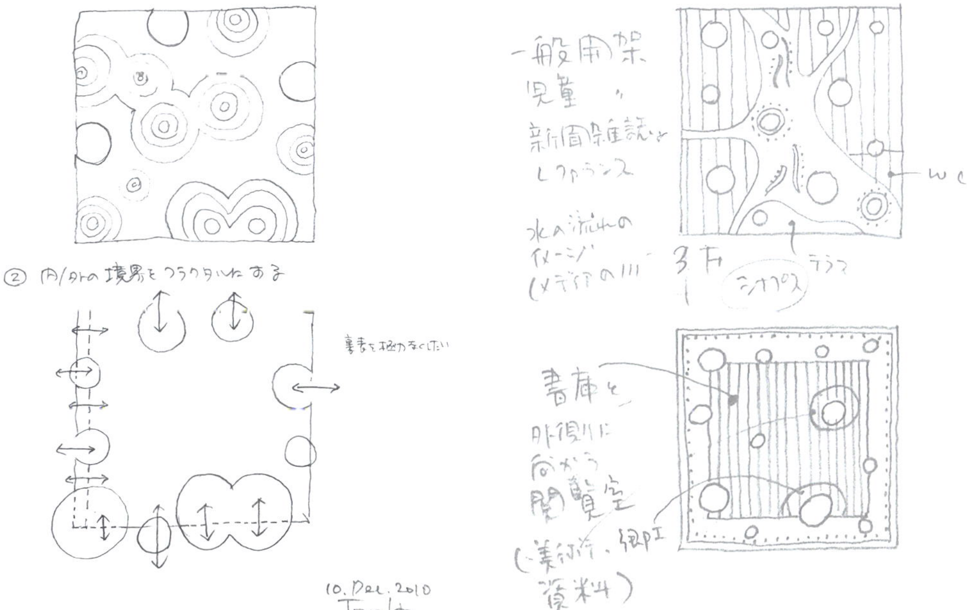

② 内/外の境界をフラクタル化する
一般開架
児童
新聞雑誌
レファレンス
水の流れの
イメージ
WC
書庫を
外側に
向かう
閲覧室
10. Dec. 2010
Toyo Ito

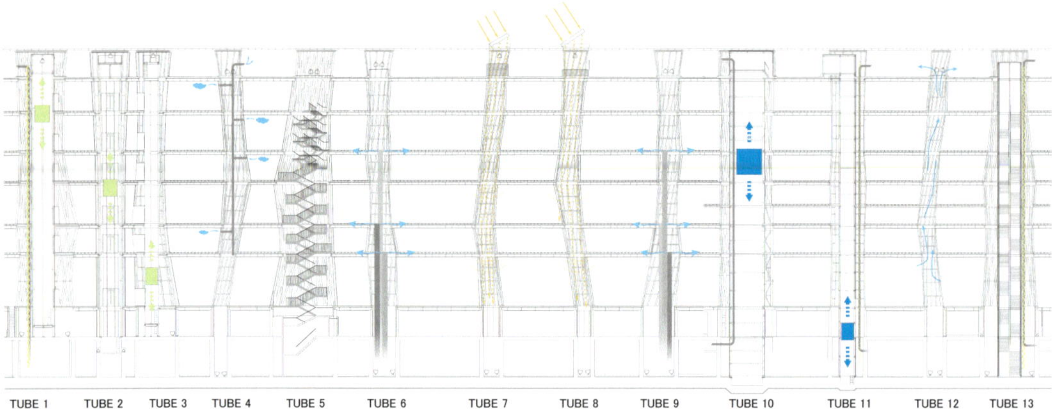

Sendai Mediatheque, Sendai, 2001, tube functions

that avenue of thinking altogether and explore a completely different route. This process repeats over and over.

How many people work at your office at the moment?
At present, we have a total of 40 people.

Let's talk about influences, relations and issues. Is there any architect whose work has particularly influenced you over the years?
I have always been a fan of Le Corbusier ever since I was a student. Lately, year by year I seem to grow fonder of his architecture. I admire his early works and his housing projects but recently I came to enjoy his later work like Ronchamp and particularly La Tourette. Those works seem to come right out of the ground; they are really organic but also have a warm feeling. Last year I visited Chandigarh and I was really blown away by it.

When you look at the Pritzker Architecture Prize laureates from the last years, including yourself, it is striking to see so many Japanese architects among them. How would you explain this interest in Japanese architects? Why is Japanese architecture so successful internationally?
I would say that Japanese architects have an advantage because Japanese clients don't usually care all that much about the architecture. They care about the budget and the timeline and as long as you keep it under budget and on time, you have a lot of freedom—you can almost create whatever you want. In Europe, clients are stricter and often have a clearer picture of what they want. Then again, just saying it is easy to build doesn't mean it will be received well by the public. That's another issue altogether.
In addition, Japanese construction companies are very good. They can build almost anything to an extremely pristine and precise quality. All my buildings have been

Sendai Mediatheque

made possible by the advanced technologies that Japanese construction companies have and they take great pride in creating and making things well. Rather than just taking orders, they work almost like craftsmen, contributing their own ideas like the other people involved in the design development. And I think it is important that everybody involved in the project also identifies with it.

That is an interesting point. It shifts the focus from the architect and his creativity to the whole process from initial sketches to actual construction. If you compare the situation in Japan today with that of, say, 20 years ago, how has it changed?
On the one hand, it has become much easier to build now. Cost is a big issue. For example when I built the "Sendai Mediatheque," it was considered a very difficult structure and very challenging for the construction companies and the workers. Today, the same design would be much easier to build. I have the feeling that as time moves on, advances in technology have made a big difference. On the other hand, there used to be more openness.
I feel that society is much more managed, more regulated than it used to be. To be more specific, so many laws and rules have become stricter than they were 20 years ago, making it hard to do public buildings nowadays. The process needs to be more open to new ideas, so that new architecture with more energy can come about again. But I think that process is happening the world over.

Let's talk about connections between generations. You could draw a line from Kenzo Tange to yourself, and from yourself to Kazuyo Sejima and then to Junya Ishigami. Is there a red line between all these people and their mutual influences?
In a recent exhibition called "A Japanese Constellation" at the MoMA in New York in March 2016, the curator was especially interested in the relationship you just mentioned.
These relationships are very special in Japan. There is this kind of link you mention but I would describe it as a network that is actually more intricate. It is like a solar system with Kenzo Tange in the middle and the others revolving around him in different relationships to one another. Japanese architects respect each other and have mutual, reciprocal relationships. This network has a kind of hierarchy which is characterized by the Japanese culture of teachers and students and a general overall sense of politeness.

In Europe, by contrast, many architects of your generation have striven to break with earlier generations and their teachers.
Zaha Hadid, for example, was a student of Rem Koolhaas at the Architectural Association in London. But she never mentioned that Rem Koolhaas was her teachers. In Japan, students seem to have greater respect for their teachers. Of course, in public they may not utter a bad word about their teachers, but in other contexts they probably do.

Is there an intellectual exchange, a debate, between architects and between younger and older generations?
There is not much in the way of discourse. But after the great eastern earthquake disaster in 2011 an initiative was started called "Home for All," where we called on

TOD'S Omotesando Building, Tokyo, 2004

younger architects to contribute to the debate about what architecture means in the context of such a disaster. That was one example where I curated a kind of debate between the different generations of architects.
When I was young, many of my contemporaries did not have that much work to do. We had a lot of free time and would meet, drink and talk to each other. A lot of very close relationships were forged at that time. Today, young architects are all very busy, they have a lot of work to do and little time to drink and socialize. There's not so much fun in that.

National Taichung Theater, Taichung, Taiwan, 2016

TOYO ITO

Biography

1941 Born in Seoul, South Korea
1965 Graduated from Department of Architecture, University of Tokyo
1965–69 Employee at Kiyonori Kikutake Architect and Associates, Tokyo
1971 Started own studio, Urban Robot (URBOT), Tokyo
1979 Changed office name to Toyo Ito & Associates, Architects
2013 Awarded Pritzker Prize

Principal Works

1971 Aluminum House, Kanagawa
1976 White U, Tokyo
1984 Silver Hut, Tokyo
1986 Tower of Winds, Kanagawa
1991 Yatsushiro Municipal Museum, Kumamoto
1993 Shimosuwa Municipal Museum, Nagano
1997 Dome in Odate, Akita
2001 Sendai Mediatheque, Miyagi
2002 Brugge Pavilion, Brugge, Belgium
Serpentine Gallery Pavilion, London, United Kingdom
2004 TOD'S Omotesando Building, Tokyo
2005 MIKIMOTO Ginza 2, Tokyo
2006 Meiso no Mori municipal funeral hall, Gifu
Hospital Cognacq-Jay, Paris, France
2007 Tama Art University Library (Hachioji campus), Tokyo
2008 ZA-KOENJI Public Theater, Tokyo
2009 The Main Stadium for the World Games 2009, Kaohsiung, Taiwan R.O.C.
Torres Porta Fira, Barcelona, Spain
2011 Toyo Ito Museum of Architecture, Imabari, Ehime
2013 National Taiwan University, College of Social Sciences, Taipei, Taiwan R.O.C.
2015 Minna no Mori Gifu Media Cosmos, Gifu
CapitaGreen, Singapore
2016 National Taichung Theater, Taichung, Taiwan

Publications—Selection

2009 *Toyo Ito*, Phaidon Press Limited, London
2011 *Tarzans in the Media Forest, Architecture Words 8*, AA Publications, London
2012 *Forces of Nature*, Princeton Architectural Press, New York
2013 *Toyo Ito 1: 1971–2001*, TOTO Publishing, Tokyo
2014 *Toyo Ito 2: 2002–2014*, TOTO Publishing, Tokyo

▲世田谷村東西面断面図／
吊り橋のような構造で住宅が成立している。
地階のＲＣ基礎部は、設計工房。１階は、今はもうない日本家屋。２階、３階が住宅部である。屋上階は庭園である

OSAMU
ISHIYAMA

Kitsch is a bad thing and a good thing

Mr. Ishiyama, you studied architecture at Waseda University in Tokyo and were a student of Takamasa Yoshizaka, who had worked with Le Corbusier in Paris. What motivated you to study with him?
In my student days, Takamasa Yoshizaka distanced himself from Le Corbusier, emphasizing that his own way was very different. I think independence is good and Yoshizaka's way was independent. His language, meaning and philosophy was very clear. Yoshizaka's theory is about discontinuity and his life, and his own style was similarly discontinuous. He had a very cosmopolitan attitude and his way of working and his lifestyle was very eccentric, but I love him that way. I learned his way of thinking, but not his style. I would say he was a very good teacher.

In 1966, as a student, you won the second prize in the Shinkenchiku residential design competition judged by Kenzo Tange, among others.
I remember meeting Kenzo Tange during the competition award ceremony. Over a drink he told me that he liked the shape of my proposal but that it would be better constructed as a structural space-frame of the kind pioneered by Konrad Wachsmann. I don't think he understood my concept and way of thinking and I replied that I didn't share his view and did not intend to change my approach.

What was it that you disagreed with about Kenzo Tange's idea?
Yoshizaka's philosophy and approach was very different to Tange's, including how he designed the shape of buildings. Yoshizaka's shapes are not so beautiful. Tange, on the other hand, was interested only in beauty! In clarity and beauty. He spoke about Japanese tradition but his real interest was beauty, as well as proportion and composition. I don't share this view.

Was there a strong countermovement against Kenzo Tange's approach and Metabolism at the time?
Most of my generation were students in 1968, at the time of the student revolts. It was also a time of experimentation. In 1968, Team Zoo emerged on the scene, along with Toyo Ito and Tadao Ando, and the effect was akin to that of an earthquake. In 1968, many young architects staked out a position that was different to that of Tange and the Metabolists. It was important for the generation to doubt the established.

After you finished your studies you started your own office which you called Dam-Dan. Why did you choose that name?
Everyone always asks me what Dam-Dan means, but I don't know. Everybody says Dam-Dan when you are an anarchist. It sounds very dangerous and I liked the sound

of the words. The name may be one reason why I didn't get any work, so it was in fact very dangerous—to my business!
The new name of my office is Gaya. It also has no particular meaning, perhaps some humor, no humor, or a type of humor... It's difficult to pin down, like Dam-Dan.

The "Villa Gen-An," one of your early projects, soon became quite well-known. What was the background to this project?
In the "Villa Gen-An" you can see my philosophy. I wanted to create the cheapest shelter possible, an industrial product with a very good price, like the social housing experiments by the architects of the early Modernist period. I tried a system for shelter buildings, but it did not offer enough potential. I wanted to achieve a specific expression, to do something interesting with the design. It's not about just achieving a simple mix, but about creating something different every time.

You mention early Modernist architects. Have you also been inspired by other building systems or approaches, for instance by Konrad Wachsmann's space-frame, as mentioned by Kenzo Tange?

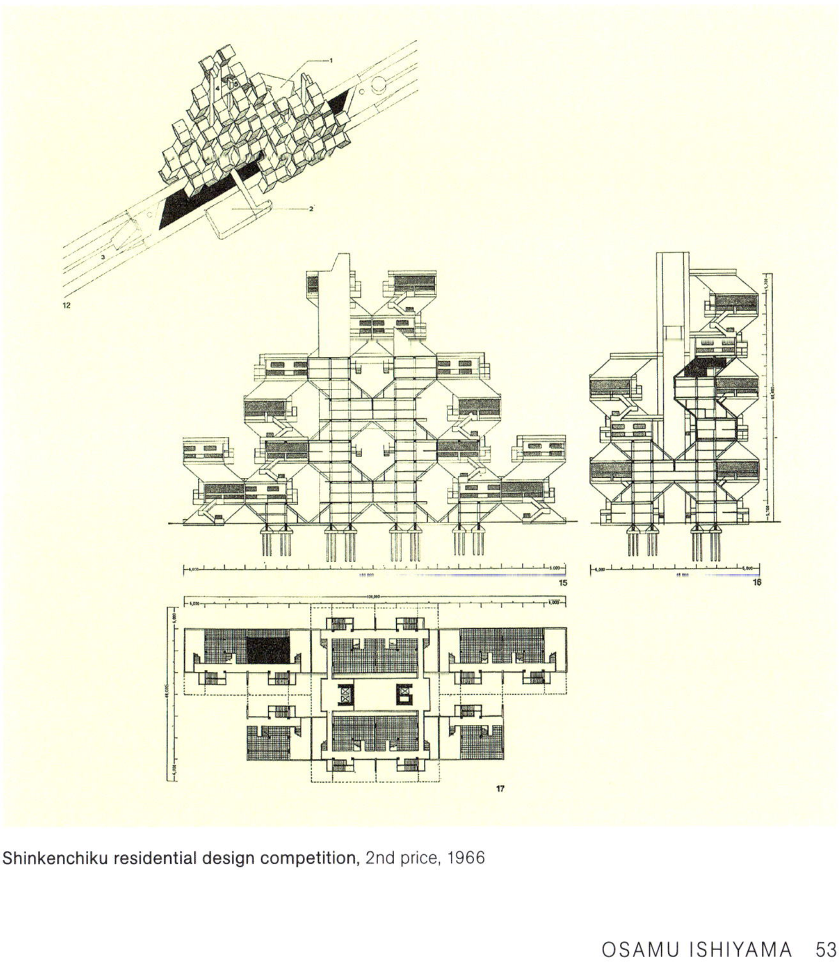

Shinkenchiku residential design competition, 2nd price, 1966

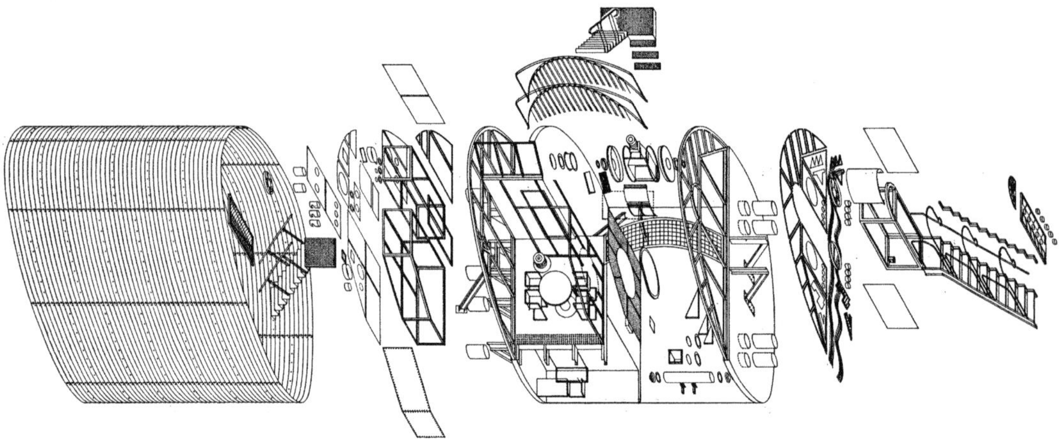

Villa Gen-An, Ohmi, 1975

I have great respect for the early Modernist architects and their search for affordable housing for everyone using the means of industrialized production, standardization and cost-effective construction. That seems an ideal approach to me. In terms of building systems, Buckminster Fuller's theories are very convincing but ordinary people cannot live in those structures. With Konrad Wachsmann's theory it is the same: pure theory but not livable.
I did once build two "Buckminster domes" and it proved to be quite difficult to realize them according to his theory. The theory is all very well, but there are so many nodes and joints in the roof that all pose problems when it rains. Buckminster's theory covers lots of things, but not the poetics of rain. Every human being has a very poetic existence. I am interested in that—and in change.

You wrote about poetics and changes in your text "Akihabara feeling" ...
Akihabara is a little world of its own in Tokyo. Originally it was known for its black market and electronic goods, but now it is known for its anime and computer goods. It struggles along changing ever so slightly every day, never staying the same. Akihabara is a lasting phenomenon but at the same time it is always a little different; every day some parts change. This is the kind of architecture I would be comfortable with.

Is there a building where you have been able to realize architecture as you have described it?

Villa Gen-An

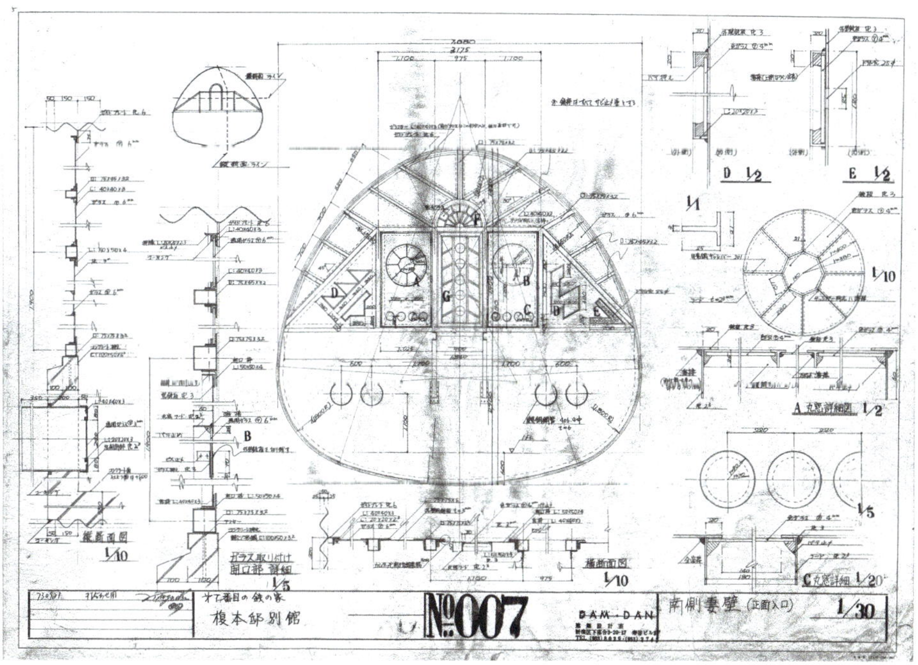
縦断面図
1/10
ガラス取り付け
開口部 詳細
1/5
横断面図
1/10
C丸窓詳細 1/20
A丸窓詳細図 1/2
D 1/2
E 1/2
1/10
1/5
オて番目の鉄の家
榎本邸別館
№007
DAM·DAN
南側妻壁 (正面入口)
1/30

Setagaya Village, Tokyo, 2001

Maybe in "Setagaya Village", my house and office. My wife and children say that they don't like this house as it is always changing. But I think it is ok and we are constantly changing it to meet their wishes. We select its "clothes," we select a funny chair, select something else and change it. This is how I think architecture should be, especially in a house.

So you change a lot in your house, "Setagaya Village" by building and rebuilding, there you have sometimes worked with traditional wood craftsmanship and in other parts you have used shipbuilding techniques. Why?

Design and artfulness is important to me. But the price–cost ratio is even more important. It is not about building cheaply, but rather finding a clear relationship between cost and price.

Shipbuilding is a case in point: construction companies have very high prices, but you can have the same item made by shipbuilders for a very reasonable price. So sometimes I use shipbuilders. Another reason is that I like curves. Shipbuilders never use flat parts; every element is curved, and they can make them very easily. The work of shipbuilders or craftsmen is in a way comparable to that of a car designer, whose work is very elaborate but also very rational and conscious of the price-cost ratio.

You refer to shipbuilders but also to carpenters and traditional wood constructions, as we see in your house. What does tradition mean for you?

Setagaya Village

Traditional Japanese carpenters are very clever, not only in their constructions, but also in making money and managing their work. This management talent in traditional technology is also to be found in general contractors. Many of the most successful Japanese general contractors are carpenters.
I think my relationship to the topic of architecture–culture–tradition is that architecture is not made by architects alone but also by contractors, craftsmen and others. The input of other people is important to me, not just in terms of simple communications, but also the influence other people bring to bear.

How do you see your work as an architect?

I have no interest in making models, drawings and writing, but I am interested in being an editor. Every element has to be assembled, and that is the principle of an editor. Making sketches is, for me, a kind of editing, a way of assembling. I never think up a form or an approach in my head; I always assemble and mix.

What are your inspirations when you are designing—or "editing?"

That changes: what inspires me today, and influences how I am and how I work can be different tomorrow. I don't have a fixed method, and small ongoing changes are very important to me. If today and tomorrow were always the same, I would not be very happy. History is always important to me, and it does not have to be Japanese history. It can also be European history. It's not as easy, but there is plenty of information.

With respect to history, you showed historic textiles in an exhibition in London in 1991 about the "The Visions of Japan."
I used parts of fishermen's textiles from the Tohoku area. That was somewhat ironic for the Europeans. You might call it kitsch, or kitsch design. For those kinds of fishermen's textiles, we say kitsch, too.

Kitsch?
It has an ironic quality, a tongue-in-cheek attitude to culture. Real kitsch can be very nice, like traditional Japanese carpentry. So, kitsch is both good and bad. The concept of kitsch, the language of kitsch can encompass both. In a review of the exhibition in the newspaper *Le Monde* they wrote with regard to the fishermen's textiles that "Japanese architecture laughs at itself."

In the "Chohachi Art Museum" you also used typical traditional plaster patterns.
Typical kitsch. In Japan the Edo period is associated with kitsch. It has a special culture, visual culture and design culture—which is very nice and also kitsch. Of course Kabuki is also kitsch, as is wood printing, etc.
In our university studies on the Edo period and its art and design, we were told that it is kitsch! Our education in Japan was something of a catastrophe. The teachers taught us that the *Tenno* is good and *Nikko* is bad, that *Nikko* is kitsch, and we were not to question that.
Bruno Taut said once that *Nikko* is kitsch. But something else that Bruno Taut said is, I think, much more important, namely that Japanese wooden houses are very good, because Japanese wooden houses, ordinary houses, have a very rational, very direct price-to-cost ratio. He understood that Japanese traditional houses have a very well-conceived system. With this system, a carpenter in Kyoto and a carpenter in Tokyo can work the same way, and the price and cost are the same everywhere. In Japanese architectural education, the professors only ever repeated Bruno Taut's statement on Edo, *Nikko* and kitsch, without ever mentioning his primary concern: that of the system of a house.
The Japanese history of architecture education is very short: about 150 years ago, one man from England, Josiah Conder, came to Japan and almost single-handedly shaped the concept of architectural education at universities. He was a very eccentric person, and it is said that he really taught Saracenic architecture! Is that kitsch?
Later the modernists dominated architectural education, teaching modern European architecture in a very simple way. The way in which Japanese architecture came to be modernized is quite difficult to understand. So it is easier to imitate, copy and replicate European modern architecture—but I am not interested in that. About ten years ago, I wrote an essay in which I said that modern design in Japan is now kitsch. Repetition, repetition, and more repetition ends up as kitsch.

How do you think younger generations of architects relate to architectural history? For instance, in the work of Sou Fujimoto, Go Hasegawa or Junya Ishigami?
Junya Ishigami, for example, is quite conservative, I think. That is not necessarily a criticism. He is, of course, mostly influenced by the Heian period of Japanese culture, which is a very nice period in which some special buildings were constructed that also have a very good human scale. You see this in Ishigami's architecture too.

Room Chaos, The Visions of Japan, Victoria and Albert Museum, London, United Kingdom, 1991

Chohachi Art Museum, Matsuzaki, 1984

But his buildings do not have a strong connection to society: his work is predominantly artistic with little social perspective. In 1968, on the other hand, our generation was constantly fighting about society.

Coming back to the generation and time of 1968. You said that it was also a time of experimentation with new input from Team Zoo, Toyo Ito, Tadao Ando and others. What do you think of them today?
Team Zoo are my friends and sometimes my enemies. I feel close to them, and then sometimes very foreign. The architects at Team Zoo were, like me, students of Takamasa Yoshizaka. One of their best buildings is in Okinawa, at the edge of Japan. I have the same problem: I have been unable to realize a big project in Tokyo, only at the edge, far away from Tokyo.

Tadao Ando, Toyo Ito and some other architects have since become famous brands. I think this brand-phenomenon will never happen again, as we have a different system today. It was different back then. In the 1970s and 80s there was a strong "paper culture." Arata Isozaki, for instance, wrote a great deal. The market for magazines and papers was very strong and there were ten or more architecture magazines. Every architect and every student read magazines. We discussed them and it contributed to our learning, to our education. Ito, Ando and other architects were very present in magazines and books.

But now that the internet has become so pervasive, there is very little paper culture for architecture. The "brands" had their basis in paper culture, and paper culture means theory and architecture design journalism. So I think such "brands" are declining along with press culture. The young generation may find this hard to understand. I wouldn't necessarily say that the situation is bad, but then again I wouldn't say it is so good.

OSAMU ISHIYAMA

Biography

1944	Born in Tokyo
1966	Graduated in architecture from Waseda University, Tokyo
1968	Completed graduate studies at Waseda University Established Dam-Dan design studio
1988–2013	Professor, Architectural School, Waseda University, Tokyo
2013	Established Studio Gaya

Principal Works

1975	Villa Gen-An, Ohmi, Aichi
1984	Chohachi Art Museum, Matsuzaki, Shizuoka
1986	Farmer's House, Sugadaira, Nagano
1990	Seaside Street, Kesennuma, Miyagi Mazda R&D Center, Kanagawa
1991	Nexus World, Collective Housing, Fukuoka The Visions of Japan, Victoria and Albert Museum, London
1994	Rias Ark Museum of Art, Kesennuma, Miyagi
1996	Kannon-ji Temple, Tokyo Venice Biennale 6th International Architecture Exhibition, Venice, Italy – Golden Lion Award
1998	Kita Incineration Plant, Tokyo
2000	Tree House, Saitama
2001	Setagaya Village, Tokyo
2006	Hiroshima House, Phnom Pehn, Cambodia

Publications—Selection

1982	*Barrack Jodo*, Sagami-Shobo, Tokyo
1984	*Idea of housing with Akihabara feeling*, Shobunsha, Tokyo
1997	*House debauchery*, Kodansha, Tokyo
2008	*Self build*, Kotsu-shupansha, Tokyo

RYOJI SUZUKI

True architecture is when nobody is living in it

Mr. Suzuki, why did you decide to study architecture? Did you have any connection to architecture during your childhood?
My father was a painter. I was surrounded by artwork, catalogs and books, so I had a good grasp of art and became familiar with it. I was interested in painting, which is two-dimensional, but I was even more interested in three-dimensional work. At school I was better in art and mathematics than in humanities. I became more interested in cultural aspects later, but initially I thought I could combine my interests in art and mathematics in architecture. That's how I chose to become an architect.

You studied at Waseda University. Which teachers were important to you?
My master teacher was Professor Yoshiro Ikehara. His field covered Antoni Gaudí, Rudolf Steiner and German expressionism. At that time French and American architecture was very much in trend, but I was more interested in Yoshiro Ikehara, Togo Murano, Kazuo Shinohara, Ragnar Östberg, Gunnar Asplund and Eero Saarinen, who were not mainstream at that time. Another professor at Waseda University who was an important influence was Takamasa Yoshizaka. He worked with Le Corbusier, but he was different to the other "Corbusier-crazy" architects.

At university you learned a lot about European architecture and its history. Did you also study the history of Japanese architecture?
At university we did also learn about Japanese architectural history, but the focus was on European architectural history. If you wanted to work in the field of design, if you wanted to become an architect, then you had to study European history. Japanese architectural history represented a comparatively small part of the courses that everybody studied. Japanese architecture became Europeanized through the Meiji Restoration.

After you finished your studies, you worked for the general contractor Takenaka and at Fumihiko Maki's office before you decided to study again.
I knew that if I wanted to open my own office, I would need certain skills, so I decided to work for Takenaka. General contractors had better technical skills than most famous architects, so I went there to acquire as much knowledge as I could on constructing buildings to a high standard. I wanted to work at Fumihiko Maki's office as he was very internationally-minded. But so did many other architects. Luckily, I had the opportunity to transfer straight to Maki's office from Takenaka, as Fumihiko Maki was working on projects with Takenaka.
Overall, I worked for about seven years for Takenaka and Maki before deciding to leave in 1973 in order to study again, this time with Professor Yoshiro Ikehara. I

undertook research into Michelangelo, Charles Rennie Mackintosh and studied Giuseppe Terragni. At the same time, I started designing houses while still at the university.

You called your office "fromnow." Why did you choose that name?
I'll risk telling you: things were changing rapidly at that time and when I started the firm, we felt as architects that there was nothing one could rely on. So I thought: we have to do things now—"fromnow"—and that is how I came to the name. It may sound funny when you see it now, but it represented a break with the past. When I started my office, I thought that the modern architectural movement was over and I felt it no longer offered a good framework within which to discuss designing architecture. I warmed to the ideas of architects like Superstudio and Archigram, who were producing new concepts and images but had never built.

Since then, you have undertaken a lot of projects: not just architecture, but also art projects and installations, as well as writing texts and making films.
Just designing buildings is not so exciting—architecture has many more possibilities. If you look back at the Renaissance, architects were also artists, art critics, sculptors and painters. Architecture is not just about building; there is more to it. But as modernization progressed, a sort of division of labor set in and different professions evolved with the result that architects just build buildings. And within that field, some architects design just factories, others just hospitals, or housing, etc.
So staying true to the "fromnow" concept, I decided to start over with a new, broader concept of architecture that encompasses a wider range of options and wider meanings. That gave me the freedom to branch out into the media of text, art and cinema—and you can find concepts of architecture in all these fields too.

Absolute Scene, Experience in Material No. 24, Tokyo, 1987

Barrack Architecture, Experience in Material No. 23, Tokyo, 1987, photo, sketch, drawing, model

And you are not only interested in writing texts, making movies and designing buildings, but—as in your "Absolute Scene" project—you are also interested in demolishing buildings. What was your interest there?
Designing and building architecture is not everything. After that, architecture takes on a life of its own. It changes with the people living in the building, and it remains when the people leave. That's what interests me about abandoned buildings. In Europe, buildings are mostly made of stone and endure pretty well. But in Japan, buildings are basically wooden structures that disappear more easily. In Tokyo, after the bombing and the fires of World War II, most buildings burnt down, but their remains lingeredå on like ghosts. I wondered what would happen to a Japanese building when it became unused and began to slowly disappear.

In your project "Barrack Architecture" you again dealt with architecture that was disappearing. What interested you about these buildings in particular?
The "barracks" I was interested in were about to be demolished. They were quite ordinary houses. I took pictures of them and started drawing them as I felt that they exhibited a certain strength in contrast to new buildings, which are different. I preserved the buildings by drawing the existing appearance of the houses before they were destroyed. Ultimately, they became the only proof that these buildings existed.

So you dealt with something vanishing, with architecture that is not in use, that is abandoned. In this context you cited Louis Kahn with his definition of architecture in relation to ruins: "But when the building is a ruin and free of servitude, the spirit emerges, telling of the marvel that a building was made." (Alessandra Latour, ed., *Louis I. Kahn: Writings, Lectures, Interviews*, New York 1991, p. 268.)
I think it is a criticism of contemporary architecture. Louis Kahn said that architecture becomes true architecture when nobody is living in it, and it really shakes the assumption that many people have of what architecture is or should be. Kahn's definition challenges the preconceived notion of architecture. I am interested in his idea because architecture has been too human-centered. I don't mean that Kahn made

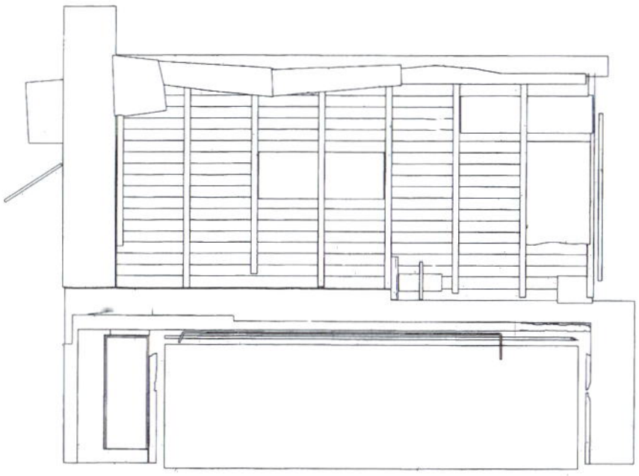

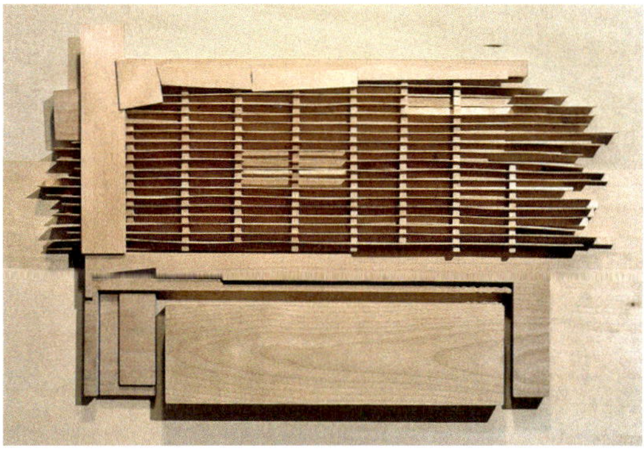

inhuman buildings—he made great buildings—but he was designing them to become ruins and I think that makes sense as well.

Concerning the meaning of architecture, what should architecture be or what should architecture provide?

It serves people, it is useful for people, but the life of architecture is longer than the life of people. It should be something that is more than just for certain people. Architecture should be a source of strength that helps people contemplate and think. The surroundings create an atmosphere which can serve people—not just for people who live now, but also for people in the future. If you only think about people in the present, it is constrictive.

So, when a building is finished, the process of its transformation starts and its end may be a ruin. But how can you anticipate this process? How does it influence your design?

Buildings are constantly changing and transforming. I have to meet the clients' needs, of course, but I see it rather as a process of discovery, because how it is actually used depends on the client. I can't control how it changes, but I do observe the aging process. So, what I can control is my choice of material. As it changes over time, I want to choose materials that will age over time according to their substance, such as stone or steel or solid wood rather than thin superficial materials. I design elements where you experience the aging of the material.

You always title your works "Experience in Material." You began with "Experience in Material No. 1," all the way up to "Experience in Material No. 57." As I understand it, material is not just material to you, but "space" as well?

It is my way of avoiding using the term "space." I prefer not to use the term space—or *kukan* in Japanese, because it is too controversial. It is a delicate term. The term space, as used today in architecture, is from the 19th century and modern times and refers to three-dimensional fixed space. The term *kukan*, which was introduced quite late in Japanese history, was widespread as a term implying space as developed from the Renaissance through to Baroque architecture in Europe. I am suspicious of architecture based on space—fixed space. I think that space is a happening, a process, as in the Japanese term *ma* for void or gap, which is older than *kukan.* Space has no limits, it does not stop. It is more than the rather shallow definition of space used in modern architecture and thinking. I am referring to movies, for example, you often see different shots of the same room, but it looks different because it changes within the film. That is something I am very interested in as a concept.

As I understand it, your building "Azabu Edge" is an interpretation of material—in the sense of your term for space—as well as of its surrounding context in Tokyo?
I think the context is part of the building. I designed the building to include the surrounding buildings which were not designed by me. There are lots of edges and gaps in the surrounding area and I recreated gaps within the building. The surrounding buildings are out of control because of their odd design, and they do not really blend in. My intention in adding the "Azabu Edge" was to unify the surrounding area into one, rather than just leave pieces be by themselves.

So when you embark on a project, how do you work on it, how do you develop the design?
When I start the design process, I want to keep as many options open as possible in my design. I don't really have a fixed idea in mind—I go to a site, meet the client and see the surrounding context, the atmosphere, the landscape, and that is what inspires my design. Building, designing and architecture is in that sense also a happening, because it does not start from a fixed idea. It is an open process which is always different. For certain projects I start with models and for others I work mostly with sketches and drawings.
With some projects, I sometimes even make additional drawings after completion to revise my work. Once built, a completed building tells us something. I am inspired by the atmosphere of the built work. For the Kohun-ji Temple, for instance, the combination of the traditional roof and the modern steel framework has an interesting impact, much stronger than I expected. I tried to capture that by making drawings after the building was completed.
In a few of my housing projects, I made models after the houses were completed. It was my way of thinking through the ideas that inspired me during the design. While I am designing I have many ideas and after completion I often revisit and revise them.

In your architecture, you deal with ambivalence and fragments, and in your texts you refer to theories by Gilles Deleuze, Michel Foucault and other texts from the 1980s. How important are these texts and theories to you?
I think that the philosophers from that period—Foucault, Deleuze or Roland Barthes, for example—were right with their ideas about illuminating the past and thinking forward, so I am very interested in their theories.

You are referring to those theories from a European context. How do you refer to the Japanese context?

Azabu Edge, Experience in Material No. 20, Tokyo, 1987

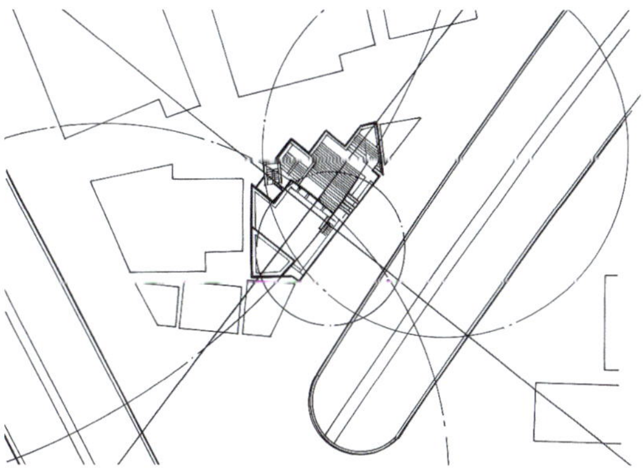
Site plan

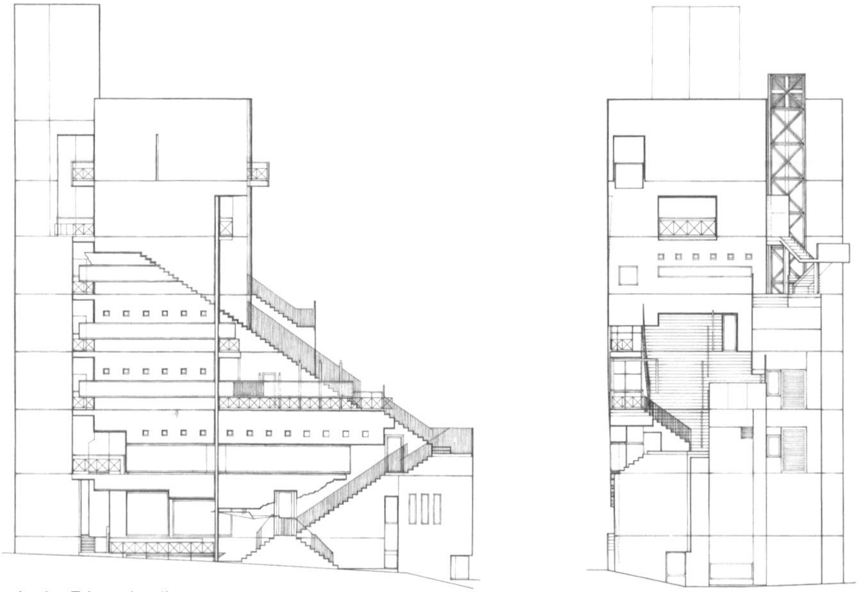

Azabu Edge, elevations

I think it is really important to look at old buildings from 1,000 years ago and to interpret them in modern terms. To properly consider Japanese architecture, you need to deal with roofs because in the past, there used to be rows of those traditional roofs, whereas now they are flat and all gone. The sloped roof is a really important aspect of Japanese architecture.

In your architecture, you mostly deal with traditional roof forms when you build temples or shrines, while other buildings have primarily flat roofs—can you explain why?
I would like to work more with roof forms, but there are not always many opportunities. With shrines or temples, it is easier to use traditional roof forms because they are part of the spiritual and symbolic background of religious buildings.
At some points before and during World War II certain roofs were associated with a nationalistic image, and were "contaminated." So, you have to be really careful when designing sloped roofs because it can also have political implications. So it is very difficult to work with that. In Tokyo there are also fewer opportunities to employ sloped roofs in the way that I have done with temples and shrines.

You mention the problem that a kind of tradition is contaminated because of the misuse at least in the 1930s and 40s. What does that mean for you?
In the 1930s and 40s, there really was a kind of unworthy architecture with nationalistic connotations. Kenzo Tange, for example, proposed projects with sloped roofs such as in the nationalistic project *Daitoa*-Memorial, a memorial hall for the Greater East Asia Co-Prosperity Sphere. A lot of architects do not like dealing with national

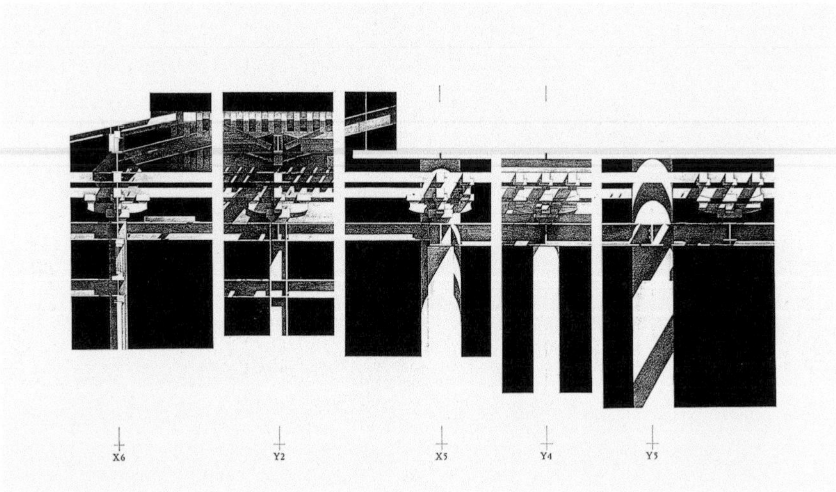

Kohun-ji Temple, Experience in Material No. 33, Tokyo, 1991, drawing after completion

or traditional architecture, because of the danger that it might be seen as nationalistic, which they want to avoid.

In order to interpret traditional Japanese architecture in a way that is not nationalistic, I start with the materials and not with the forms. I combine traditional materials and traditional Japanese architectural methods with steel, which is not found in traditional Japanese architecture, but blends well with it. For the Konpira Shrine project, I looked at old drawings to study traditional roofs. The design was inspired by buildings from the 14th and 15th century. I was not taught this at the university—I learned how to design a traditional roof from scratch because I thought it was the right approach to designing a traditional temple.

Why do you refer to the 14th and 15th century in particular?

In the history of Japanese architecture there were two periods when culture and architecture really flourished: one was the Nara-period, when Japan imported a lot of culture from China, and the other was the Kamakura Muromachi-period.

I was asked to design two buildings for the Konpira Shrine, so I designed two roofs: one refers to the Kamakura Muromachi-period and the other to the Nara-period. In these two periods, temples and shrines were made by great master-carpenters, who were not architects but very skilled craftsmen. A lot of very good buildings evolved during those two periods. I wanted to use these old traditional buildings as a reference, while at the same time taking care to avoid it becoming kitsch. You can't just rebuild historical architecture.

We've been talking here about architecture from the past. What do you think was of importance in the development of architecture in Japan in the 19th and 20th century?

Project Konpira, Experience in Material No. 47, Kotohira, 2004

In general, people think modern architecture in Japan starts with Tange in the post-war period. But I think it started in the pre-war period. I am very interested in Michizo Tachihara. He was a year senior to Kenzo Tange and they studied at the same university. He was well known in his teens for his poetry—which is as magnificent today as it was then—besides his genuine talent as an architect. He wrote a lot, for example about ruins and had similar ideas about architecture as Louis Kahn—and he also wrote about buildings without people. He was uniquely talented, but unfortunately died at the age of 24. He is one example of a pre-war modern architect, and of other interesting movements and people who are not as well known as the Metabolists became later.

Do you think that the architects today refer to the architectural developments before the 1960s in Japan?

No, they don't! Japan was destroyed after World War II and Kenzo Tange and other architects went about creating new buildings and rebuilding the country in a very aggressive way, advocating the Metabolist group and the World Expo. I think it is really important to go back to the pre-war period and look at non-aggressive architects like Michizo Tachihara.

When I look at recent architecture in Japan, I see a tendency towards a quite calm architecture focused on shape and form. Ten or 20 years ago, the tendency in Japan with Atsushi Kitakawara, Makoto Sei Watanabe and others was more about chaos, about an architecture of collision and confrontation. I think this tendency has now passed and the younger generation is by comparison rather quiet.

I think, there are two reasons for this: first, there was the economic bubble, which were festive days. The party is now over and people are gradually settling down.

Perhaps we are now re-examining our modern architecture. In my view, if we are to revise our idea of modernism, we should begin with the pre-war period—before it all began with Kenzo Tange and all that followed from that—and instead look to Michizo Tachihara and his ideas for an architecture of generosity.

The second reason is that Japanese architecture has matured in a way, but in the process has also become more rigid. This is probably because a lot of great teachers have gone on to influence a whole generation of architects who studied under them, resulting in work that has become very similar. So while one might say, the architecture in Japan has matured, settled down and become calmer, it has also become flatter and less diverse.

RYOJI SUZUKI

Biography

1944	Born in Sendai and raised in Tokyo
1968	Bachelor of Engineering, Department of Architecture, Waseda University, Tokyo
1968–73	Employee at Takenaka Corporation
1970	Established fromnow, Tokyo
1970–71	Employee at Maki and Associates, Tokyo
1977	Master of Engineering, Department of Architecture, Waseda University, Tokyo
1982	Renamed practice Ryoji Suzuki Architects & Partners, Tokyo
1997–2015	Professor, Waseda University, Tokyo

Principal Works

1987	Experience in Material N. 20, Azabu Edge, Tokyo Experience in Material N. 23, Barrack Architecture, Tokyo Experience in Material N. 24, Absolute Scene, joint work with Shigeo Anzai and Kyoji Takubo, Tokyo
1990	Experience in Material N. 31, Expo Osaka, Folly 4, Osaka
1991	Experience in Material N. 33, Kohunji Temple, Tokyo
1992	Experience in Material N. 34, Clairière, Creux, Vide (Installation), Gallery Ma Experience in Material N. 35, Clairière, Creux, Vide (Film)
2003	Experience in Material N. 45, House in Jingumae, Tokyo
2004	Experience in Material N. 47, Project Konpira, Kotohira
2006	Experience in Material N. 48, House in Nishiazabu, Tokyo
2011	Experience in Material N. 50, House in Shimoda, Shizuoka
2012	Experience in Material N. 52, Dubhouse (Film), with Kei Shichiri
2014	Experience in Material N. 55, Bridge, Kotohira Experience in Material N. 56, Muzeum (Installation), 21st Century Museum of Contemporary Art, Kanazawa

Publications—Selection

1988	*Architecture in Drawings, Space & Concept: Several Experiences in Material*, Dohosha Publishing, Kyoto *Experience in Material N. 28: Dis-Architectural Considerations*, Chikuma Shobo, Tokyo
2001	*Architettura Anno Zero*, Chikuma Shobo, Tokyo *Essay on Houses by an Architect*, Kajima Institute Publishing, Tokyo
2007	*Experience in Material N. 49: Ryoji Suzuki Complete Works 1973–2007*, Inax, Tokyo
2013	*Material Suspense: Architectural Cinema*, LIXIL Publishing, Tokyo
2014	*Architecture of Generosity*, Misuzu Shobo, Tokyo

RIKEN
YAMAMOTO

Changing the order between public and private space

Mr. Yamamoto, you were born in Beijing, China. Your mother studied traditional herbal medicine and your father was an electrical engineer. What was your motivation to become an architect?
My father had a big table and drawing equipment, so I was familiar with planning things. But he died when I was five years old and I have only a very vague image in my mind. I entered university just as the Olympic games were taking place in Tokyo in 1964. Some of the buildings were very popular, such as the "Yoyogi Olympic Gymnasium" by Kenzo Tange. I think his buildings were a strong reason why I wanted to be an architect.

You entered Nihon University and graduated in 1968. Who were your teachers?
At Nihon University, I was part of the Department of History and Mr. Kobayashi Bunji was our teacher for Western architectural history. He wrote a very good book about Western culture and architecture from the Greek culture to the 20th century. After that, I joined Tokyo National University of Fine Arts and Music, also in the Department of History. My professor was Gakuji Yamamoto—same name, different family—who was both a modernist and a communist. His course could be described as something between architecture and engineering. I was very influenced by both of them. While at Yamamoto's department, I wrote an article about modern housing, and especially the dramatic changes in modern housing after World War I in Germany as a result of the Bauhaus, CIAM (Congrès Internationaux d'Architecture Moderne), Mies van der Rohe, Le Corbusier, Taut and others.

After your master's degree at Tokyo National University of Fine Arts and Music you joined Hiroshi Hara's Research Laboratory at the University of Tokyo, where you did quite a lot of travelling.
Yes. It was around 1968, the time of the student uprising against the government. During my graduate studies, I was not at university very often and frequently took part in the demonstrations against the government and its policies. After graduating, I didn't want to work for a company, so I asked Hiroshi Hara about doing research into housing. I travelled with him all over the world and became very interested both in travelling and seeing vernacular housing. The evolution of modern architecture from the 19th to the early 20th century is only part of the story. Vernacular housing is very different to modern housing, especially with regard to strong relationships within the village community. A house is not independent of other houses but is strongly connected to both the village community and the inhabiting family. We wanted to investigate how these relationships are supported through architecture.

How long were you abroad?
Each tour was almost three months and I visited the Mediterranean region, Central and South America, the Near East and the Middle East, India, Iraq and Iran. We were ten students in all, travelling together in two rental cars, both of which were pretty damaged after the tour.

How do you think all this travelling influenced your architecture and especially your later design work?
In the "Yamakawa Villa," my first project, you can probably sense the influence of my experiences of small villages. It is a very small house on a mountainous site. My early works are, I think, quite influenced by my studies of vernacular architecture.

What do you think about the Metabolist movement in Japan in the 1960s and 70s? Did it influence you?
I was a student at the time, but I was not so strongly influenced by it. We noticed, of course, that they were doing something different. Their theory focused on infrastructure and about how to attach everything to infrastructure. The attachments can easily be changed and infrastructure remains. For me that's the main idea of the Metabolists. However, after travelling around the world, I realized my own ideas were far removed from theirs.

You started your own office in 1973. Have you worked in an architectural office before?
No, I hadn't (*he laughs*).

And while you were at university you had focused more on research, so you had limited design experience: how did you get on when you started your own business?
Friends and staff who had already worked in architecture offices helped me. Makoto Motokura, who is now a professor at Tokyo University of the Arts, was a great help. We graduated at the same time and he had worked in Maki's office. He taught me many things about detailing and architecture and remains a good friend to this day.

That was again an unusual way of doing things: learning from one's staff and not the other way round.
Even now I learn many things from my staff (*he laughs*).

That's nice to hear. But you are also a teacher and have taught at several universities. Do you emphasize knowledge of history in your teaching, as was your own experience, or do you focus primarily on design?
Of course, it is a design studio, but I don't just focus on the architectural object itself. Nowadays it is easy to create a three-dimensional object with a computer and to switch scales. But designing architecture is also about considering the cityscape, the urban environment and the people in the city—and how to make a connection between the city and the architecture.

How would you describe the importance of knowing about the society in general when designing architectural spaces?

Shibam, Yemen, journeys

In my studio, we focus on the scale of the "Local Community Area." Students design, for example, a center for a local community, such as a library. Often they design only the shape and volume of the library, and the result is more like an object, a sculpture. I tell my students that it is very important to think about architecture in relation to the community and that is the main issue in my studio.

When you think of a local community, do you have a certain number of people in mind? Is this size of local community applicable in every culture?
It is not about a precise number. What is important is that we not only propose housing, but also a mix of shops, restaurants and public facilities. There are economic relationships at work here too. This system can be found anywhere: I have travelled to many countries and have never seen examples that were, for example, only housing. There was always some economic relationship.

When you teach your students about the "Local Community Area," what literature do you recommend?
I ask them to read *The City in History* by Lewis Mumford. And recently I wrote a very theoretical book called *The Space of Power and the Power of Space*, which is heavily influenced by Hannah Arendt. Her text *The Human Condition* is very interesting. In it, she writes about the relationship between the Greek city and the house. Most Greek *poleis* had a grid pattern because they were colonies, and maybe that was a good way of creating equality among the people. Greek houses also had an *andron*, which was part of the house and the public space—each house had some public space. The *andron* is where symposia were held, meaning discussions, eating, drinking and coming together. This is very relevant and I drew a diagram that stands for one house. Hannah Arendt divided into the private and public realm. The *andron* is in-between, but belongs to the public space. This is very different from modernist houses. Arendt calls it "no man's land;" I call it the "threshold between

Housing in Chibaysh, Iraq, journeys

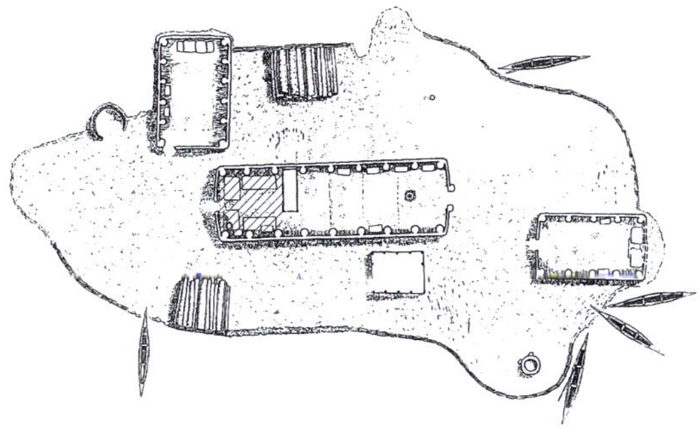

Housing in Chibaysh, floor plan

outside and inside." I investigated this further and tried to identify this theory in traditional villages and I was amazed by her investigations.

We see examples of threshold spaces in Greek houses and in your own projects. Does it work the same way in different cultures? Is it the same system?

Yes, it is always the same system. For example in Iraq, there are similar houses on an artificial island in Mesopotamia that also have a place that corresponds to the Greek *andron*. In Spain this place is like a foyer. The Spanish people call it *respido*. In India it is very similar too. And in Japan we call this place *sashiki*, which is a public space, even in a small house. Of course they are different in material and shape, but as a diagram they all work in more or less the same way. Modern housing instead is in many respects unusual compared with earlier times. The modernist movement started only about a hundred years ago but it resulted in a new system of housing—especially in Germany, at the Bauhaus or CIAM—that is still basically now the predominant system. It is actually close to Ludwig Hilberseimer's idea of the "*Hochhausstadt*" from 1924. The scale is, of course, different, but the system is the same. Every family's house is separate, and there is no public space, no "threshold between inside and outside," only space that is controlled by the government. This is now the most common form of housing, and it is very different to the housing forms I investigated in my research.

Why do we make these kinds of houses?

I think to a large extent it is a product of the nation state and the idea of the family unit. In Japan and many European countries, we have a nation state and the family unit remains the dominant entity for housing, more so than housing for individuals. In Japan, the family is very important for the government because it is very useful for controlling the country. In Europe things are already very different: Europe is more open to the needs of independent people.

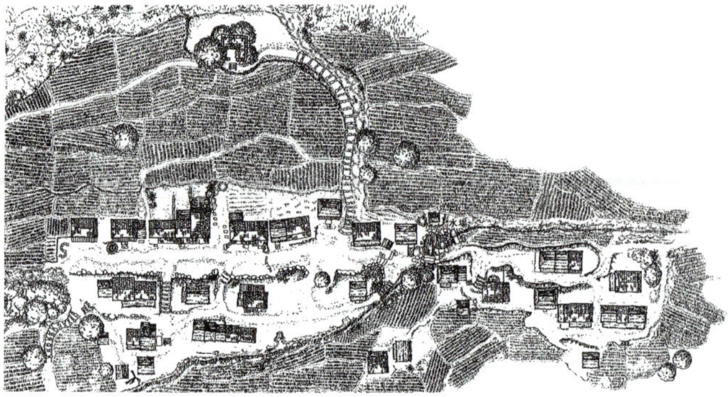

Nakagaon Nakhsa, Nepal, journeys

What do you think about public space? Is it the same in a city and a village, and has it remained the same over the centuries?
The meaning of "public" has changed greatly between the 19th century and the 20th and 21st century. "Public" in the modernist city means that it belongs to the government: streets and plazas are controlled by the government; electricity and infrastructure are controlled by the government. The modernist city is a bureaucratic system, and the street is therefore defined by this system.

What can we, as architects, do to change that?
I think we need to change the order of public and private. Currently, it is very rigid, but it is easy to change. We need to resurrect these in-between spaces; spaces that are changeable. Shops, boutiques and bodegas are part of the public realm but are also private spaces. In the medieval city, in Japan as well as in the West, houses had small shops on the ground floor and the interface between them and the street facilitated interaction between public and private. These are the kinds of situations I am interested in.

Which of your projects best illustrates your ideas about the relationship between public and private?
The "Pangyo housing" in Seongnam City, South Korea, shows my idea of the threshold very well, I think. It is very open: there is a common deck for every ten units. From this deck you enter the entrance space, which is very transparent and also comparably large. There are three stories. The family living room is on the first floor, the bedrooms are on the third floor. In-between, on the second floor, is a big glazed entrance space—the threshold space. It can be used however the inhabitants like: some use the place as a public coffee place, or as a guest room.

And when you are designing, how do you work most of the time? With models, sketches, drawings or texts? How do you design?

Yamakawa Villa, Nagano, 1977

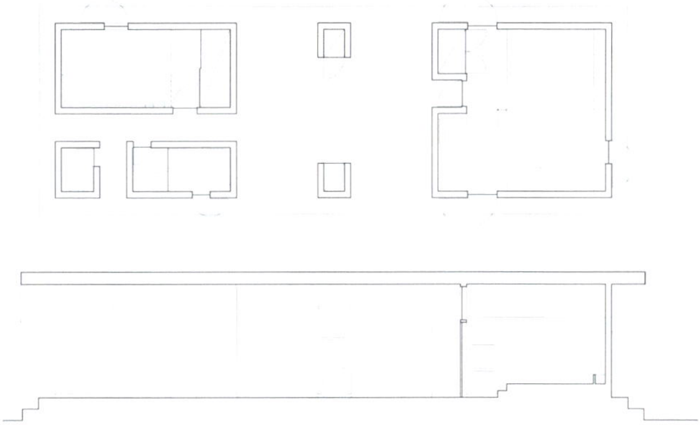

Floor plan, section

Pangyo housing, Seongnam, South Korea, 2010

Floor plans

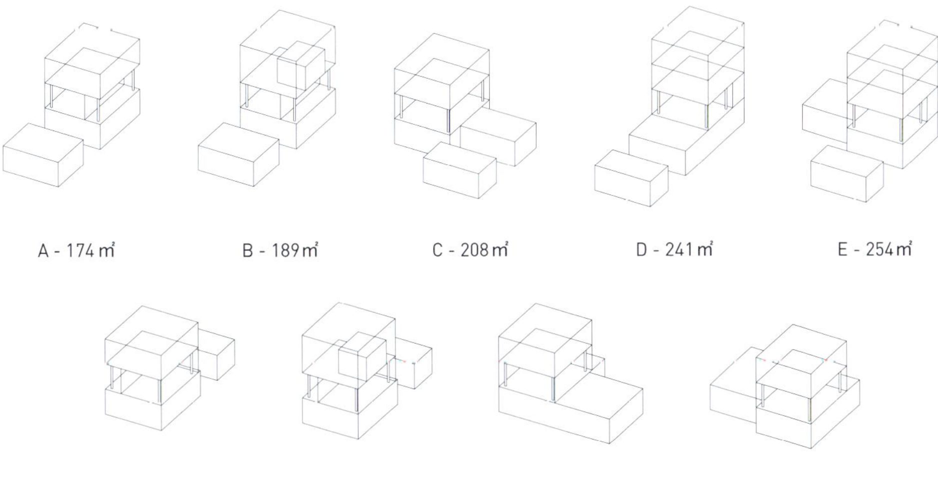

Isometric drawing

Pangyo housing

Mostly with models. We make numerous models for one project, at almost every conceivable scale. We begin, of course, with small-scale models and over time work up to a scale of 1:20 or even 1:10. Models help us to do detail work. We find it easier than using computer graphics. If a project calls for it, we even do 1:1 scale models.

We remember the models and drawings of the "Local Community Area" project you did with students with lots of small units, shops, ramps, etc. Are you still working on that?
I proposed something similar in Tokyo, but it is very difficult to realize.

Why do you think it is so hard to realize? If you look at traditional areas, that is exactly what you see. Your model just gives this pattern a modern shape.
Yes, that's right, but the government does not see that kind of space as a good space. They think they are dangerous spaces in terms of earthquake protection, due to the old, wooden houses. Instead, they propose concrete structures and high-rises.

What responses have you had to your proposals?
Many of my projects have been commended in competitions and the judges have agreed with my proposals, but discussions afterwards with the municipality were

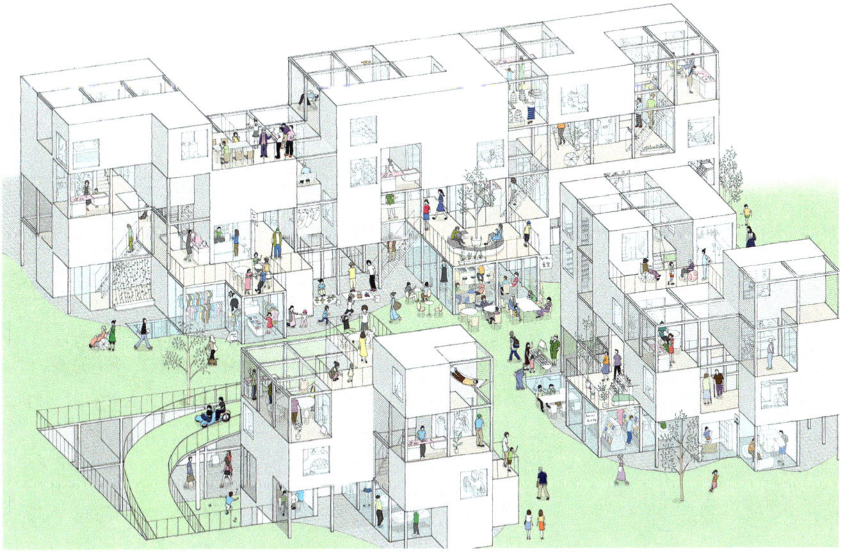

Local Community Area, project, 2012

always a struggle. Right now, we are negotiating about a primary school I designed. Educational bureaucracy is very entrenched, and the authorities prioritize being able to control the students. They would like to see a long gallery where one can monitor the students… like in a jail. My proposal is completely different.

In recent years you have realized several projects outside of Japan—in China and in Korea. Do you think it is easier to bring your ideas to life, even in a reduced way, outside of Japan?
I think so. Presently, it is very difficult to propose new ideas in Japan. Outside of Japan there are fewer hurdles in discussions with clients and governments. Things began to get more difficult around the year 2000, when neo-liberalism came to Japan. The government changed its attitude. Now the prime minister and his ministers are strange people. Very conservative, very right-wing.

You are quite critical of the government.
Yes, I quite often am (*he laughs*).

Does this go back to the time of the student uprising in the 1960s?
I think so, definitely

Local Community Area, model

RIKEN YAMAMOTO

Biography

1945 Born in Beijing, China
1968 Graduated from Department of Architecture, College of Science and Technology, Nihon University, Tokyo
1971 Master of Architecture, Graduate School of Fine Arts, Tokyo National University of Fine Arts and Music
Research Student, Hara Laboratory, Institute of Industrial Science, University of Tokyo
1973 Established Riken Yamamoto & Field Shop
2002–07 Professor, Department of Architecture, Faculty of Engineering, Kogakuin University, Tokyo
2007–11 Professor, Yokohama Graduate School of Architecture
2011 Visiting Professor, School of Engineering Science, Yokohama National University
Specially-appointed Professor, College of Science and Technology, Nihon University, Tokyo

Principal Works

1977 Yamakawa Villa, Nagano
1986 Gazebo House, Kanagawa
1988 Hamlet housing, Tokyo
1991 Hotakubo housing, Kumamoto
1992 House in Okayama, Okayama
1996 Iwadeyama Junior High School, Miyagi
1999 Saitama Prefectural University, Saitama
2000 Future University of Hakodate, Hokkaido
2006 Yokosuka Museum of Art, Kanagawa
2010 Pangyo housing, Seongnam, South Korea
2014 Seoul Gangnam housing, South Korea
2017 The Circle at Zurich Airport, Switzerland, under construction

Publications—Selection

1993 *Theory of Dwelling*, Heibonsha Publishing, Tokyo
1997 *Riken Yamamoto*, Kashima Publishing, Tokyo
2006 *Potential of Architecture: Riken Yamamoto's Imagination*, Okokusha Publishing, Matsudo
2012 *Riken Yamamoto*, TOTO Publishing, Tokyo
2015 *The Space of Power and the Power of Space: Designing Between Personal and State Spaces*, Kodansha, Tokyo

HIROAKI KIMURA

Prefabrication for Individuality

Mr. Kimura, you grew up in Osaka. Did you have any kind of relationship to architecture during your childhood? Why did you decide to study architecture?
I always liked making things, but I had no family background and actually no real reason why I chose architecture. I was 16 years old when I started my education at a college with architectural courses, but it was mostly technical aspects. It took five years to learn the basics about architecture.
What was very influential for me was the Expo '70 in Osaka. I worked at a kiosk at the Expo Station, so I was often in the exhibition. Initially, I didn't know Archigram, but when I saw the capsules in Tange's big roof, I was very impressed and quite fascinated. You know the "Tower of the Sun" by Taro Okamoto? Inside it showed the history of mankind, beginning at the base of the tower, a spiral escalator ascended within it. There were also escalators in the arms of the tower figure and at the end you could see the capsules of Archigram and the others.

What did you do after you graduated in 1973?
After graduation, I worked in a local architectural office. I had hoped that they would teach me, but it was just work. At the age of 24 I travelled around Europe. After four months, I returned to Japan to continue work but soon realized that I wasn't learning anything and that I wanted to study again. I looked at books and magazines of *Japan Architect* and I very much wanted to become an architect. So I joined the Mackintosh School of Architecture in Glasgow.

Why did you decide to travel and study in Europe, and not, for example, in the United States, China or India?
I never thought about going to India or China. At that time, it was out of the question. America was a possibility but it is a very large and expansive country, so the structure of the cities is very different to that of Japan. I had travelled in Europe and understood how in Europe the scale of the cities is more comparable to those in Japan, as there is also a very old tradition.

Why did you choose to go to the Mackintosh School of Architecture in Scotland?
I wrote letters to the Architectural Association, to London Polytechnic and to Glasgow, describing my motivation and ideas for studying abroad. The letters from London came back with an application form. But the letter from Glasgow came back with the application form and a personal letter with kind words and not just the formal application. So I decided to study there.

Who were your teachers in Glasgow and what did you study?

One of them was Antony G. Vogt. At that time, I was already an architect in Japan because of my work experience after graduation from technical college. So in Glasgow they said that as a professional I should start the master course, which was more about research and not about designing. Tony asked me, "What are you going to do?" In the beginning, I meant to do some research on Charles Rennie Mackintosh and after that I wanted to do some drawing and design work. Tony thought I should study Mackintosh and that was the beginning of my Ph.D.

So you didn't officially learn how to design?

Not while doing my research, but I had discussions with other students about design and together we thought about architecture. I also came to a clearer understanding of Japan because I was able to consider it from afar. I had a lot of friends in Japan and we influenced each other, but abroad I had to think about things on my own and learned to look at things differently. Before I went abroad, I thought that Japan and Europe were different in their points of view. Of course they were, and still are, but not when it comes to decisions about the quality of architecture.

Before going abroad, I couldn't decide what was good or bad—I think every student faces that problem. But from talking to others I realized that my ideas weren't bad at all. That gave me the confidence to do my own work when I returned to Japan.

Steel Truss, Nara, 2009

After you came back from Europe, you started your office in 1983. At that time, in the 1970s and early 80s, it was an interesting period in the development of architecture in Japan. What were your particular interests?
In the 1970s there was a change in Japanese architecture. A new generation of architects was emerging in the wake of modernist architects like Kunio Maekawa, Kenzo Tange or Kiyonori Kikutake. These included Toyo Ito, Osamu Ishiyama, Monta Mozuna and also Tadao Ando, who were all quite well known in Japan. At that time, they were around 40 years old and I was about 30. So, I was able to observe their architectural approach.

What did you think about the very different approaches of Ito, Mozuna, Ando or Ishiyama?
In 1970, people were reexamining what architecture really was. Before, modernism had changed and by 1970 it was mostly gone. Ito, Ishiyama and Mozuna, thought about the basics of architecture: Ito, for instance, said that architecture is like a human body—a thin surface, the skin, separates inside from outside. Ishiyama said that true architecture arises without architects—just like a nest. Architecture is something original made essentially to satisfy basic emotional and functional needs using things and materials at hand. Mozuna thought more about the cosmos, about the mental connection, and was more mystical, spiritual. He thinks that the origin and basis of architecture has to do with mysticism. And Ando had started working in the Kansai area. We knew Ando's work very well. He was always making simple concrete buildings—and this soon became a fashion.

It was also the time of postmodernism and deconstructivism. Were you interested in that?
At that time, or maybe some time later, Frank O. Gehry's buildings and Bernard Tschumi's deconstructivist projects were starting to become more well-known. My generation looked more at Gehry and Tschumi, not so much at "classical postmodernism" but at deconstructivism.

So at that time you were interested in Ishiyama and Ito, and in Tschumi and deconstructivism. What was it about them that interested you?
It was the freedom! As a student, our education was all about modernism. Everything was about order; everything was perfect. But postmodernism as well as deconstructivism was different. Compared with modernism, it was more like junk. A front is a front and a back is just a back. If you make a timber building, why not make it look like concrete? I think it is about freedom. It freed up architecture to be many things. This open mindset was important for us: anything goes! This was my starting point when I came back from England and started my office in 1983.

But after the early 1990s your architecture changed.
In the beginning, I used many materials, not just steel or concrete. I found some materials in the city, like billboards—or even cheaper materials than that—and also more temporary materials. In European cities, buildings are built to last. In Japan, it is different. After 30 years or so, the buildings are gone. The urban landscape is always changing. Initially, that informed my ideas on architecture. Over time I changed and my architecture became more stable and not so temporary.

Docomo Shop Hikone, Shiga, 2007

During this time, in Japanese architecture as well, the influence of deconstructivism began to wane and buildings became more subdued. Why do you think this occurred?
The times grew more conservative. I became more conservative and more interested in the essence of architecture. In the early days, I used very thin metal sheets, maybe 2.6 millimeters thick, which is cheap and can be bent easily, but later I used 9-millimeter sheet steel, which was not easy to bend but very stable. Architecture became calmer through the way it was constructed with stronger materials.

Let's talk about one of your projects. Your teahouse is a good example of how you dealt with this kind of steel structure.
The teahouse could be produced anywhere; it is easy to make and almost a kind of product. It is made out of a single sheet, doesn't have columns, and is just two *tatami* mats large. It came in two parts and was welded together on site. It looks wide but, on the other hand, it is also small. The highest point is just 170 centimeters, although it looks bigger.

In the teahouse you also deal with the history of Japanese architecture. When did you become interested in historic Japanese architecture?
When I was 30, I was not so interested in historical Japanese architecture, roof shapes or Japanese culture, only as I grew older, maybe 40. We are lucky: compared to architects in Tokyo, we are very close to Kyoto and Nara and we can always see old buildings and visit gardens. You can feel the atmosphere and also the sense of scale. Gradually, I became more interested in traditional architecture. Before then, I looked more to Western architecture.

Steel sheet teahouse and farmhouse, Osaka, 2004

I also became interested in Togo Murano, an architect who dealt with modern and historical Japanese architecture from the 1930s. He built quite a lot in Osaka and in the Kansai area. I studied books on Murano quite often, tracing the height or the scale, learning from his drawings, and this fed back into the design of my buildings too.

What was the design process for the teahouse?
Before designing any house, I go to the site. Before that, I don't think about it, so my first ideas start to develop only after my first visit to the site. With the teahouse it was very much about the location. I looked at the garden and wondered how I could open the teahouse as much as possible to the garden. Initially, it was about how to make a tearoom and about the site, then questions of openness and closure became important.

How was the design of the tea house related to the tea ceremony?
In the beginning, I didn't know much about the tea ceremony. I began by placing the building at the outer corner of the grounds. The area behind the site is not very pleasant, so I placed the house as a screen to block the sight. The windows face onto the garden, so the back of the site is completely out of sight—from the house

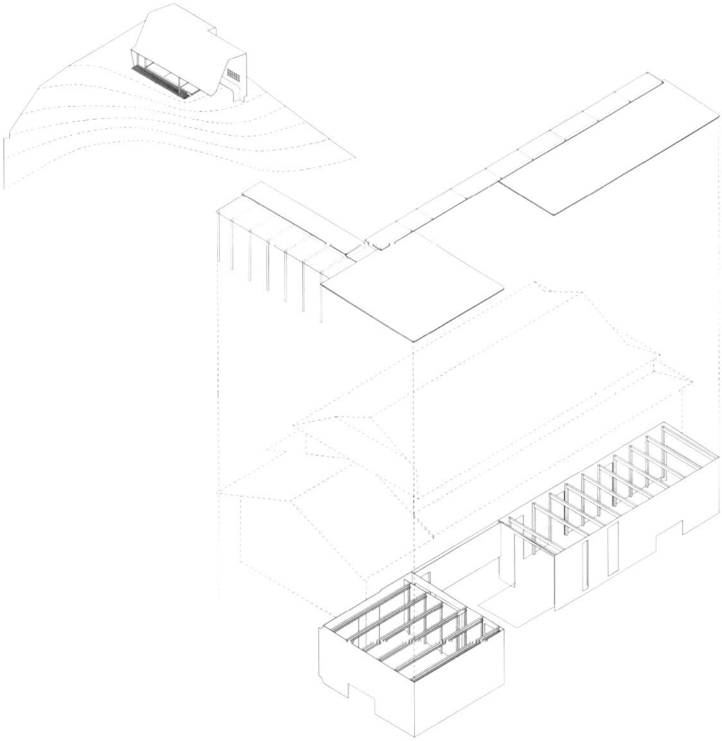

Exploded view

as well as from the teahouse. There is a small entrance and another door. And there is a waiting space. Normally, guests have to wait until being called by the tea master before being allowed to enter. And you don't use the normal door, but the small door to enter. When you drink tea, the window is closed, and you do not talk. After drinking, the window is opened and you talk and laugh and relax. The atmosphere of the space changes with the different parts of the ceremony.

How do your houses and architecture relate to historical Japanese architecture?
In Japan, there are very good craftsmen for every material. It is interesting to talk to them and learn from them.
The atmosphere of some buildings also relates to Japanese culture—they are finer and have certain details. When I plan a house, I rarely use *shoji* and timberwork, but I do use sliding doors. Also, I understand the relationship between outside and inside—how to use it and define the boundaries between inside and outside.
In some buildings, I have used a cantilever to define a space beneath it as something between outside and inside. Like an *engawa*, it creates an individual space between outside and inside but in a more Western way. The purpose is the same but it comes from a mix of influences.

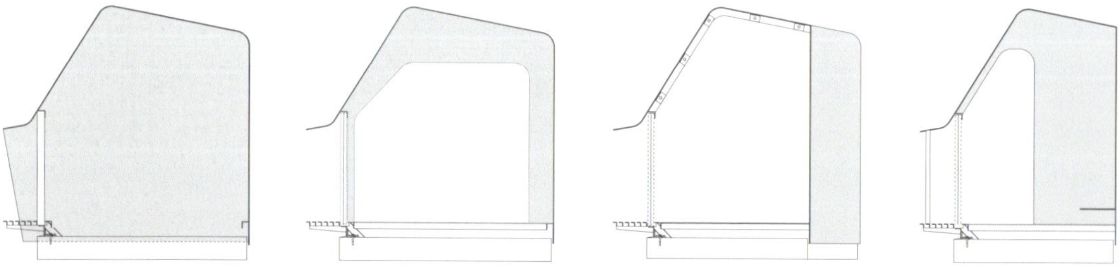

Steel sheet teahouse, sections

Tower House, Shiga, 2006

I assume you work with models and sketches?
Of course. I make drawings and also three-dimensional renderings, but these are just in our minds, not in reality, so I also make models. Nevertheless, I always check on site during construction, in case changes still need to be made.

You change the design during the construction?
Yes, sometimes. Of course, I do not destroy things that are already finished, but during construction I am on site, watching and changing before the next stage, if necessary. The scale 1:1 is simply the best we have. For example, if I think a window is too small, I make it larger. The teahouse is very small, so I could control everything.

Can you tell us about the development of your steel sheet houses? You could use steel the "normal" way with columns and beams, but instead you use it as sheet. Why is that?
In the beginning, I was more interested in steel as a structure with a thin metal skin around it. In the Kansai area, the material is important. In Tokyo, people are more

interested in the concept. I think that in Kyoto and Osaka, people are more interested in material and less willing to accept cheap buildings. I tried to thicken the steel, to make it more substantial, so that it cannot be bent or perforated easily. The quality is better if you use thicker steel as a skin for a building. In the beginning I used 2.6-millimeter-thick aluminum; now I use 9-millimeter steel and that works well as a monocoque structure.

Traditionally, architecture was constructed of columns and beams. In industrial times, with the building of ships and cars, a new system using monocoques was introduced. Why not use that for architecture as well? Okay, architecture is larger, but the technique has improved and it is much easier to implement today.

I think that in future, the use of steel will increase still further. Progress is being made in all aspects. Even paints are getting better; cars don't rust anymore.

What do you think about prefabrication, standardization and individuality?

Metal, of course, has to be fabricated in the factory, not on the building site, so it is to some degree a prefabricated product. Since you have to transport it to the site, it cannot exceed the maximum size you can load onto a truck. You have to think about the individual sections and the way they are connected. In this sense the prefabrication idea is very important. But architecture must always be individual and belong to the site. So, although I am using prefabrication, I am using it to make unique buildings.

If you look at Mackintosh's buildings, they are completely individual and he designed almost everything from the architecture to the interiors and the furniture. I think architects should work like this—creating something unique for each site, each building.

What influence did your own studies of Mackintosh and the Arts and Crafts movement have on the way you design?

In the Arts and Crafts movement, everything had to be individual. Nowadays, everything is made in a factory. Windows are delivered ready-made to the site. Who made them? We don't know! But Mackintosh or later Aalto designed everything themselves. Everything they did was individual—including the furniture and the light-fixtures. That is what made it a Mackintosh or an Aalto building. The unique feeling of the space—what makes it an "Aalto-" or "Mackintosh-space"—is because of that. Nowadays, architects often forget that. Everything is ready-made and just assembled and has little individual feeling. Using ready-made elements may give a building or interior a sense of our times—of being contemporary—but it is not the same as an architectural concept.

So you think all things should be handcrafted?

I'm not saying that everything has to be handcrafted, but that the building should be individual. You can use ready-made elements, but there should be architecture involved to make it individual, to create a quality of space. The more factory-made elements are used, the more impersonal it becomes. The idea is not necessarily to make it in a Mackintosh way—to handcraft everything individually—which is not feasible anymore, but I try to get as close as possible.

Did you use any ready-made elements for the teahouse?

No, everything was individually designed just for the house.

Kyoto Institute of Technology 60th Anniversary Hall, Kyoto, 2010

So this project does come close to your Mackintosh ideal!
Yes, exactly.

Let's talk about the different ages and different mutual influences. Mackintosh was influenced by Japan and there were European influences in Japan as well. How would you say it is today?
Nowadays, through the internet, it seems like we look at things at the same time. No one special region has a singular influence, because information comes from all over the world more or less simultaneously. Everyone is watching interesting architectural developments all the time and it is hard to trace influences, because there are so many of them! We are closer nowadays. Back in the 19th century, it was completely different: they wanted to know about each other and influenced each other more strongly than today.

So, although we have more possibilities today, you think the mutual influences are not as strong as they were in the 19th century?
Yes, I think back then, a few architects were influenced by each other. Nowadays, we do not so much influence one another as explore together to find out what is interesting. We talk to each other and attempt to jointly elaborate the future of building. It is no longer about influence, but about thinking and working together as a world community because it is now so much easier to talk to each other and to travel.

So what challenges are architects facing today?
When I was 30 years old, I tried to explore and absorb the complexity of the city to create something. This is still what being an architect is about. Society needs architects and ideas. The situation within society pushes architects to create something new.

And how do we judge whether "new" architecture is good architecture?
By trusting one's impression. Go there, look at it, feel the atmosphere and look at the scale, materials and design. After that, you'll be able to make a judgement.

Kobe Shinsei Baptist Church, Kobe, 2005

HIROAKI KIMURA

Biography

1952 Born in Osaka
1973 Graduated from Department of Architecture, Osaka Technical College
1979 Mackintosh School of Architecture, Glasgow Art School and Glasgow University, United Kingdom
1982 Ph.D., study on Charles Rennie Mackintosh
1983 Established Ks Architects, Osaka
1986 Established Hiroaki Kimura + Ks Architects
1997 Associate Professor, Dept. of Environmental Design, Kobe Design University
2000 Professor, Dept. of Architecture and Environmental Design, Kobe Design University
2006 Professor, Dept. of Architecture & Design, Kyoto Institute of Technology
2015 FRIAS Fellow, The Royal Incorporation of Architects in Scotland

Principal Works

1987 Toki No Fune (Forest building), Osaka
1990 Toki No Meikyu (House of labyrinth), Hyogo
1991 Common City Hoshida community hall, Osaka
1995 3 in 1 House, Hyogo
2000 Ta House, Hyogo
Mo House, Kobe
2004 Steel sheet teahouse and farmhouse, Osaka
2005 Kobe Shinsei Baptist Church, Kobe
2006 Tower House, Shiga
2007 Docomo Shop Hikone, Shiga
2009 Steel Truss, Nara Prefecture
2010 Kyoto Institute of Technology 60th Anniversary Hall, Kyoto
2011 Steel Wall, Kobe
2013 Machiya of Arts & Crafts House, Hyogo
2015 Kyudo club house, Shiga University, Shiga

Publications – Selection

1982 Ph.D. Thesis: *Charles Rennie Mackintosh, Architectural Drawing Catalog & Analytical Design Catalog*, Mackintosh School of Architecture, Glasgow
1986 *Charles Rennie Mackintosh* (Process architecture 50), Tokyo
1992 With others: *New Style of Houses. Charles Rennie Mackintosh*, KBI-Shuppan, Kyoto
1993 With others: *Europe – Beginning and End*, Exhibition catalog, Japan Art Culture Association, Tokyo
1998 *Charles Rennie Mackintosh*, Exhibition catalog, Hida Takayama Museum of Art, Nagano
2002 *Steel Sheet House*, Amus Arts Press, Osaka
The World of Mackintosh, Heibonsha, Tokyo
2007 *Vivid Technology*, Gakugei Shuppansha, Kyoto
2008 With others: *Japan Living*, Tuttle Publishing, Tokyo/Rutland
2009 With others: *Steel Structure Houses in Detail* (The Japan Architect 75), Tokyo

MAKOTO SEI WATANABE

Natural life and science fiction

Mr. Watanabe, you were born in Yokohama and you began your architectural studies there. Why did you decide to study architecture?

When I decided to go to university, I had two choices: to become an architect or to become a biologist. I liked biology very much, but my biology teacher at high school told me that it would not pay enough to live on. That was before ecology became an issue. I was actually more interested in bionics than in biology, but at that time there was no way of studying bionics.

So, because I also liked to draw, I chose to study architecture—which for me is a combination of arts and sciences—in my home town, Yokohama. My interest in biology has, however, continued to the present day and it is probably the main reason why I started Induction Design for computer-generated architecture. It is an attempt to identify essential algorithms in nature and to transfer them to the computer to achieve better designs.

Who were your teachers at the university in Yokohama?

In those days the architects at the university were not so famous. One person, Koichi Nagashima, did make an impression on me. He had returned from Harvard to Japan and went on to become the chief of Fumihiko Maki's office. He brought a fresh perspective to our studies.

Whenever I finished design projects that I felt were very good, some of the more conservative professors were not amused: "That isn't architecture," they said. Nagashima on the other hand said, "That's excellent and great." He encouraged me and that was very important. Now, as a professor myself, I try to discover the hidden talent in my students and encourage them to develop that.

Was there a focus on design at your university?

There was little focus on design in Japanese architectural studies in those days. There were lots of teachers for other aspects such as research, theory, structural engineering, planning and so on. In Yokohama, for example, there was a large number of professors for structural engineering, because the architecture department belonged to the faculty of technology. In Japan, many architecture faculties have their roots in engineering and few faculties come from an arts background. One positive effect of this is that Japanese architects have both design skills and a good knowledge of structures. That may be one reason for the good reputation of Japanese architects.

Which architect or architecture interested you most when you studied? What was your inspiration?

I was fascinated by Arata Isozaki because he seemed to be an outsider and innovator in the architectural field. I liked his early work, which was why I joined his office after my studies. Later he became mainstream. But when I was a student, he sought new ways of creating architecture, bringing it closer to art or films, novels or manifestos. That echoed my sentiments about architecture, which I thought should be seen from many different aspects.

Did you work in Arata Isozaki's office immediately after graduating or was there a break in-between?
Before I graduated, the Japanese economy was prosperous, but in 1976 the oil crisis hit Japan. Just as I finished my master's course, the major architectural firms stopped hiring new staff. I went to Isozaki's office and met him but he said: "I can't hire anyone. Look at the office—the entire staff is reading books." So I went to work in another architect's office, one of the Metabolists, Masato Otaka. I worked there for three years but I couldn't forget Isozaki, so I sent him a letter with sketches I had drawn over those three years. My package came back almost immediately and I thought that was it: he wasn't going to hire me. But when I opened it, I found a letter inviting me to come to his office. And that's how I started working for Isozaki. He had just got his first big commission for the "Tsukuba Civic Center," a project that I worked on for five years—from the first designs to the supervising of the construction site, the completion and the publications.

What was the starting point for establishing your own office? Did you have a project—or did you feel you had worked long enough for Isozaki and that it was time to try something new?
For me, the completion of the "Tsukuba Civic Center" was a kind of second graduation. I felt ready to take on projects by myself and by chance I received a commission almost immediately. However, when my office was really up and running, the commission evaporated and I lost my direction. So I shifted to interior design. I designed a club in Aoyama, projects for the Toto company and so on.
Then, one day, I saw the announcement for an international competition for the "Aoyama Technical College" in a magazine. I sat down and developed a design within five days, because the deadline was six days later! In the end it became my first architectural work and the building was completed in 1990.

The "Aoyama Technical College" is quite unique. What were your architectural and historical references? How did the tendencies of the time—postmodernism and deconstructivism—influence you?
I don't think those tendencies influenced me directly, but it is possible, having lived and worked during that period, that I was affected subconsciously. As I mentioned before, what I found most inspiring about Isozaki was his way of seeing architecture from different fields.
Concerning historical references, many Japanese architects of my generation—and even those who followed—refer to Le Corbusier. Isozaki has said that older European architecture is a strong foundation of his work, but not for me. Of course, I like ancient European architecture and I respect Le Corbusier's concepts and designs, but I am not so influenced by what one might call regular works of architecture. I am more influenced by nature or clouds, crystals or science fiction.

Iidabashi subway station, Tokyo, 2000

What kind of science fiction?
Recently, I have been particular drawn to the work of Ted Chiang, a Sino-American author. Or Ken Liu, who is also Sino-American. More popular examples are well-known movies like *2001: A Space Odyssey* or *Blade Runner* because they convey iconic images of the future and of the city imagined for that era.

So architecture rarely serves as a basis for your work? What do you think then about the developments in Japanese architecture?
After postmodernism and deconstructivism, minimalism came back in fashion, and now more or less everything exists in parallel. There are different streams—Ito, Sejima, etc. I respect their work, they are different, but they share a common taste for simple forms. They are partially open, but their vocabulary is a bit limited. In general, the spectrum of architectural positions is nevertheless fairly narrow.

Is there a reason for this tendency?
I don't think this is something new. Even if there seems to be diversity, the foundation is narrow. Japan has one kind of common sense or culture. Ito has his roots in this culture, Ando too. Of course their buildings look different in terms of their shape and materials, but in principle, they share the same tendency (of course, they may not agree). Their foundation is the same, derived from the Japanese tradition. This traditional tendency transcends all fashions, trends and "-isms" in design.
If you look at original Japanese wooden architecture such as Shinto shrines (but not temples), their essence is in my view about being simple. Another obvious example

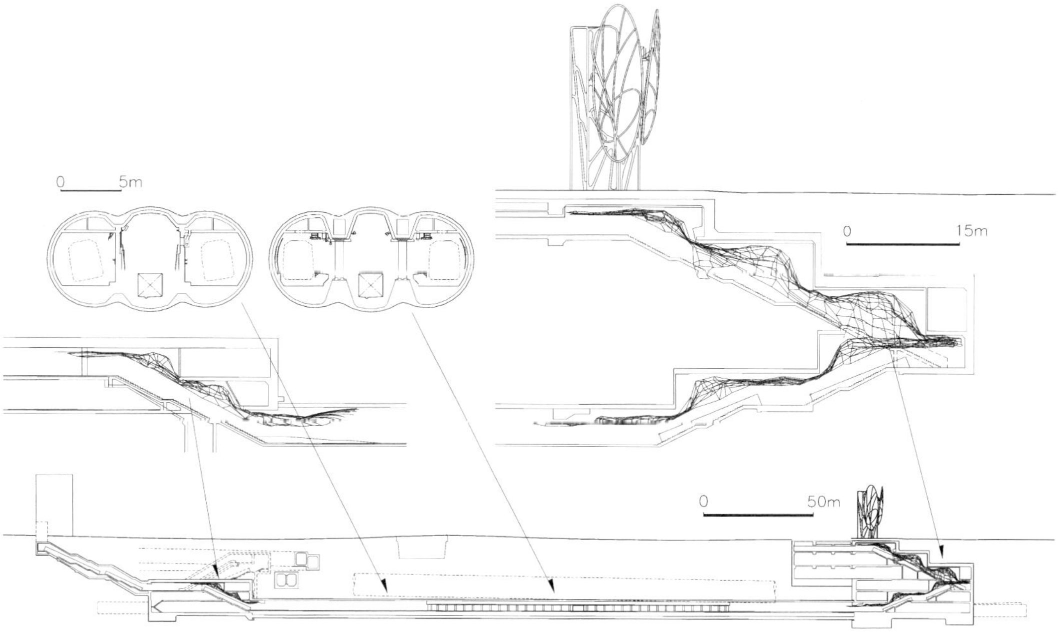

Section

are *hashi:* chopsticks. A knife and fork have different shapes that correspond to their different functions. Japanese people, of course, are familiar with these utensils but rarely use them at home. They love using a pair of simple straight bars for almost all purposes. A knife is, of course, better for cutting meat than *hashi*. But still, Japanese prefer to use *hashi*—but why? One reason may be that Japanese Wagyu beef is very tender.

But the actual reason is that Japanese people don't like using a sword or a spear at the table. *Hashi* are functional and purpose oriented, wild and not elegant. Japanese people prefer abstract objects that need not be explicitly functional. Instead of demanding a tool to serve a singular purpose, they prefer to require themselves to have the skills to manipulate tools that can be made to serve several purposes. Simplicity is still the foundation of Japanese culture. On the surface, it may seem diverse and widespread, but the underlying basis is very simple.

When you designed "Aoyama Technical College," was it intended to oppose this kind of simplicity in Japanese tradition? Was it a provocation?

Yes, it was a statement against mainstream trends. I didn't want to walk with the crowd. I do not want to be part of one of those periodic waves that wash over and then pass away. That is my personal criticism. As I mentioned before, embracing simplicity is one aspect of Japanese character. At the same time, the Japanese also have a contrasting character. We can see it in Japanese cities: many cities in Japan look quite chaotic, but they still work well—i.e. are safe, clean, and functional—and they are lively and exciting. They are not arranged according to some overarching plan, but organized by many small individual relationships. I want to make this

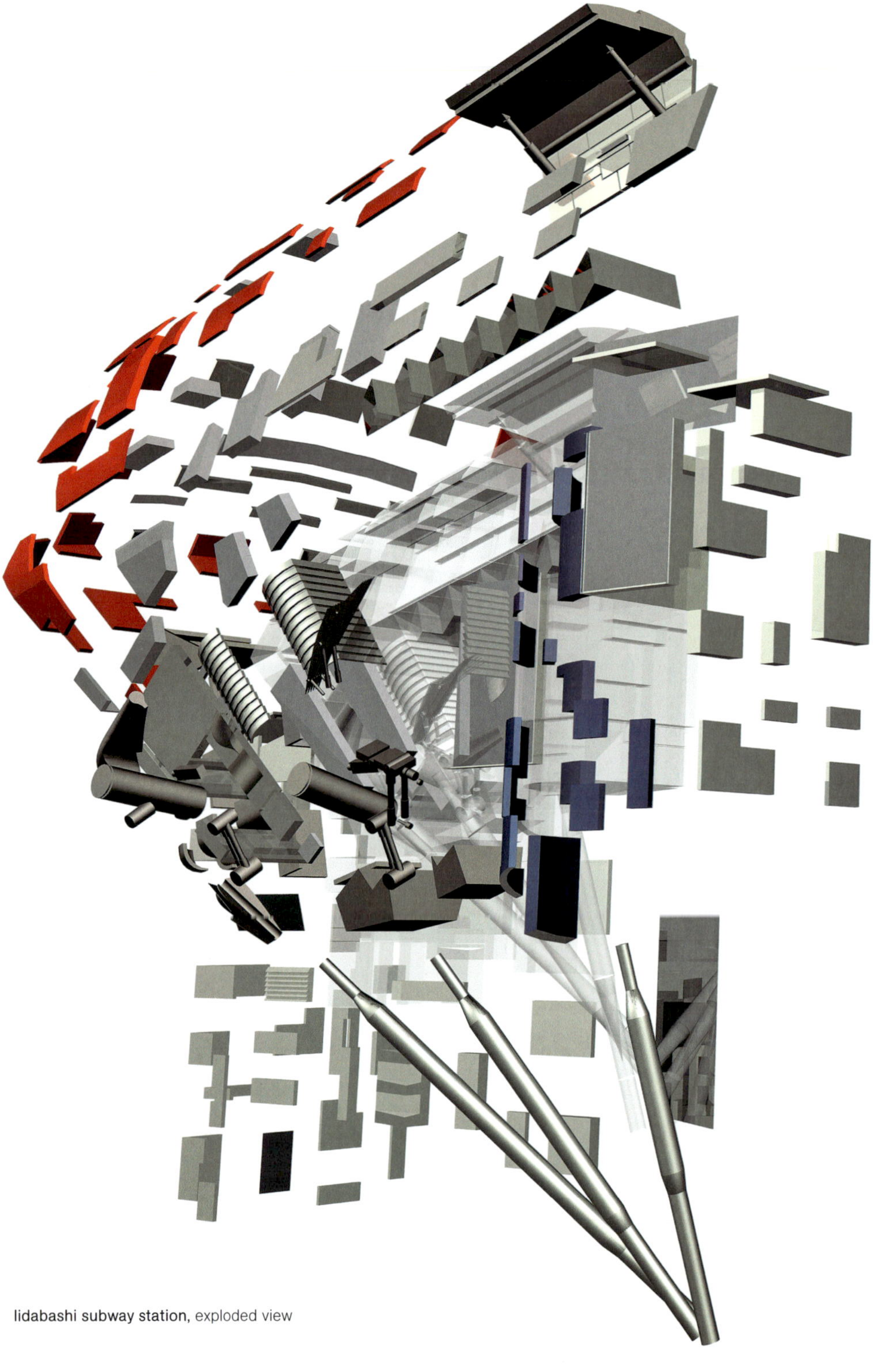

Iidabashi subway station, exploded view

Aoyama Technical College, Tokyo, 1990

Aoyama Technical College

approach possible for use in design. "Aoyama Technical College" was the first experimental manifestation of this idea in an analog form.
I then started to identify these algorithms in cities and nature and to translate them into computer programs. That is what led to Induction Design and Algorithmic Design.

Why did you win the competition for the "Aoyama Technical College?" Who was in the jury?
The jury comprised Riken Yamamoto, one other architect, the owner of the building and another person. I think Riken Yamamoto pushed my proposal, as did the owner who liked Japanese science fiction movies and obviously responded to that.

So you were quite fortunate to win. Did you know that the owner was a fan of science fiction?
No, I wasn't aware of that at the time. I don't usually have that kind of strategy for a competition but do what I like. It was similar with the competition for Iidabashi subway station. Again, I didn't think about the jury, I just designed what I felt would be right, and they chose me.

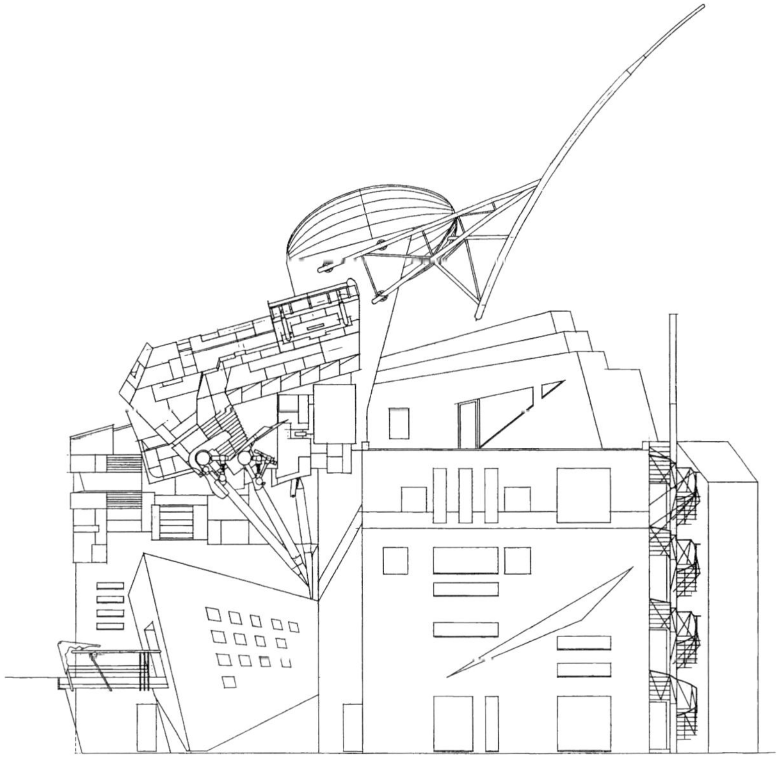

Elevation

Did you consciously decide not to build too much? Was it a deliberate decision not to have a really big office?
I like doing everything myself, so I don't want to organize a big office. I prefer to concentrate on my work and, if possible, be involved in everything myself: the basic concept, site supervising, every detail and so on. It is possible to take on large projects with a small office if the team spirit is good and cooperative. With some smart footwork, the core team can be very small.

In the 1990s you started experimenting with the potential and possibilities of computer-generated and digital design. You were one of the first architects in Japan to use the computer not just as a technical instrument, but to actually explore its capabilities for design.
I devised the first program to generate architecture more than 20 years ago in 1994 and called it Induction Design. At that time some architects used computers, but only as an extension of their hand. I wanted to use the computer as a brain. The human brain is splendid, but it can't handle lots of complex conditions concurrently. If three people talk to you at the same time, you will not be able to understand all of them at once. For computers that's easy.

K-Museum, Tokyo, 1996

With design it's similar. When designing you need to consider lots of demands and conditions. Our brains are not able to manage them all at once, so we simplify the conditions to make them manageable. This simplification can lead to important possibilities being excluded with the result that they have no impact on the solution. On the other hand, of course, a computer can't dream.
Brains and computers have different strengths and weaknesses, but by combining the two we can achieve better solutions and better designs that are neither restricted by simplification nor in their freedom of expression and individual diversity. That is how I intend to refine Algorithmic Design.

The computer can generate forms that comply with all of those input parameters. But what about scale or materiality? Can computers take these into account and what are the limits of designing using computers?
You can think of it like self-driving vehicles. If your aim is to travel from your home to your office, your need is to reach the destination quickly and safely. You're not concerned with the experience of driving to work. In such cases, you can click the autopilot button and sleep for a while.
But if your purpose is not to reach a particular destination but to enjoy the sensation of driving a car, it is better to switch off autopilot.
When to use a computer program and when to use our own free will depends on the respective aim. The intention of Algorithmic Design is not to make an automatic designer, but to extend the possibilities of design. Algorithmic Design can be

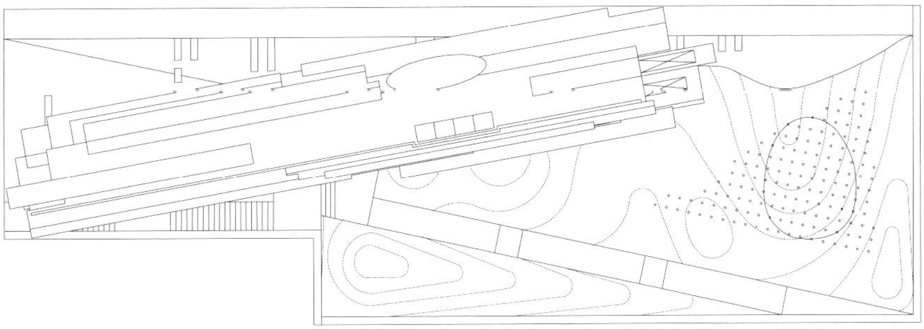

Site plan

called "AI," by which I mean not only Artificial Intelligence but also Architectural Intelligence.

Who designs how the computers run? Do you do that yourself or do you work with specialists?

Originally, I wrote the programs myself, but it has become so complicated that I now cooperate with a professional programmer, so it is a cooperative venture.

Let us turn to the Japanese architectural scene. How much exchange do you think goes on in the profession? Do you communicate with colleagues and exchange opinions?

When I was younger we took part in conferences and exhibitions together. We were of the same generation, the same age, and we talked a lot and cooperated occasionally. Since then, we have spread out and are all independent now.

How do you see the current architectural situation in Japan? Is there still room for experimentation?

For many years, the Japanese government's public architecture programs or civil engineering projects were a great way of fostering good architecture. State taxes were used for public projects and that was a good way for architects in Japan to obtain commissions. Of course, most commissions went to large firms and very few went to smaller architects' offices. Since the decline in the GNP growth rate, the government has changed its ways. Public spending has been cut, but even so Japan

Shin-Minamata station, Minamata, 2004

realizes many more public buildings than the United States, for example, and this has an impact on young architects. Young architects have fewer chances to gain public commissions than we did in the 1980s and 90s, but on the other hand, many local governments now know the power of good design. While state-initiated competitions are still comparatively rare and young architects are finding it hard to come by public projects, there has been slow but steady growth in the use of such mechanisms. That suggests there is hope for the future.

MAKOTO SEI WATANABE

Biography

1952 Born in Yokohama
1976 Master of Architecture, Yokohama National University
1976–79 Employee at Masato Otaka
1979–84 Employee at Arata Isozaki & Associates
1984 Established Makoto Sei Watanabe / Architects' Office, Tokyo
1988–97 Lecturer, Graduate School, Yokohama National University
1994–95 Lecturer, Kyoto Seika University
1997–2005 Lecturer, Tokyo Denki University
2005–10 Professor, Tamkang University, Taiwan
2013 Professor, Space-Generating Lab, Faculty of Urban Life Studies, Tokyo City University

Principal Works

1990 Aoyama Technical College, Tokyo
1995 Mura-No-Terrace, Gifu
1996 K-Museum, Tokyo
2000 Installation Fiber Wave, Venice Biennale, 7th International Architecture Exhibition, Venice, Italy
Iidabashi station, Tokyo
2004 Shin-Minamata station, Minamata
Shanghai House, Shanghai, China
2005 Kashiwanoha-campus station, Tsukuba
Kashiwa-Tanaka station, Kashiwa
Tokyo House, Tokyo
Ribbon, exhibition "Chikaku – Time and Memory in Japan," Graz, Austria
2009 Ribbon, Outdoor Theater, Taichung, Taiwan
2011 Web Frame-II, Tokyo

Publications—Selection

1998 *Conceiving the City*, L'Arca Edizioni, Milano
2002 *Induction Design: A Method for Evolutionary Design*, Birkhäuser, Basel
2007 *Makoto Sei Watanabe*, Edilstampa, Rome
2009 *Algorithmic Design*, Kajima Institute Publishing, Tokyo
2012 *ALGODeX: ALGOrithmicDesign Execution and Logic*, Maruzen Shuppan, Tokyo

JUN AOKI

A dematerialized feeling

Mr. Aoki, how did you decide to become an architect?
I had always imagined becoming an architect but it was just one option. When I was a child, I liked to draw plans of houses in a very traditional Japanese style, not creative at all. Later, when I was a senior high school student, I came across a picture of Gaudí's architecture in the school library and was quite stunned by how impressive it was. Architecture, I thought, is very interesting, because we can create the world.
I had three options in mind: to become a film director, a novelist or an architect. But as I had no idea how to become a film director or how to become a novelist, I decided to become an architect. That was very simple: I could go to a school of architecture. So I embarked on an engineering course at Tokyo University and after two years was able to choose a specialization. That was when I began to study architecture, and I found it very interesting to design and wished to keep on designing.

Can you tell us something about your experience at university and which teachers were important to you?
My first professor was Yoshinobu Ashihara, and one year later Fumihiko Maki also joined the university. I should also mention Hisao Koyama and visiting professors such as Arata Isozaki and Kazuo Shinohara. I was very influenced by all of them.
I was also interested in foreign architecture. The first architecture magazine I purchased at the university was a special issue of *Space Design*, published in 1978, on European formalism and contextualism, featuring Oswald Mathias Ungers, Rem Koolhaas, Leon Krier and Joseph Paul Kleihues. I remember reading this magazine over and over again, as well as the following issue, which was mostly about Aldo Rossi.

The positions of those architects were quite different to what Maki or Shinohara did at that time. Do you think that there was any link?
Maki's work is very different to formalism or contextualism; indeed, he is very much a modernist. But Shinohara's starting point was pure geometry. In my view, there is not so much distance between his work and that of Ungers or Rossi. I see some relationships between Rossi and Shinohara. For Rossi, memory is very important, while Shinohara pays no attention to memory. But the form and order behind architecture are important to both of them.

In the 1980s and early 90s, a lot of architects from abroad came to Japan—Aldo Rossi, David Chipperfield or Philippe Starck for instance. What effect did that have on the architectural scene in Japan?

Fukushima Lagoon Museum, Niigata, 1997

I remember that Michael Graves also came to Japan and built some buildings as well as Aldo Rossi. But their architecture was not so important for Japan. Postmodernism had a quite limited lifespan in Japan. After the "Tsukuba Civic Center" even Arata Isozaki abandoned the postmodern style.

You worked in Arata Isozaki's office after your studies. Why did you decide to join his office?

When I finished my university studies, I had two options. one was to go abroad to England to work with James Stirling, the other option was to go to Arata Isozaki. In the end I entered Isozaki's office. At that time he was designing the "Tsukuba Civic Center" in a postmodern style, but I was not involved in this project. The project I worked on most in his office was an entry for the Tokyo City Hall competition, which was eventually won by Kenzo Tange. The other project was the "Mito Art Tower," which I was in charge of for four years. After that, I needed a change and decided to go abroad. I went to Istanbul and lived there for several months. I found it very interesting because Istanbul is neither West nor East but an amalgam. But when the Gulf War started, I came back to Japan and founded my own office in 1991.

How did you start your office? How did you get your first big break?

Typically, the first project a young architect does is a housing project for relatives. Since I had experience of working on bigger and more complex buildings in Isozaki's office, I was asked by the mayor of the small city of Niigata to design two public buildings: a swimming pool and a museum. At the same time I also designed the "Mamihara Bridge" in Kumamoto. Arata Isozaki was the commissioner and he

Aomori Museum of Art, Aomori, 2006

selected the architects for the projects of "Kumamoto Artpolis." This project was special in that the time span for the design work was very short: I was asked to design the bridge in February and had to finish in March. The design was over in one month and it became my first realized project.

When you look back over your work from 1991 until now: which are good examples of your way of designing?

The early projects—the bridge and the museum in Niigata—are very important to me, because at that time I concentrated on developing architecture from the circulation spaces. For example, the bridge is just a circulation space, it is one road that splits into two and comes together on the other river bank. The museum is based on the idea of a spiral: you ascend in spiral galleries and come back down via a spiral staircase. In Japanese cities, there are no *piazzas*. Everything happens on the road—that was my reference and the spiral refers to this sense of movement. After completing the building, I felt that the experience and sequence was very interesting, but also that the configuration compels you to move in a certain way. From then on, I wanted to create spaces that are freer, that do not anticipate people's activity but encourage people to follow their own impulses and ways of using the space.

My most important work to date is the "Aomori Museum of Art." It is located at an archaeological site and my idea was to dig into the earth and make a grid of trenches. The structure of the museum galleries hovers above this artificial land scape. The bottom of this floating structure and the surface of the artificial landscape vary creating positive and negative interstitial spaces between them. These spaces are more site-specific and white cube spaces more art-specific. Visitors experience the earth-bound galleries and the white cube spaces a bit like a chessboard. What is figure and what is ground alternates: sometimes it's the white areas, sometimes the black areas.

Your projects in Niigata and Aomori follow quite different design strategies. When you start a project, how do you find a certain strategy? How do you deal with the requirements and how do you develop your own concept?

We begin, of course, with a study to find out how we can organize every requirement, but the most important aspect for the design is the key idea. The Aomori Prefecture, for instance, wanted to have a museum on the location of an archaeological site. My primary concern was: how can this museum be related to the archaeological site? We developed one diagram that covered all the requirements and it became the primary concept around which we organized the form.

Aomori Museum of Art

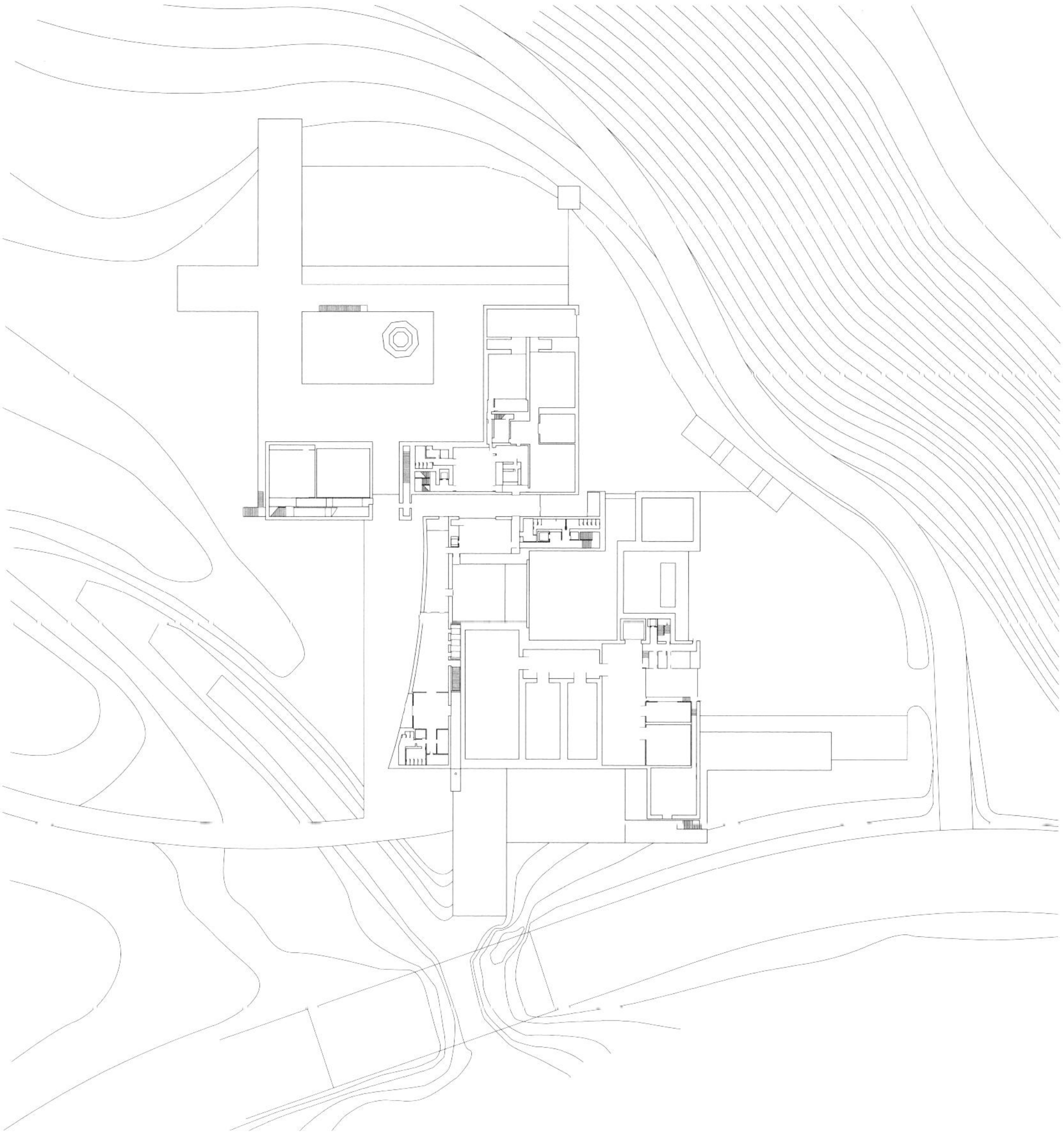

Ground floor

Louis Vuitton Matsuya Ginza Store, Tokyo, 2013

Your projects for Louis Vuitton are different from the buildings you have mentioned up to now. Here you focus on the surface, on ornament, on cladding. What is the potential of the façade? Can you explain your major concern?
When we design for fashion brands, the internal composition of the building is less important because they re-arrange the internal space every four years. The internal space needs to be flexible. The shop is very much like a box, and that frees us up to just work on the surface. How can we design this box to be a work of architecture? This was the challenge we faced when designing for a fashion brand the first time. My first project for Louis Vuitton was in Nagoya. I wanted to create a building with the quality of aerogel—a material that is almost made of air. The box should be like a volume of air, different to the ordinary spaces around it. I found a way to achieve this quality by overlaying two patterns to create a *moiré*-effect. That was my first approach to making architecture by concentrating just on the surface of a building.

So for you the surface of a building is not just a wall or boundary but also has depth. Why did you decide to try and give an otherwise flat surface this idea of depth?
Japan can be very humid sometimes, and fog and mist are very common. If you look at the mountains, you can feel their silhouette but not see their details and the trees. It is a blurry feeling and it is this that influenced my idea of the design and dealing with depth and layers.
Once you have a certain depth, you can play with the layers. One layer is merely ornament. Two layers allow you to create a more complex sensation. This is why I

Louis Vuitton Nagoya Store, Nagoya, 1999

often design with two layers. With one layer, you know exactly what material it is—you feel the materiality of just one layer of glass. But if I use glass, I don't want you to feel that it is glass. My goal is to dematerialize it, to create a feeling of depth that cannot be achieved with just one layer.

By way of example: if a person's make-up is done well, you are not aware of the cosmetics of the make-up, you see just the face. The cosmetic treatment brings out the quality of the underlying face, or in our case of the "internal space"—this is the function of the surface or of the ornament. Ornament serves to express the internal space within. If you can feel that the façade is made of glass, then it is not successful. But if you sense its depth, if you can see the world within, then it is successful.

To date you have built nine buildings for Louis Vuitton and every building has a different surface. Are these responses to the respective site or did this come about because you are interested in experimenting with different expressions for the façade?

It's primarily because the sites are different. When I design, I want to relate the building to the city. Diversity is also very important for Louis Vuitton to attract travellers—if every store looked the same, there would be no need to visit another store.

Your design for the "White Chapel," a room connected to a hotel that can be rented for wedding ceremonies, has certain similarities to your Louis Vuitton projects.

White Chapel, Osaka, 2006

The starting point of the idea was to make a space out of air that is different to the air around it. Here too, my wish was to design a building that evokes a similar feeling to that of aerogel, but developed in a more architectural way. The intention was to create a building of "solid air," which we achieved by constructing a very porous three-dimensional structure made out of steel rings. The connected rings generate a truss-like structure. The entire "White Chapel" is a truss structure and the circles are therefore not ornament, but structure.

Is there a semantic dimension to the rings? They resemble engagement or wedding rings. Surely this was not by chance.
When I proposed this idea for the chapel, the director of the hotel was most pleased because they evoke associations with the notion of infinity or of engagement rings. The idea itself, however, arose outside of this project. I have used the same structure or ornament in other projects without these specific associated meanings.

There are many definitions of ornament. What is an ornament for you?
In the case of the wedding chapel, one could say that the building is both structure and ornament. An ornament imparts a feeling, mood or atmosphere. If a structure also communicates a feeling of infinity or softness or some other feeling, it also serves an ornamental function. For me, an ornament is a function which materials or elements can also fulfill.

On the one hand, you have worked with ornaments such as paintings of very large flowers in art installations. And on the other, you say that structure can also impart an atmosphere and function as an ornament. Does that mean a very thick concrete wall could also be an ornament?

Yes, concrete can also be an ornament. When we design architecture, we aim to convey a particular atmosphere—we control the characteristics and meanings of the elements of space and with that their ornamental function. The white paint of modernist architecture is, for example, also an ornament as it conveys the meaning and atmosphere of purity and neutrality. Every material can have this kind of ornamental function.

You create both art installations and architectural projects. Is there a difference for you between art and architecture?
Of course! Art and architecture are very different, because architecture has to fulfill functions. But the design of architecture and the making of artwork are similar processes, because in both my primary concern is how to treat the material and create a good composition with the elements. This is, of course, just one part of architecture.

Sometimes, you work together with artists. What gives rise to these collaborations and how do you work together?
I have collaborated with artists on a few projects. I like working with artists because it is stimulating to get to know how other people sense a space or feel the architecture. For the exhibition "The Red and Blue Line" in the Nagoya City Art Museum, a postmodern building by Kisho Kurokawa, I worked together with the artist Hiroshi Sugito. Over a period of almost one year, we discussed how we should grasp the space and transform the architecture. We discussed architecture, we discussed space and we discussed art.

Let's talk about the way your office is organized and how you collaborate with your staff members.

The office comprises myself and eight staff members. The staff members can stay in my studio for four years, like at a university. It depends, of course, on the the project, but usually they stay for four years. Most are very young—almost everybody enters my office just after the university.
With regard to the work process, one person is usually in charge of one project, so if there are eight staff members, we have eight projects. Every project is a collaboration of one staff member and myself. We discuss the design, the solution and idea suitable for the project. My staff make models, which we then discuss together. I encourage them to bring in their own ideas, and often these act as a springboard: they propose an idea, I have another idea which they then take further and so on. We always work with physical models, not computer models.

In the contemporary architectural scene in Japan, do you see much collaboration or exchange between architects of different generations or at least within your generation? Or does everybody work for himself?
There isn't always much time to communicate with one another, especially between architects of the same age. Every time I have the chance to talk, for example, to Kazuyo Sejima, it rarely takes place in Japan, but somewhere else, for example when we give lectures at the same symposiums in Europe or the United States. But discourse with younger architects is always very interesting, because they have different ideas about architecture, and wherever possible I try and visit their realized works and discuss architecture with them.

The Red and Blue Line, with Hiroshi Sugito, Nagoya City Art Museum, Nagoya, 2013

JUN AOKI

Biography

1956 Born in Yokohama
1980 Bachelor of Engineering in Architecture, University of Tokyo
1982 Master of Engineering in Architecture, University of Tokyo
1983–90 Employee at Arata Isozaki & Associates, Tokyo
1991 Established Jun Aoki & Associates, Tokyo

Principal Works

1995 Mamihara Bridge, Kumamoto
1997 Yusuikan, Niigata
Fukushima Lagoon Museum, Niigata
1998 Mitsue Primary School, Nara
1999 Snow Foundation, Niigata
Louis Vuitton Nagoya, Nagoya
2000 Louis Vuitton Matsuya Ginza, Tokyo
C House, Tokyo
2002 Louis Vuitton Omotesando, Tokyo
2003 Louis Vuitton Roppongi Hills, Tokyo
2004 Louis Vuitton New York, New York, United States
Louis Vuitton Ginza Namiki, Tokyo
2005 Louis Vuitton Hong Kong Landmark, Hong Kong
2006 White Chapel, Osaka
Aomori Museum of Art, Aomori
2007 J House, Tokyo
2008 SIA Aoyama Building, Tokyo
2010 Maison AoAo, Tokyo
2011 Louis Vuitton Fukuoka Tenjin, Fukuoka
2012 L'Avenue Shanghai, Shanghai, China
2013 Louis Vuitton Matsuya Ginza, Tokyo
2014 Omiyamae Gymnasium, Tokyo
2015 Miyoshi City Hall "Kiriri", Hiroshima

Publications—Selection

2000 *Jun Aoki 1991–99*, Shokoku-sha, Tokyo
Atmospherics, TOTO Publishers, Tokyo
About Houses: Dialogues with 12 persons, INAX Publication, Tokyo
2004 *Jun Aoki Complete Works 1: 1991–2004*, INAX Publication, Tokyo
Harappa to Yuuenchi, Okoku-sya, Tokyo
2006 *Jun Aoki Complete Works 2: Aomori Museum of Art*, INAX Publication, Tokyo
2008 *Architectural Creation: Peter Märkli and Jun Aoki*, The National Museum of Modern Art, Tokyo
Harappa to Yuuenchi 2, Okoku-sya, Tokyo
2013 *Jun Aoki Notebooks*, Heibonsha, Tokyo
2016 *Jun Aoki Complete Works 3: 2005–2014*, INAX Publication, Tokyo

HIROSHI NAKAO

Giving darkness and depth

Mr. Nakao, why did you decide to study architecture? Was there anything in your childhood that inspired you to become an architect?
When I was a child, I loved football. I played football all day long. I chose to study architecture when I was at high school. At that time, I saw some beautiful buildings: the Hillside Terrace Buildings by Fumihiko Maki and the bank in Fukuoka by Kisho Kurokawa. I was inspired by Maki and Kurokawa. This is top secret, but Kurokawa's bank is very beautiful.

You studied architecture at Kyoto Institute of Technology and continued your studies at the Institute of Art at the University of Tsukuba. Why did you decide to study at these different universities?
I decided to go to Kyoto Institute of Technology because you were able to study the design of architecture from the first year on, without first doing foundation years. After that, I went to the Institute of Art at the University of Tsukuba, as I was also very interested in art.

Which teachers were important to you at university?
Our studies at Kyoto Institute of Technology were very strange. We rarely saw any professors and discussed projects with them just a few times in four years. We were very free and had to decide everything ourselves. We mostly went to school after midnight, spending the daytime in coffee shops. So we learned and made drawings and models on our own.

How did you learn at the Institute of Art at the University of Tsukuba?
I went to Tsukuba about once a month. I lived in Tokyo and I studied mostly in Tokyo on my own and with friends, artists, art critics and philosophers. I guess I wasn't a model student.

At that time, which artists, philosophers and architects interested you most?
During my years of study, the most important philosopher for me was Henri Bergson. In the arts, I was interested in some of the Arte povera artists, especially Jannis Kounellis and his cultural environment. I very much liked his sense of material. Also Eduardo Chillida is a very important artist for me. I think his works, even his paper works, are architecture. He studied architecture and played football as a professional goalkeeper before becoming a sculptor. To me, that sounds like an ideal life. Among architects, I was interested in Adolf Loos, of course, Jože Plečnik and Sigurd Lewerentz as well as in the baroque architects Borromini and Bernini. But the most important architect for me is Louis Kahn. I believe he treats space and light as a

liquid body, like Mark Rothko does too. And I have always been inspired by some film makers, for example Orson Welles, Andrei Tarkovsky, Robert Bresson.

After your studies, how did you start your own office?
I started my office when I got my first project to design a house, the "Weekend House" in Osaka, my first black house. Before then, I had not worked in other architecture offices. At the same time, I also started teaching to earn a steady income. I taught at small colleges with students of about 18 or 19 years old. I really enjoy teaching.

If somebody wants to understand your way of working and what you are interested in, which project would you choose to explain your ideas and concepts?
I think the "Weekend House" in Osaka is interesting as well as the "Black Maria" installation and the "House with a Studio" in Tokyo.

Concerning the "House with a Studio", you wrote in the book *Leib – Raum – Plan* in 2003: "The house is (...) an outside injected into the world, turned indoors and closed (...)" Could you describe what you mean by that?
Usually, we think of architecture as defining inside. But I think architecture should define outside too. As Hannah Arendt described, the social territory of modern ages has deleted the "outside," the public territory or space, that once guaranteed freedom for the individual. As the power of modern society grew stronger, the former "outside" became controlled like in a huge household, organized in a manner of

House with a Studio, Tokyo, 1996, series of prints

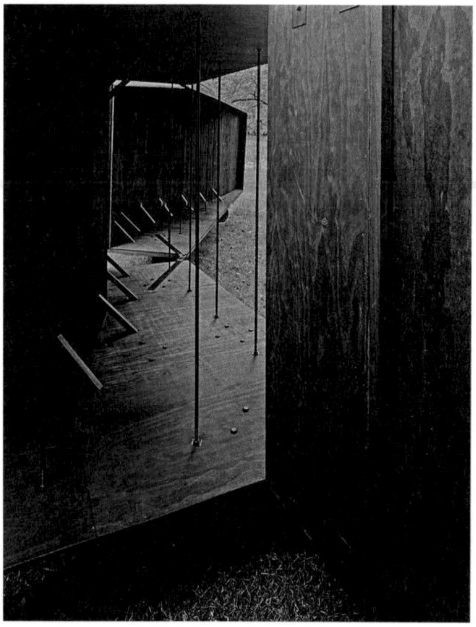

Black Maria, Sezon Museum of Modern Art, Karuizawa, 1994

"housekeeping." Society became one large interior where everyone is "at home," always engaged in social dialog, as Theodor W. Adorno described in his book *Minima Moralia* in 1951: "Not to be at home in one's home is part of morality."
If you consider that seriously, architecture should react and provide space for the individual itself. In the past, architecture defined borders between public and private space, but this aspect has declined in modern ages. I think that architecture should return to its original function and define borders and edges to public and private space. The task of architecture is not to protect the "inside" from the "outside," but rather to protect the "outside" from the "inside." I want to contribute a space that is "outside," another place, which is not controlled by society, but provides space for individual freedom. And to create that I define edges, by giving it a dimension of depth or hollow in the interiorized space, the "inside."
(*Hiroshi Nakao draws a sketch on paper beginning with the inside and shows us how to define an outside by tearing a hole in it*).
This space is "an outside injected into the world, turned indoors and closed," as in the "House with a Studio" in Tokorozawa or in the "Weekend House" in Osaka.

So the space you create is a kind of special space of its own. Can you describe the space you want to create?
My intention was to make a "body space" (*Leib-Raum*), a space to be by oneself, a space for the self that is apart from society. Walter Benjamin said in his text "Surrealismus," that the *Leib-Raum* is a totality, an actuality, that has no living room (*Gute Stube*), no room where society can exert its power over private space. The *Leib-*

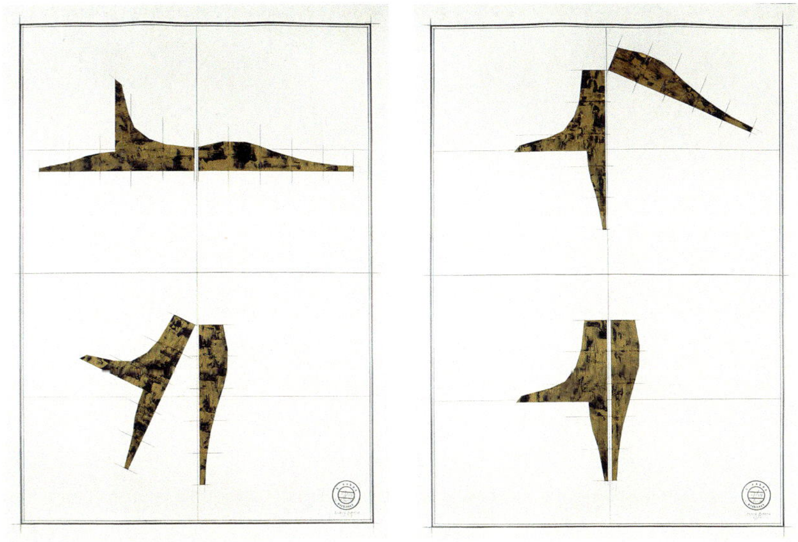

Black Maria, series of prints

Raum is a space where one can be by oneself, a space of self-awareness. It is also a space where you feel your body as well as depth and materiality within the space.

In which way do you think perception, space and materiality are linked?

I think that space and materiality are not only linked through perception, but that space itself can have a quality of materiality. I do not mean materiality in the sense of brick, wood, floor, wall or ceiling. What I mean—and what I hope to feel and create—is the materiality of the space. I think, in the German language *Raum* has this sense of materiality.

(*Hiroshi Nakao shows us his huge blackboard*).

For example, the Latin word *spatium* embodies, I think, a sense of extension. The Japanese word *ma* is very much related to body-sense. They are each a little different.

The German word *Raum*, for example in Adolf Loos' interpretation, is connected with volume and materiality. In my interpretation, materiality means the intention of space: Space intention.

What does that mean? How is intention connected with material and space?

Every material has an intention. For example, hard or soft materials, materials with different structures. Every material has specific characteristics or intentions. Louis Kahn also wrote about materials, their intention and their connection to forming and designing space. In this sense, I think materiality means space intention. So I like to work with this intention in my projects.

Weekend House, Osaka, 1991

So, which kind of materials are you interested in?
I often design with wood, nearly black wood. On the one hand, it is inexpensive, and on the other, it has the quality of a simple material while being a sensitive material. I also like steel: my second house in Tokorozawa is covered with steel, and because the surface is always changing, it has several colors and surface qualities over time. Brick is another favorite material.

You use wood, and especially black wood, which was painted or glazed black, in your houses—what interests you especially about black?
People often say that black has negative connotations. But for me, black is a very sensitive color, especially in architecture where it reacts to light and shadow in a variety of different ways. Sometimes things disappear in black space. One's perception changes in dark spaces, and darkness can evoke a lot of associations.

But doesn't that also happen with white?
In a different way. White gives you very clear light and shadow, not the depth and variety that darkness affords, the kind of deepness where things become associative. I think we need more black, more darkness and depth today, as the spaces become flatter and lighter, and especially in Japan, spaces are getting bright. I hope to provide darkness and depth.

Another project, the "Stawell Steps" you did with students from Monash University in Melbourne. There is no inside and outside. What were you interested in with this project?
The "Stawell Steps" are also a kind of body space. The Japanese concept of *ma* connects time and space with ourselves, our body. Steps embody this perfectly—the connection of time, space and ourselves. Steps are of course stairs, but they also move the body in time and space, like dancing on stairs. I wanted to work with that idea in the "Stawell Steps." This thinking is connected with the Japanese sense of space that you also find in Japanese old gardens. One of the most important things in the design of old gardens are the standing stones. They were designed without any sketches or drawings. The creators of the gardens came to the site and designed where the stones should be then and there, marking them with wooden plugs beaten into the earth. The design of the garden was a kind of performance, the sound of beating in the plugs resounding like a kind of percussion. The design of the space sounded like music. In our project we wanted to make a space sound—by making steps.

So, in this project you dealt with steps, with people moving, with sounds as well as with landscape. Are the "Stawell Steps" landscape, art or architecture?
There is a matrix on this subject in the text "Sculpture in the Expanded Field" by the art critic Rosalind Krauss. Rosalind Krauss works on land art and the question how land art can be interpreted: as landscape, art or architecture—or in reverse as not-landscape, not-art or not-architecture. It is interesting for me to challenge and go beyond received definitions and classifications.
The "Stawell Steps" are therefore not just architecture, not just landscape, and not just art. We have tried to make a work that is both architecture and not-architecture, both landscape and not-landscape, both art and not-art.

Let us talk about the "Coups de Sonde," an art project in which you also challenge perceptions. How did the project get its name?
The name is French for "plumbing the depths". The "Coups de Sonde" are chairs that fold the landscape and create depth in the back of the people sitting in the chairs. The people sitting may become a *sonde* themselves through the depth of the chair and the landscape.

Do you work or design differently when approaching an art project or an architectural project or is it the same for you?
I approach both the same way because, for me, architecture and art are the same thing. The purpose and the issues are the same for me in art and architecture. I am interested in body space, in perception and creating depth, creating an "other place," an "outside."

Weekend House

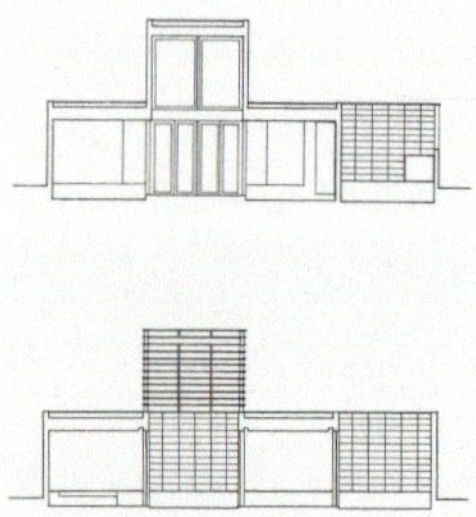

Section and elevation

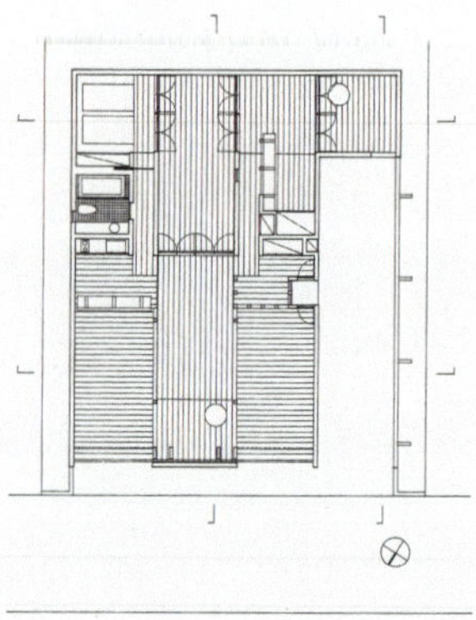

Ground floor plan

In 2001 you were asked by Arata Isozaki to design some 30 apartments in Gifu but you turned down the project. Why?

I left the project very quickly of my own accord as I was not interested in it. Several architects were invited to design dwellings, but the brief was given—kinds of apartment blocks—and I did not want to design these kinds of controlled spaces. I am more interested in "other spaces."

How do you work when designing your projects?

I almost always work with drawings when designing. Prints are interesting too, as I am quite interested in color. When printing, you can work differently with colors, as the colors are absorbed deeply by the paper.

In your work, you refer to art, texts and theories from abroad—you mentioned Theodor Adorno, Walter Benjamin and Adolf Loos and you have also studied the theories of Maurice Merleau-Ponty, Sigmund Freud and others. Are there theories from Japan that you are also interested in?

I don't feel the same need to refer to philosophy from home. For me, European thinking is always very stimulating and surprising, and these new ideas interest me more than the old ones I know from home. Maybe Europeans feel the same about Japanese thinking. The exchange is what makes it stimulating. People grow up with the traditions and thinking of their culture, and so I cannot free myself from the Japanese way of thinking. To find fresh ideas, I have to look beyond my own boundaries.

So, when you use dark wood or deal with depth or darkness you are also referring to Japanese tradition in architecture?

I cannot be free of Japanese culture and tradition, so my sense of material or color is inevitably connected with that. At the same time, I think it is also a very normal sense.

In Europe, people like Augustin Berque, Günter Nitschke and others write about Japan, about Japanese thinking, about the "other" as seen from Europe. What do you think about what they write?

I have read Augustin Berque's books, but I am not interested in them. Berque's interpretation, for example, of the Japanese landscape is very normal.

What do you think, for example, about Roland Barthes' book *The Empire of Signs*, which also refers to Japan, even though he says in the foreword that he is not writing about Japan?

Roland Barthes' eyes are perceptive. He portrays small scenes, writes very deep texts and is careful to avoid the clichés and cultural generalizations that beset the work of others. I do not believe that cultures are distinct and can be described on their own. I also don't think we need to describe or understand Japan or Europe as separate cultures. I think, it is impossible to understand another culture in its entirety, but we can still meet and have exchanges with other cultures. For example, I like to read what Theodor Adorno or Hannah Arendt have written, because I find their ideas very interesting, but I do not think that I fully understand their thinking in detail. My ambition is not to understand their entire thinking but to consider their new ideas.

Stawell Steps, Stawell, Australia, 2012

On the subject of new ideas, what do you think about more recent developments in architecture?
There was an important movement for instance in the 1960s in Vienna. I love, for example, the work of Walter Pichler and also John Hejduk, because it has poetry. By that I mean radical, incisive thought, not in the romantic sense. We have since lost a lot of the poetry in architecture, I think. That has happened all over the world, but in Japan especially.

Where do you see this poetry in Japanese architecture?
For example, in *haiku*. A long time ago, Japanese architecture was imbued with a sense of *haiku*. *Haiku* is very simple—five, seven, five—a very simple structure that can convey very rich meaning. Ancient Japanese architecture embodied that, and you can see it, for example, in stone gardens too. It was present in the Middle-Ages but began to disappear, I think, in the Edo period. But I sense it again, for example in Jannis Kounellis' work.

What do you think about the development of recent architecture in Japan?
Nothing.

Coups de Sonde I–IV, project, 1990

HIROSHI NAKAO

Biography

1961 Born in Kobe
1985 Bachelor of Architecture, Kyoto Institute of Technology
1989 Institute of Art, Graduate School of University of Tsukuba
Established own office
2012 Visiting Artist, Monash University Art Design & Architecture, Melbourne, Australia
2015 Professor, Shonan Institute of Technology, Fujisawa, Kanagawa

Principal Works

1988 Chairs for a photographer I–IV, Project
1990 Coups de Sonde I–IV, Project
1991 Weekend House, Osaka
1994 Black Maria, Sezon Museum of Modern Art, Karuizawa
1996 House with a Studio, Tokorozawa
1997 Gisant / Transi, Sezon Museum of Modern Art, Karuizawa
2001 Slaughterhouse (with witness room), Sezon Art Program, Tokyo
2002 Projection booth for an artist, The Ciccillo Matarazzo Pavilion, São Paulo, Brazil
2006 Nobody Home, Aichi Prefectural Museum of Art, Nagoya
2012 Stawell Steps, with Nigel Bertram, Stawell, Australia

Publications—Selection

1994 *Creating a Hollow*, Gallery ROM, Oslo
1997 "Weekend House / House with Studio," in: *AA Files 33*, Architectural Association, London
1998 *Critic 4: Hiroshi Nakao*, Tatsusuke Uehira, Osaka
2000 "Not to be at home / Creating a Hollow," in: *Quaderns 226*, Association of Architects of Catalonia, Barcelona
2003 "House with Studio / Weekend House," in: *Hiroshi Nakao: Leib—Raum—Plan*, Junius Verlag, Hamburg
2016 *Monash Steps / Stawell Steps*, Monash University Publishing, Melbourne

SOU FUJIMOTO

A balance of order and disorder

Mr. Fujimoto, what made you decide to become an architect? Did you have a particular connection to architecture during your childhood?
Well, architecture was just one option for me (*he laughs*). Before I chose to study architecture, I was more interested in physics and mathematics. In high school, I read books on Einstein and physics theories from the 20th century and I was really fascinated by the revolutionary way of thinking and Einstein's new concept of space and time. At that time, I wasn't so interested in architecture.
But ever since my childhood days, I was interested in creating things, although not necessarily architecture. At university, I soon learned that physics and mathematics are quite difficult (*he laughs*). It's a different world, and I gave up. I'm still interested in new theories about the universe, like string theory, but that is beside the point.
It was then that I chose architecture. I was at a university where one could choose between mathematics, physics, different kinds of engineering, technological and scientific studies, but architecture was also an option.
At that time, the only architect I knew of was Antoni Gaudí; I didn't know any others. At Tokyo University, our studies began with a review of modern architecture. It was then that I realized that at the beginning of the 20th century—almost at the same time as Einstein—Le Corbusier, Mies van der Rohe and other modern architects were creating innovative projects that changed the concept of architecture completely. Those kinds of really fundamental, conceptual innovations have always attracted me and I was quickly drawn in and began to really enjoy it.

Who were your teachers at university?
Hisao Koyama and Hidetoshi Ohno were at the University of Tokyo. Ohno was from the school of Fumihiko Maki, but was already working independently at the time of the course. He was interested not only in architecture but also in urban strategies. Koyama focused more on architectural design and was from the school of Louis Kahn. It was a nice balance and I learned from both of them. There were no big names like Fumihiko Maki, Kenzo Tange or Tadao Ando, and our studies were more open as a result. We could do whatever we liked and did not necessarily have to follow in the masters' footsteps.

What did the architectural history courses focus on, for example Western modernism or traditional Japanese architecture?
There was a class that taught traditional Japanese architecture and we had a study trip to visit the traditional architecture of Kyoto and Nara. So, I knew about that, but I wasn't really interested in it at the time. Later, after university, I became more interested in traditional Japanese culture and architecture.

Since I didn't do a master's course, my time at university was quite short. The first half-year was about how to draw lines and the history of modernism – Mies, Le Corbusier and so on. During the next two years, we had six or seven design classes. I really enjoyed those, because we could make almost anything we liked.

You graduated in 1994 and opened your office in 2000. What did you do in the intervening six years?

After school I was afraid of everything, because I was young and rather naive. I thought about applying to Sejima's or Ito's office, but I was afraid they would not find my portfolio very interesting! (*he laughs*) That would have been the end of the world for me.

So, it was mostly a period of thinking. I worked on six projects of my own and also realized two projects for my father. But for me, it was more important to think about architecture, the architecture of the future, calmly, for five or six years.

Did you travel a lot?

Not very much. Actually, I should have travelled a lot. In my last year of school, I went to Europe for the first time and saw buildings by Le Corbusier and Mies, and visited France, Spain and Italy. The following year, I went to Greece and Turkey to see older buildings: classical Greek architecture and Turkish architecture, that's all. But I didn't travel the world.

Children's Psychiatric Rehabilitation Center, Date, 2006

During the time when you were thinking about architecture, did you read books, write texts or sketch drawings?
Something like that. There was one very important book that I read, written by Ilya Prigogine. It is like a counterpart to modern order thinking, more like a soft order, a more dynamic order, just on the edge of chaos, and I was very influenced by it.

Then you established your own office. Was that because you won the second prize for the "Aomori Museum" competition or because of the hospital project for your father?
Winning that second prize was a very big thing for me, because Toyo Ito was a juror. After the competition, Ito mentioned me as one of an interesting young generation of architects. Then I won a small ideas competition and was invited to take part in some small exhibitions. No real projects, but I thought that it was a good time to start my own office officially and to settle my mind. And then everything slowly began falling into place.

The relationship between landscape and architecture is one of your recurrent design themes. Why does this idea interest you so much?
Architecture is of course architectural, but it is also half nature. Inside there is architecture, outside nature. In Japanese architecture this transition is blurred. The question here is how to deal with the relationship between nature and architecture, between inside and outside? We have to think about the boundary, not just install glazing or a beautiful window but try to create a sense of layering and graduation. At the very beginning of the process for the "Aomori Museum," I tried to create new geometries in order to mix nature and architecture, complexity and simplicity in a

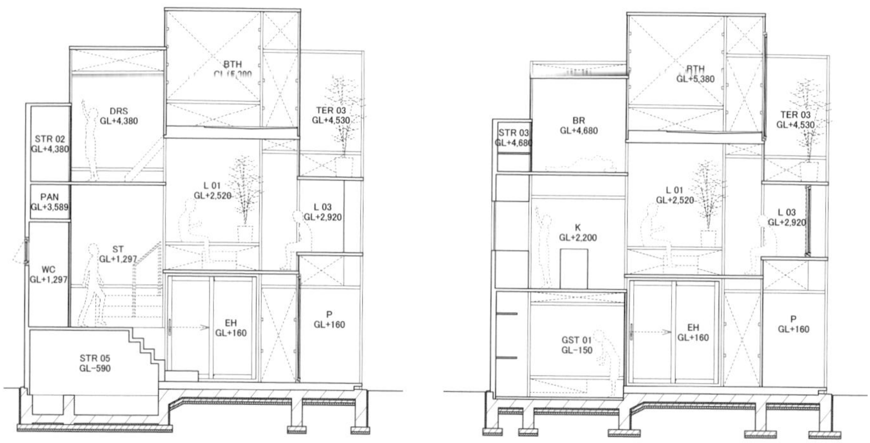

Sections

House NA, Tokyo, 2010

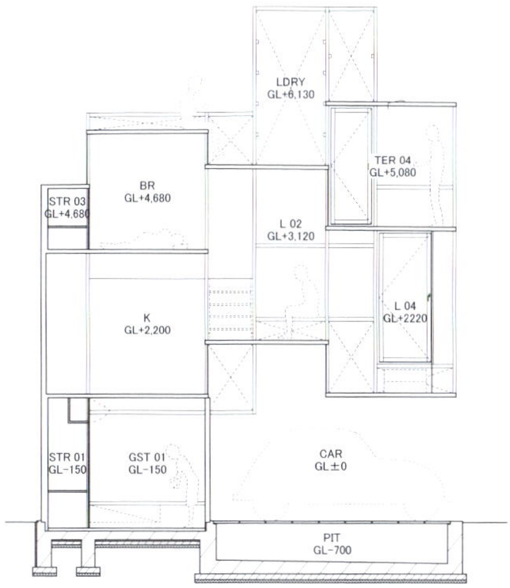

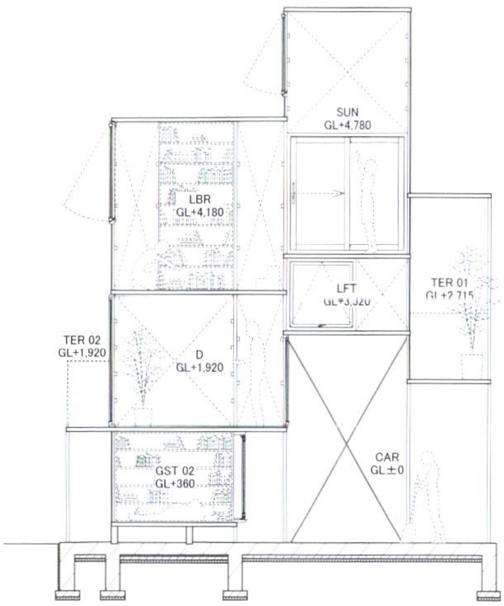

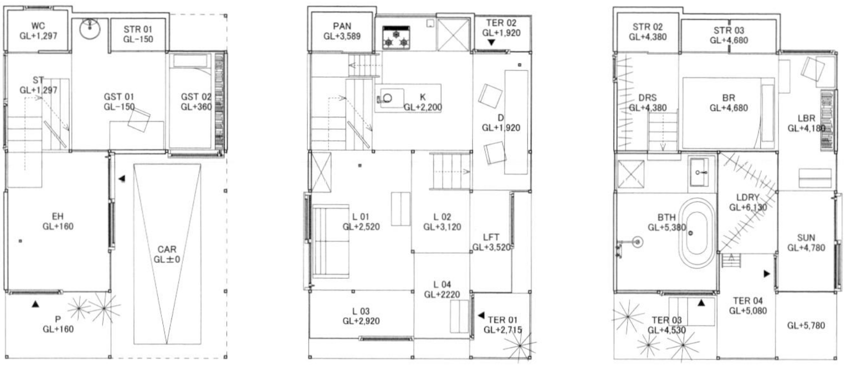

House NA, floor plans

single geometrical pattern. Recently, I have become more interested in not only using geometries but also several different themes to deal with a new kind of mixture between natural things and architecture. For example, the "Serpentine Gallery Pavilion" can also be regarded as landscape. I am also interested in the crossover of scales: from the human scale, the scale of furniture, the architectural scale, and the scale of the landscape to the urban scale. My aim is to find a new way to mix not only architectural elements, but to bring nature or urban elements into the architecture. For me this incredible mixture is a really exciting theme – it's the core of my architectural thinking.

Like many Japanese architects, you decided to set up your office in Tokyo. What does the experience of the cityscape of Tokyo mean for you?

I grew up in rural Hokkaido and later came to Tokyo, which is completely different. But it also provides a similar kind of comfortable feeling when you walk through the small pathways of the residential areas of Tokyo. The basic fabric of space is, I think, almost the same. In the forest, you are surrounded by many, many different things of small or medium scale that together form a territory. You feel protected, but at the same time it is not defined – you can choose any path you like. In Tokyo the materials are artificial, but you still have the small scale. Being in the middle of a small street in Tokyo is almost like being inside a forest. It is an artificial forest; you are surrounded by many, many small things, and it is an open space but still not completely open. This kind of similarity between the natural and the completely artificial in Tokyo really surprised me, to the extent that it served as a starting point to think

Musashino Art University Library, Tokyo, 2010

about how we can integrate such different situations and about how we can understand that quite different things can have a similar quality of space. Then I tried to create in-between spaces, a mixture of city, architecture and smaller, tiny things in Tokyo. It was a really nice transition of scales. Walking around Tokyo, I gradually established that way of thinking as a basis for my architecture.

Tokyo consists of small neighborhoods with small buildings. For many of your projects, these everyday buildings are the immediate surroundings. How do you deal with this condition?
I try to create something like Tokyo itself, no matter what kind of surroundings it may be in. If a building can represent Tokyo itself, then it is fitting for the Tokyo situation. Again, scale is very important: if the old small houses in Tokyo are replaced by medium-size buildings, Tokyo will lose its scale. I really dislike that. For example, for the "House NA," which is in the middle of a typical Tokyo neighborhood, I tried to create a grouping of small things—thin slabs, thin columns. It is not so much inspired by the surroundings as by Tokyo itself. We have to save Tokyo by creating good representations of Tokyo. The "Tokyo Apartments," for example, are a small group of small houses. If it were one big box, it would destroy the scale of Tokyo, so I tried to articulate the building using small parts.

Another recurring element in your architecture is the use of a grid, a kind of structure in different dimensions. That is, of course, a common topic in architecture — a basic principle of architecture not only in the present but also in the past. You referred to chaos earlier, and the grid would seem diametrically opposed to that. How do you work with this element?

Before the "Serpentine Gallery Pavilion," I almost never used a grid. In fact, I tried hard to do something other than a grid. The "Children's Psychiatric Rehabilitation Center" consists of a random layout of boxes, for example. One can see it as a counterpart to the grid; it is more like a straightforward translation of Prigogine principles or the layout of a Japanese garden. The "Aomori" project was something in-between: based on the grid but generating something non-grid-like to create an interesting mixture of order and disorder. This balance of order and disorder interests me. "House N" has a very simple ordering principle: a box in a box in a box — but the positions of the openings are very varied, introducing a sense of disorder.

In more or less every project there are contrasting aspects of order and disorder, or simplicity and complexity. This, of course, relates to natural and artificial things, because nature is in a sense ordered, but also very complex. In the case of the library of the Musashino Art University, the bookshelves have a rigid order, but the plan is more freely-shaped and the openings in the walls are varied and random; so again, the whole is a balance of order and freedom.

With the "Serpentine Gallery Pavilion," the size of the grid is much smaller and we found a new relationship between the order of the grid and something beyond that order. So, while I worked with the grid, the grid was not the theme. The theme has always been the balance between simplicity and complexity, or order and disorder. I wasn't entirely sure how this balance could be achieved with a grid, and up until completion I was worried the grid would be too dominant. But when it was finally built, I thought: "Wow, what an amazing balance!" Seen from further away, the order of the grid disappears and it becomes like a cloud. This experience opened the door to grids for me.

Does the grid also give you a way of combining different scales? You started with small-scale buildings, but nowadays you are working on several large projects.

Crossing between scales is an exciting challenge. Sometimes large-scale structures need to be broken down into subscales, substructures, or subforms. And sometimes it is possible to employ a particular form or way of thinking for a building design that already works at a small scale. One starting point, for example, is simple, strong local rules.

What I learned from Prigogine is that local situations are more ordered, but the whole is less ordered. A single grid for everything is boring. A thousand grids, on the other hand, means there is no controllable overall situation, and the result is almost chaotic, fractal-like. The same applies from small to large scale: if you look at one box of the "Children's Psychiatric Rehabilitation Center," it is not particularly exciting, but 20 or 30 boxes grouped in a random way create lots of different dimensions.

How do you achieve randomness? For example, in the case of the "House N," is the placement of the windows and openings really random?

Yes, there were no defining organizational rules for them, if that is what you mean. While the shape of the "House N" was defined as a golden section, we were free to position the openings where we wanted them. There are reasons for their placement: we tried to create a nice sense of distance and enclosure. We blocked views from outside, while keeping it more open from the inside.

Do you sometimes change the design during construction?
Sometimes I do, sometimes I don't. It depends. In the case of "House N" I changed the position of the window frames during the construction phase. When I saw it on site, I wasn't happy with the arrangement. So I removed some elements and put them on the opposite side. That kind of thing.

You once compared a house with a ruin or the outer shell of a ruin. What is the notion of the ruin for you?
Ruins have both order and disorder. Somebody designed the original building according to a particular concept, but later, when the roof is gone, it collapses and falls into ruin. It starts ordered, then gradually gets more disordered until it is completely disordered and then finally ceases to be a ruin anymore—because it has returned to nature. But nature has its own order, a different kind of order. Nature is like a perfect order, so as one order disappears, the other order surfaces. Ruins lie somewhere in-between. They are like a crossing point—a balance of order and disorder. Ruins have something amazing, something unexpected about them: they are beyond time and beyond artificial thinking. It is quite fascinating.

Arata Isozaki showed his projects in a state of decay. Is there a specific Japanese approach to thinking about ruins?
I don't know. Back in his day, Louis Kahn talked about the ruins in Rome and Egypt and tried to create ruin-like architecture. I think Isozaki was influenced by Louis Kahn, and I was influenced by Koyama, who had contact to Kahn. On reflection, I don't think it is just a Japanese way: throughout history ruins have evoked a romantic feeling for people. In Germany, there are many ruined castles that tourists from all over the world like to visit. This fascination with ruins is international.
Coming back to Japan, the Japanese garden is, in my view, like a ruin. It changes over time but still retains its general structure. So that may explain why Japanese people also like these kinds of romantic things.

The Metabolist movement was also interested in the combination of general structure and changeable elements. What do you think about that? Is it still of relevance to you?
Well, I think that it was an amazing time, because it gave rise to so many crazy futuristic visions. The idea behind Metabolism still exists but maybe the key lies in how we understand organic principles. After the modern movement, the Metabolists tried to understand architecture in a more organic way. But their organic thinking was based on a hierarchy that I am uncomfortable with. In the 21st century, we now have the internet and our understanding of organic systems is more complex: it is more like a network with no central core and many mutual relationships, like a brain. The organic thinking of the Metabolists was, by contrast, more like the body. So, then as now, we continue to probe how we understand organic concepts as a counterpart to architecture, and how we can take architecture further. Some of Kurokawa's proposals provide me with inspiration, and in general, I think we are

Serpentine Gallery Pavilion, London, United Kingdom, 2013

repeating history, but in a different way, adding new concepts to the organic principles of the past. I like to respect all phases of history, because we can always find something to learn from.

Let us turn to the contemporary architecture scene in Japan. There are quite a few successful architects in your generation who have also had considerable success outside of Japan. Is there an exchange between your generation and the older generation or does everyone fight for himself?
I have a good relationship with Kazuyo Sejima, Ryue Nishizawa and Toyo Ito, and from time to time we have a drink together, but we don't talk much about architecture *(he laughs)*. Maybe it is different to Ito's younger days. Ito said that in the past, architects were constantly talking, arguing and debating, but now it is calmer. Most of the architects of my generation are friends and we meet up, maybe once or twice a year, but not especially to talk about architecture.
Japanese architecture has acquired a good reputation, especially due to some big names, but they are still individuals who pursue their own style and try to escape the typical image of Japanese architecture. In our generation, we are very varied and hopefully we can find our own unique way, like Kazuyo Sejima, Kengo Kuma or Shigeru Ban have done.

How would you describe the situation in your office? Who are your clients?
I am fortunate to have more and more projects abroad. Perhaps this is because the Japanese economy is not as strong as it was, but most of the general contractors and big design offices still have enough work. There are few interesting architectural competitions at present, which is a pity, but smaller projects—interesting projects—for private clients are still being commissioned, and not just for houses, but also for commercial or small public buildings. So, at present I feel there is still potential to try and create interesting architecture through smaller projects, while large architecture projects are becoming more and more boring.

École Polytechnique Learning Centre, Paris-Saclay, France, project, 2015

SOU FUJIMOTO

Biography

1971 Born in Hokkaido
1994 Bachelor of Architecture, University of Tokyo
1994–95 First journeys to Europe and Turkey
2000 Established Sou Fujimoto Architects, Tokyo
2012 Golden Lion for the Best National Participation for the Japanese Pavilion at the 13th International Architecture Exhibition, Venice Biennale of Architecture

Principal Works

1996 Seidai Hospital annex, Higashigakura, Hokkaido
2002 Shijima Cottage, Nagano
2003 Dormitory for Mentally Disabled, Date, Hokkaido
2005 House T, Gunma
2006 7/2 House, Hokkaido Island
Children's Psychiatric Rehabilitation Center, Date
Nursing home, Noboribetsu
2007 House O, Tateyama
Apartment, Tokyo
2008 House N, Oita
Final Wooden House, Kumamoto, Kyushu Island
2009 House H, Tokyo
House before House, Utsunomiya
2010 House NA, Tokyo
Musashino Art University Library, Tokyo
2011 Garden Gallery, Sculpture Park, Cologne, Germany
2012 House K, Nishinomiya
2013 Serpentine Gallery Pavilion, Hyde Park, London, United Kingdom
2014 The Miami Design District Palm Courtyard, Miami, United States
White Tree Skyscraper Project, Montpellier, France (under development)
House of Hungarian Music (1st price competition), Budapest, Hungaria (under development)
2015 Mirrored Gardens, Vitamin Creative Space, Guangzhou, China
École Polytechnique Learning Center, Paris-Saclay (1st price competition), France
with Manal Rachdi OXO Architects and Nicolas Laisné Associates (under development)

Publications—Selection

2008 *Primitive future*, Inax, Tokyo
2009 *Sou Fujimoto, 2G N.50*, Editorial Gustavo Gili SL, Barcelona
2010 *Musashino Art Museum & Library*, Inax, Tokyo
Sou Fujimoto 2003–2010 (El Croquis 151), Madrid
2012 *Sou Fujimoto: Sketchbook*, Lars Müller, Zurich
Sou Fujimoto: Futurospective Architecture, Verlag der Buchhandlung Walther König, Cologne
2013 *Serpentine Gallery Pavilion*, Koenig Books, London
Sou Fujimoto: Recent Work, A.D.A Edita, Tokyo
2015 *Sou Fujimoto: Architecture Works 1995–2015*, TOTO Publishing, Tokyo

RYUJI NAKAMURA

Gravity is the key

Mr. Nakamura, what was your initial introduction to architecture? Why did you want to become an architect?
When I was in elementary school, I liked looking at houses. Not the ones designed by architects—I didn't know what architects were at the time—but houses probably designed by local builders. That's how I became interested in architecture as a small child. My parents owned a liquor store, so my father wasn't a businessman who left the house to go to work; he was always at home. That might have influenced me to choose a profession that doesn't require commuting every day like a businessman. I became familiar with the situation of not having to be away from home in order to work.

You grew up in Nagano Prefecture. What kind of houses surrounded you as you grew up?
I grew up in Ina. The houses there were mostly traditional houses, unlike in Tokyo. Our bathroom, for example, was a separate outbuilding built by my father and was old-fashioned. You only had hot water when you made a fire. So, I learned how to make a fire and felt the cold in winter and the heat in summer in that short distance between the main building and the bathroom, whether I liked it or not.
The houses had traditional roofs made out of Japanese *Kawara* tiles and I enjoyed looking at the different designs of roofs. The tiles had a very mysterious form and I was fascinated that they were practically the same shape and color on every house but that each roof was similar but different because the plan of each house was different. These slight differences interested me. Some of the roofs had a slight curve, and I liked that in particular—especially after I learned it was related to the strength of the roof. I also experienced how our own house was rebuilt—with *Kawara* tiles, of course. I found that fascinating and exciting. Later I moved to Tokyo to study architecture, experienced a large city and learned about different viewpoints on beauty or art. For the first time, I understood why I had looked so intently at the *Kawara*-tiled roofs as a child.

You studied Architecture at Hosei University and at Tokyo National University of Fine Arts and Music. In 1999, you graduated and started to work at Jun Aoki's office. Why did you choose this particular architectural office?
I was very taken with Jun Aoki's "L" house. I visited it and read an article in a magazine entitled "Itareri Tsukuseri de Naikoto," which means "not too perfect." Both the article and the house made a big impression on me. It looks like a mass of concrete, like an earthenware pipe, laid on a vacant lot. The functions of the house appear and disappear depending on one's viewpoint. I knew that function and form need

hechima chair, 2005

not accord perfectly in architecture, especially in housing. In fact, some distance between form and function is important, because it creates comfort and imagination. At Jun Aoki's office I was put in charge of the "Y" house, which took a similar approach to the "L" house. The client lives in a mass of concrete that has the appearance of a civil engineering construction, but turns out to be a house. Unfortunately, it was never finished, but it had a big influence on my designs for houses and exhibitions. After that, I was in charge of "Farm" (farm and shop), the "Mitsubishi Motors Showroom" and "Louis Vuitton Roppongi." In "Y" I learned about the importance of distance between form and function, and through the other projects I gained an interest in the phenomenon of aggregation. I thought carefully about the relationship between the whole and its parts and especially about size, material and structure. For example, for the "Louis Vuitton Roppongi" project we created the big façade using about 20,000 delicate glass tubes. I knew that the relationship between the whole and the individual parts would have a great impact on the resulting effect. I also became interested in heterogeneity in homogeneity. The more delicate and homogeneous the parts, the more its heterogeneity comes to the fore. That would later have an influence on my own installations. In the "Louis Vuitton Roppongi" project, however, I was not able to establish essential relationships between the whole and the parts, and this regret also influenced my work on later installations. Through these projects, I also gained an interest in transparency.

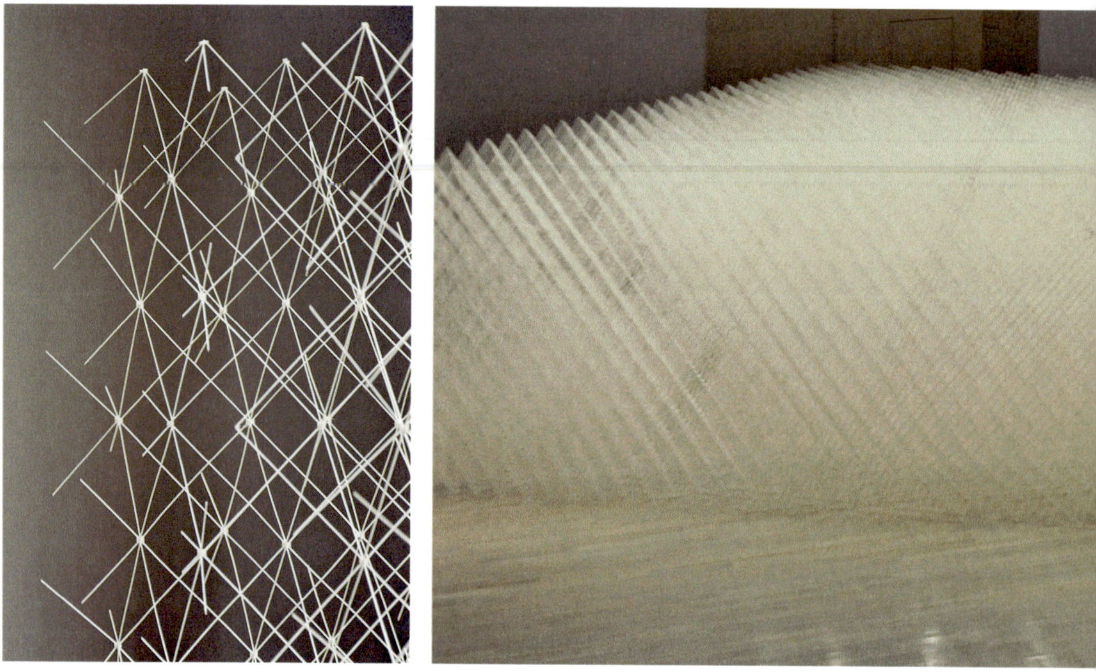

cornfield, Tokyo, 2010

You established your own office in 2004. What was the starting point for setting up on your own? Did you have your own commission?
There was not an exact starting point, but Jun Aoki encourages his staff to "graduate" after four years and leave the office—just like in college. I had finished the "Louis Vuitton Roppongi" project, so that was a good point to start something new on my own.

So you started your office without having a client or a project?
That's right. No client.

What did you do during that time?
In 2004–05, I was fortunate to win the Daikanyama Installation competition, which awarded money to actually build the winner's proposal. It was basically the structure of the hechima chair made out of wood. The hechima chair is now made out of paper. After the Daikanyama Installation, Jun Aoki asked me to work with him on the interior design for a chain store for spectacles. It was published in a magazine and after that things got going and I went on to do several stores for them and other brands.

At the moment you are taking part in international art exhibitions with Tomás Saraceno and Ólafur Elíasson. Which contemporary artists are you interested in?

The photographer Takashi Homma. In his book *Tanoshii Shashin* (Enjoyable photography) he writes about photography and talks about different perspectives on making things. I find his work both interesting and very inspiring. Photography and making things seem unrelated, but his perspective serves as a useful reference. I also like the work of Herzog & de Meuron, especially their early works, and I feel quite influenced by them.

Are you influenced by Japanese architectural history as well?
I like old temples because of the roofs. They have fascinated me since childhood. It may have nothing to do with history, but I was also always interested in making things out of smaller objects, for example stacking small pebbles on top of each other, or assembling bricks into bigger structures. Traditional Japanese architecture is strongly related to the garden or has a strong relationship between outside and inside. I think the relationship between a window and the outside is very important. But that is something that applies not just to Japan, but probably also to Europe as well. I wouldn't say that is particular to Japanese architecture.

How about the Metabolists? What do you think about the influence of this important Japanese architectural movement? Is it still relevant today?
I think it is important in terms of its historical relevance, but times have changed. The methods of the Metabolist approach have since changed and are more varied. Initially it was the idea of capsules, but now there are many different ways and pos-

bang, Tokyo, 2011

sibilities of considering Metabolism. We are beginning to see different approaches that may not look like they are influenced by Metabolism but still embody the idea. For example, the renovation of old houses is a kind of Metabolism, even if it does not go by that name. The original concept of Metabolism interpreted the concept of Metabolism very literally. Current approaches to Metabolism, as seen for example in the renovation of old houses, utilize a previously existing form for a different purpose and interpret its meaning anew. I think this is related to the distance between form and function that I mentioned before in the "L" and "Y" houses.

Let's talk about your projects and your way of designing. If somebody wants to understand your way of working, your way of designing, which project best communicates your ideas and concepts?
I think that would be the "cornfield", "bang" or "catenarhythm" projects, and also the "beam" project.

Is there a project where you were surprised by the outcome? Something you didn't expect?
In the "catenarhythm" project I used ribbons hanging from the ceiling which formed catenary curves to divide the space. People had to step over the ribbons to enter. I was aware that people might trip over the ribbons and that was intentional. If you stepped on one, it would bring down the ribbons, so I designed it so that it would be easy to put them back. But I didn't expect the space to have so much tension as the viewers entered and stepped over the ribbons and walked around the space. When I designed it, I thought mostly about the visual aspects of the ribbons, and not about the interaction between visitors and ribbons.

Most of your work is either white or polychromatic. How important is color to your projects and when do you use color instead of white?

catenarhythm, Tokyo, 2008

I often use white. I like white, because it is affected by its natural surroundings. For example, in the morning white has kind of a blueish shade and in the evening turns more orange, affecting the inside of a house or project. If you paint something red, all you feel is red and it is hard to sense the other colors. It would be difficult to feel blue in a red environment. I think it is good that a space is influenced and affected by its surroundings and this works best with white.

Why do you choose to use color, for example in your "bench" project?
That project is painted in such a way that it changes color as you move around it. Its color changes in relation to people. What was important here is not so much the color but the distance and relationship between object and people and how it changes within this framework.

Some of your designs, like the "spring" project, push the boundaries of materials. What interests you particularly about that?
I don't feel like I am pushing the boundaries. If anything, I am on the boundary itself, and that is what interests me. For example, if I consider weight when I am on the boundary then it is possible to evoke a sense of both lightness or mass. Something that is on the border between two states can be both depending on the situation. My work therefore often has fine lines, but it is not because I think the finer the better. I guess gravity is the key here. When a material is thinner, the effect of gravity becomes more visible in the material.

Have you ever designed something hard, solid, and heavy? And how does "being on the boundary" work in such a project?
The "blank room" project is heavy in a way. Here the bent metal strips are very hard and solid when they are short, but when they are long, like seven meters, they become soft. That is a good example of the idea of being on the boundary: it is the

same material but its state depends on its length. I consider "beam" a heavy project, too. A single beam weighs 200 kilograms but seen from a certain distance and angle, the beam acquires a graphic quality. Its depth is reduced to two dimensions. The three-dimensional becomes two-dimensional, loses its solidity, its weight, and becomes soft.

What I find interesting about art is that you don't fully understand how to interpret it. Art actively tries to be on the border between things or states. Take a chair for example: if you create it in a form that is not immediately recognizable as a chair, it could also be seen as a table or a cushion. It is harder to interpret what it is, and that is what I mean by being on the border. The work of art itself tries to be something that can be seen either way.

You have undertaken a lot of installations and artworks. Is there a difference between doing architecture and artwork? What are the relationships between installations and architecture?

I think installations and architecture are the same in terms of space. For architecture there is the land you build on, and for installations there is the gallery space which has its own characteristics and you extract those characteristics in order to produce an artwork. So in that sense, at least, they are very similar!

Your designs for houses seem very different to your installation work. Where is the common ground between designing houses and designing installations?

I mentioned gravity in my installation work, but gravity is a key aspect of my architectural designs too, because it affects the structure. Gravity is definitely a common

blank room, Tokyo, 2010

beam, Tokyo, 2011

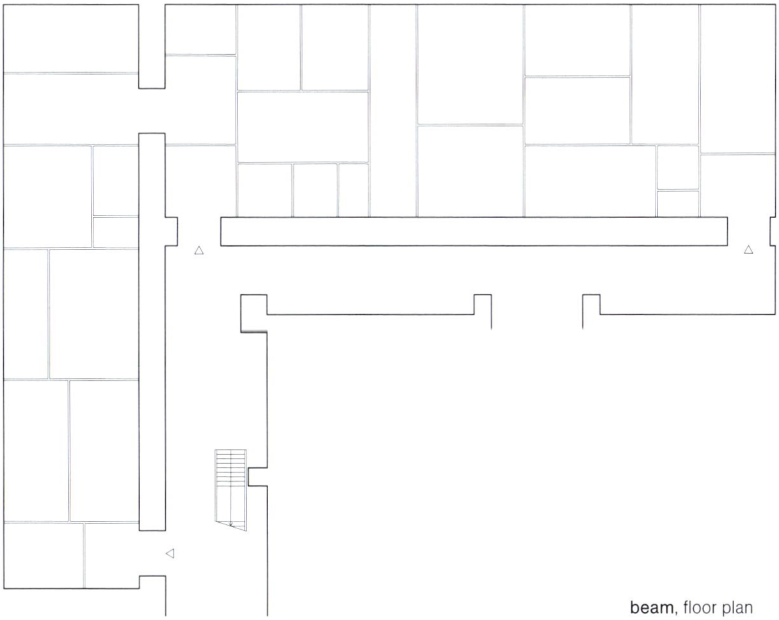

beam, floor plan

spring, Milan, Italy, 2012

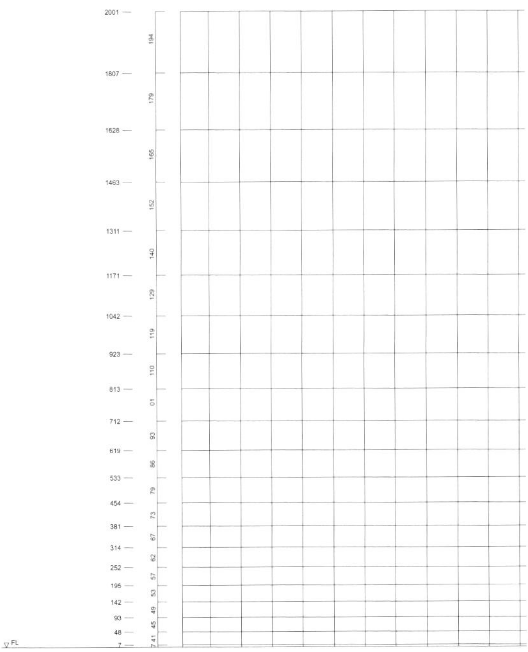

Elevation

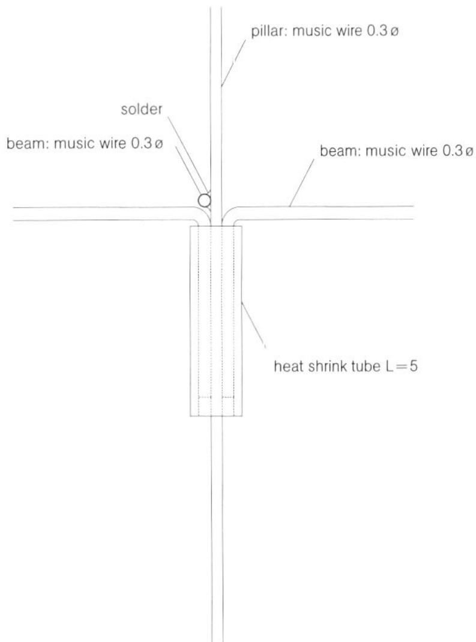

Detail

ground. Another common ground is size: architecture is big and my installations are big, so I am always thinking about how to create something big. Unlike a small object, like this cup for example, which can be made out of a single piece of material, a space like this room is impossible to make out of a single material. When you create something large, it must be made as a collection of pieces.

Are your designs dependent on a scale? Is a structure you design imaginable in another scale?
I start with a small piece. It can get bigger and I want my work to be able to grow to a larger scale. It can extend horizontally, but if it has a vertical emphasis, gravity again becomes an issue. As something expands vertically, its base has to adapt to sustain the forces and you invariably need to change the width of the base of the structure. I can imagine a change of scale for a project such as "spring." I would be interested to see it outside at a larger scale. What if one of these beams was the size of a building?

"Spring," in particular, seems extremely complex in terms of its construction. How important is the development of details in your work?
I can't deal with things that are too complicated. The designs I create come about through the process of my understanding of how things work, which can result in installations that might seem comparatively simple. When an installation is very big, I cannot build it myself so I need to come up with a system and details. I experiment with the system until I feel confident that it will work. When I draw a design, I also need to consider that my assistants, who are mostly students, also need to understand the system. Some of my assistants are good in handiwork, some are not. Others are very fast workers and some are very slow workers, so I need to come up with a system that everyone can follow. So the system and details are very important, and you can often observe this method in the resulting design.

When you design, how do you come up with your initial ideas? Is it by sketching, by drawing, by modeling or perhaps, sometimes, even by playing?
Actually, sometimes an idea may arise when I'm in a bookshop looking through books and magazines. The ideas come while I am relaxed, perhaps walking around, or browsing. Sometimes I simply play with paper or some other material and an idea arises. The more relaxed I am, the more concrete the idea becomes.

RYUJI NAKAMURA

Biography

1972	Born in Nagano Prefecture
1999	Master of Architecture, Tokyo National University of Fine Arts and Music
2000–03	Employee at Jun Aoki & Associates, Tokyo
2004	Established Ryuji Nakamura & Associates, Tokyo

Principal Works

2005	hechima chair, Daikanyama Installation, Tokyo
2008	catenarhythm, Tokyo
2009	blossom, Nagano
	atmosphere, New National Theatre, Tokyo
2010	blank room, Tokyo
	cornfield, Tokyo
	pond, Tokyo
	bench between pillars, Tokyo
2011	beam, Tokyo
	bang, Tokyo
2012	spring, Milan, Italy
2014	bench between pillars 2, Tokyo

Publications—Selection

2013	*Controlled and Uncontrolled Lines* (Contemporary Architect's Concept Series 16), LIXIL Publishing, Tokyo

JUNYA
ISHIGAMI

A world of possibilities

Mr. Ishigami, why did you want to become an architect?
I decided to become an architect because I felt it was an occupation that would allow me to contemplate numerous issues both extensively and from a variety of different perspectives.

You studied at Tokyo National University of Fine Arts and Music. Who were your teachers there? Did they influence the way you work?
I studied under the mentorship of Professor Yoshihiro Masuko. Of course, all of us students were influenced by our teachers and learned a lot from them. But rather than being strongly influenced by one particular thing, I have always been influenced by a vast range of issues.

After graduation you worked for Kazuyo Sejima. Why did you choose to work there?
In classes and assignments at university we presented proposals for architecture but there was never the opportunity to actually build any architecture. I found this to be somewhat lacking in stimulation. I wanted to actually think about architecture and observe with my very own eyes the process by which these thoughts are realized. For this reason, I began working at Kazuyo Sejima's office while I was a student. There was a very free atmosphere that permeated the office, and even as a student I was naturally given the opportunity to partake in various projects. In fact, I encountered many experiences at the office during my student days. I think that I spent more time there than I did at university. To actually have the chance to be on site and to witness the real circumstances in which architecture is created helps you to recognize the things that you can and cannot do in architectural practice. At the same time, at university I conversely began to think more deeply about themes in architecture that cannot be considered within the context of actual practice. In retrospect, I feel that the cycle of working at Kazuyo Sejima's office and attending university helped me formulate a very multi-dimensional way of thinking about architecture.

Which of your projects do you think is most suitable for understanding the way you work and design?
I consider all my projects to be equally important. I feel that it is only possible to comprehensively understand my thoughts on architecture by taking into account all of my projects in their entirety. That is, I believe, one of the most important themes I deal with when thinking about architecture in the current context: the issue of "diversity." To articulate in extremely broad terms, until the 20th century, everyone had worked towards realizing a single major goal under the pretext of a shared vision

for the future. It had thus been an era in which it was possible to pursue a sole theme that corresponded to a mutual vision or image. In this sense, in particular within the context of modernism, it could be said that it had been important to provide prototypical solutions. In our current times, however, it is very difficult to work towards a single goal and propose a single solution that will answer all the concerns of the day. The issues and demands of contemporary society are multi-dimensional and span numerous value systems. Under such circumstances, contemporary architects are indeed called on to think of means for creating a diverse myriad of variations. I believe that the key lies in how one can freely expand the scope of architectural thought and further devise a means to apply architecture to the many values that exist. I therefore constantly strive as far as possible to provide different responses and solutions for each project. In this respect, it is very difficult to try and understand the way I work by singling out a particular project.

In a lot of your projects the structures are very thin and the issue of lightness seems to be important. Your lightweight structures are exceptionally light, and at the other end of the scale your heavy structures seem to be exceptionally heavy, as in the house and restaurant project.
I do, of course, employ a lightweight structure in some of my projects, but this is not a focal aspect of all my work. There are particular projects where I have opted to use a heavy structure. When thinking about architecture through themes with various values, the scope of possible solutions naturally tends to expand.

Your work also seems to be inspired by a fascination with certain aspects of nature. In your book *Another scale of architecture* (2011) you talk about forest, air, rain, horizon and clouds as inspiration. How are architecture and nature related?
Traditionally, architecture has been contemplated and built for the sake of human beings. In considering the diversity of architecture, however, certain difficulties arise if the reason for the existence of the building is merely limited to the human being. We must think about why architecture exists from a much broader perspective. If we expand our scope of thought in this way, the boundary between what we define as the artificial environment and that of the natural environment becomes ambiguous. In current times, human activity indeed exerts a form of influence on the natural environment, and as a result allows remarkable changes to emerge within it. I believe that when building architecture, we need to consider the fact that this very artificial act simultaneously impacts to a greater or lesser degree on nature, and brings about inevitable changes. In this sense, I feel that, when speaking about architecture, it is also necessary to articulate my thoughts as if also speaking about nature itself.

Is this the reason for integrating plants in your buildings as a part of the architectural design?
Architecture had originally been something like a shelter that created a comfortable artificial environment that was isolated from the harsh natural environment surrounding it. A shelter is essentially a barrier that separates the interior from the exterior. We therefore generally consider the interior as the human territory and the exterior as the territory for everything else. Personally, I do not want to think about the interior

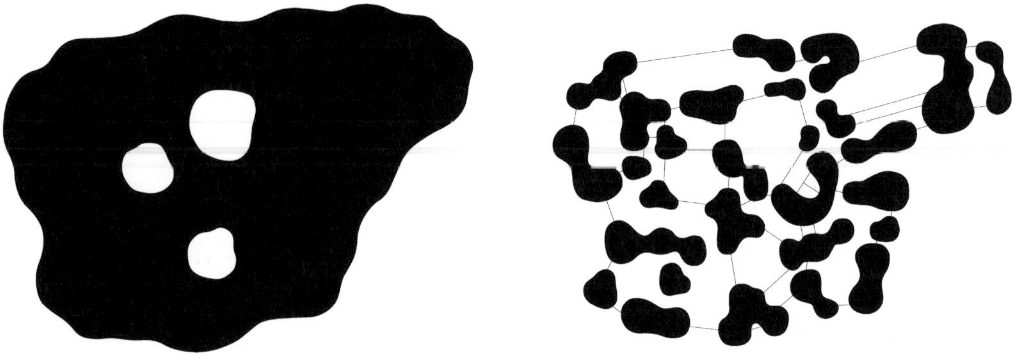

House and restaurant, project, Yamaguchi, 2015, horizontal sections

of architecture as simply being a territory solely for human beings. In other words, rather than considering human beings as the absolute inhabitant of architecture, I believe that the future role of architecture is to establish a new relationship between human beings and everything else within an architectural interior. To achieve this, I like to consider an interior in a more relative light — as an "environment that is different to the existing external space." Incorporating plants into my architectural designs is something that emerges from this train of thought. Nevertheless, it is just one element of many that allow me to pursue this concept, and not a specific concern in itself.

In the book *Another scale of architecture* there is an essay by Taro Igarashi. He mentions that in discussions between yourself and your associates you use the term "cute." How do you relate to that?
I think that architecture should be as open and as friendly as possible. I constantly aim to create an environment that allows everyone to experience enjoyment and comfort and at the same time has an atmosphere almost like air — an environment that is as modest and as unintimidating as possible, so much so that people forget that the architecture is there. In striving to realize such architecture, I feel that a cute, accessible and cherishable atmosphere is an extremely important element.

Do you think that a friendly building has any influence on society?
Friendly buildings do indeed have some form of influence on society. I believe that it is very important for contemporary architecture to possess a sense of flexibility that allows anyone to both access and use it easily. More architecture of this kind would dramatically expand the places that we can all inhabit and engage with. I feel that creating friendly architecture is synonymous to widening the scope of our current world. Furthermore, one of the important things for architecture of any era is that it continues to exist over a long period of time. In this sense, it is important

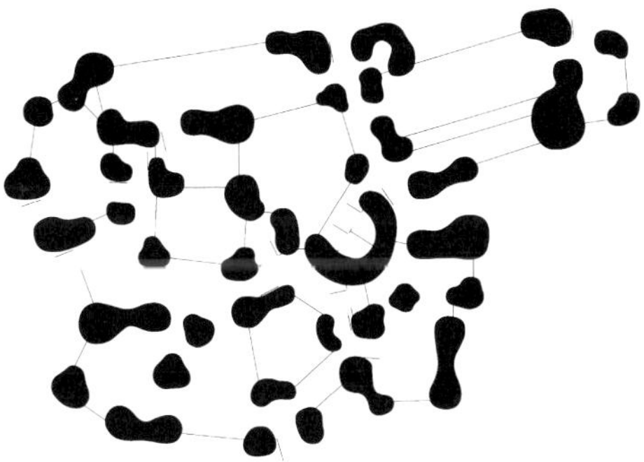

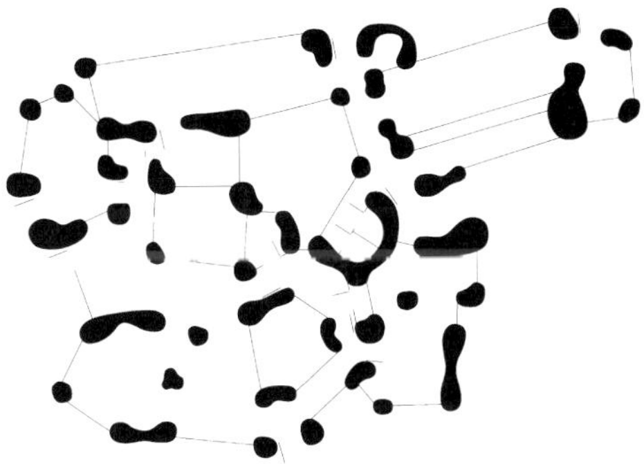

for everyone to feel some sort of attachment towards a building. If a building is not appreciated by everyone, then it inevitably will cease to exist. Friendly architecture transcends the boundaries of time, countries, individuals and groups, and is a driving force that serves to expand our existing world.
I consider contemporary architecture as belonging to society while at the same time being strongly linked to individuals. This again relates to what I mentioned earlier, as it is my understanding that the vigorous diversification of values in our current era will not cease, but will in future further permeate our entire world. In this sense, I feel that it is gradually becoming difficult to distinguish between that which is special and that which is not. One thing that might be the norm for someone may in fact be considered very special to someone else. This is an issue that I find myself experiencing on a daily basis, and something that I think is characteristic of our current times: different values co-existing ordinarily and pluralistically within the context of day-to-day society. What is important is not whether a particular building is special or not, but rather, the kind of values that its existence responds to.

You refer to the role of architecture for society and at the same time to nature as a role model for your architecture, as seen in the forest-like architecture of the KAIT workshop. What is it that interests you about these role models?
For the KAIT workshop I attempted to incorporate a spatial principle or a spatial configuration that exists within the natural environment into the context of architecture. In general, the composition of space in architecture is strongly connected to functions and roles, and these aspects typically define the plan. For example, one can often easily determine that a column or wall is positioned in a certain place for functional and/or structural purposes, and it is through such reasons that many people come to understand how to use the building. However, at the same time, one could say that these very forces in architecture also have a tendency to strongly limit the activities of its users.

Japan Pavilion, 11th International Architecture Exhibition, Venice Biennale, Italy, 2008

Within a forest, a variety of different spaces are created between each of the trees. When we visit a forest on a camping trip for example, we intuitively recognize these pre-existing spaces and accordingly establish an appropriate spatial arrangement such as a place for setting up a tent, a place to make the bonfire, etc. Needless to say, these spaces were not intentionally created for the purposes of setting up a camp, but they were already there in the first place. The users themselves create various spaces by determining the optimal use and role for the gaps between the trees in an immediate and ad hoc manner. Moreover, the trees that define these gaps may appear to be randomly arranged, but they are most certainly positioned based on a rationale produced by complex conditions. In other words, the positions of the trees in the forest are not truly random, but are the product of an invisible system. Various spatial qualities are formed by this invisible system, even though we as humans are unable to understand it. Nevertheless, I attempt to consider and appropriate the space itself that emerges within this context from a variety of interpretations.
Similarly in the KAIT workshop, the proportions and directions of the more than 300 columns are each different, and are determined based on various conditions such as architectural planning and structure. These decisions were made one by one as a result of numerous studies implemented using a dedicated program as well as building a series of models at a scale of 1:3 of all the respective areas. In other words, the proportions, directions and positions of the columns that at first glance seem unintentional, have in fact been planned with a deliberate sense of arbitrariness. There is indeed the presence of an invisible system, but because this system is transparent, the users are unable to clearly, or at least consciously "read" it. As a consequence, it subconsciously evokes various actions and at the same time grants possibilities for users to find means of intentionally utilizing the space in ways that go beyond what we as the architects anticipated.
In the project for this building I wanted to create a new sense of flexibility that is not found in previous architecture. When I say flexibility, I am referring to the spatial flexibility and level of freedom that is inherent within the natural environment. It is within this context that various creatures have been nurtured, various activities have emerged and a variety of relationships formulated. The spaces of the natural world offer us such complex and multi-dimensional functions and roles. I wanted to realize these spatial conditions through architecture.

Many of your projects show a new way of thinking about or developing architecture. What can the future bring?
I always engage in designs with a mindset that hopes to bring about even the slightest change to our world through architecture. I believe that the role of the architect is to constantly create new environments that correspond to contemporary values through architecture and to further continue developing and updating them accordingly. Needless to say, it is not possible for one person alone to change the world, but I would like to play a part in its course. We as human beings are always seeking a new "sense of comfort." This is perhaps similar to our fundamental human desires. The desire to open up a new world and to live as comfortably as possible within it is indeed something that we as human beings always arrive at. To give an extreme example from our current times, one could describe a space station as being the most innovative environment for humans to inhabit, conceived by bringing

KAIT Workshop at Kanagawa Institute of Technology, Atsugi, 2008, model

together the very best of contemporary science. But it is not architecture because, for the moment at least, it cannot be considered an environment that can be inhabited by everyone comfortably. A space station might therefore be a collective complex of innovative facilities, but it cannot be referred to as architecture. For example, our role as architects is to transform these kinds of places into comfortable environments. It is to broaden the scope of our existing world and to create new and comfortable environments. The certainty that it is possible to create a new sense of comfort in this new world is what helps us attain a sense of security with respect to the vast and limitless future that lies ahead of us.

You talked about the future: how do you relate to certain historical aspects of architecture in Japan? Is that of any importance?

I grew up in Japan and have been very influenced by its environment, so I would definitely say that it is in some respects important. The key issue is that these influences, in my case, relate to notions of nature. I also feel a certain sense of familiarity towards the history of Japan as it has been nurtured since ancient times and the many events that have been conceived throughout the course of its progression. This is something that instills me with a feeling of calmness. As such, I feel that it is extremely important for me to contemplate the reasons and factors for sensing comfort in nature while continuing to think of means for creating new architecture. What is important is that, as opposed to the reality that we can see and touch now

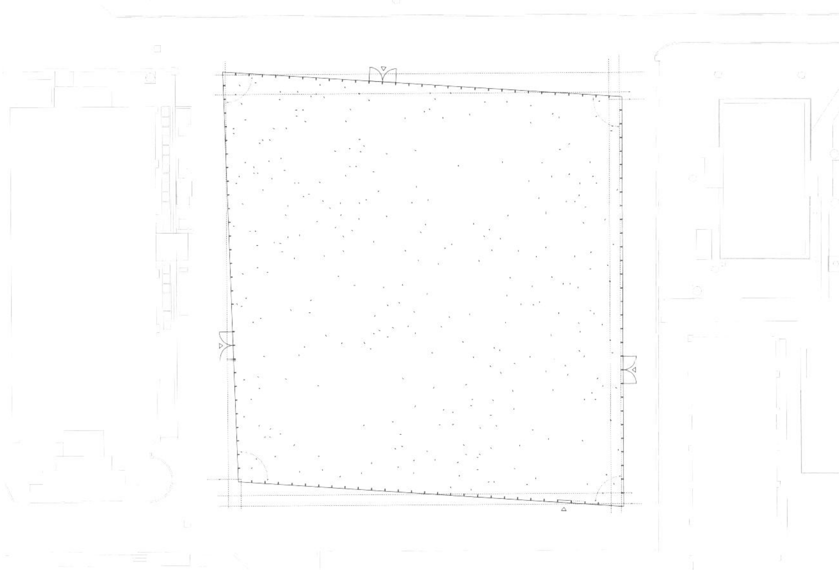

Plan

and that denotes this point in time, the past (history) and the future are both equally uncertain and at the same time embody an equivalent level of possibility. I consider both as infinite sources of information that extend from our current times. I believe that it is absolutely necessary to explore and optimally utilize this infinite array of information when thinking about new concepts for architecture. In other words, the past just like the future is important to me from the vantage point that it is a world of possibilities that expands endlessly from the current.

In the history of aesthetics and architecture in Japan, you have certain definitions of space. Do you make reference to these kinds of spaces?
Speaking in terms of the particular qualities of Japanese space that influence me personally, I am drawn to ways in which the conditions for maintaining the architecture and the conditions of the architecture itself are integrated to create a variety of unique characteristics. For example, one could mention a condition of architecture as seen in the *Sengu* ceremony of the *Ise Shrine* where the buildings are rebuilt every 20 years on the adjacent site, and the manner in which the gardens of Zen temples and the bare grounds of a tearoom have been constantly maintained on a day-to-day basis over hundreds of years so as to adjust their balance. Or alternatively, a space that may seemingly appear maculate may in fact be something that has been kept very clean, and thus could potentially lead to a particular sense of beauty. These examples illustrate that some Japanese architecture is, to a certain extent, only

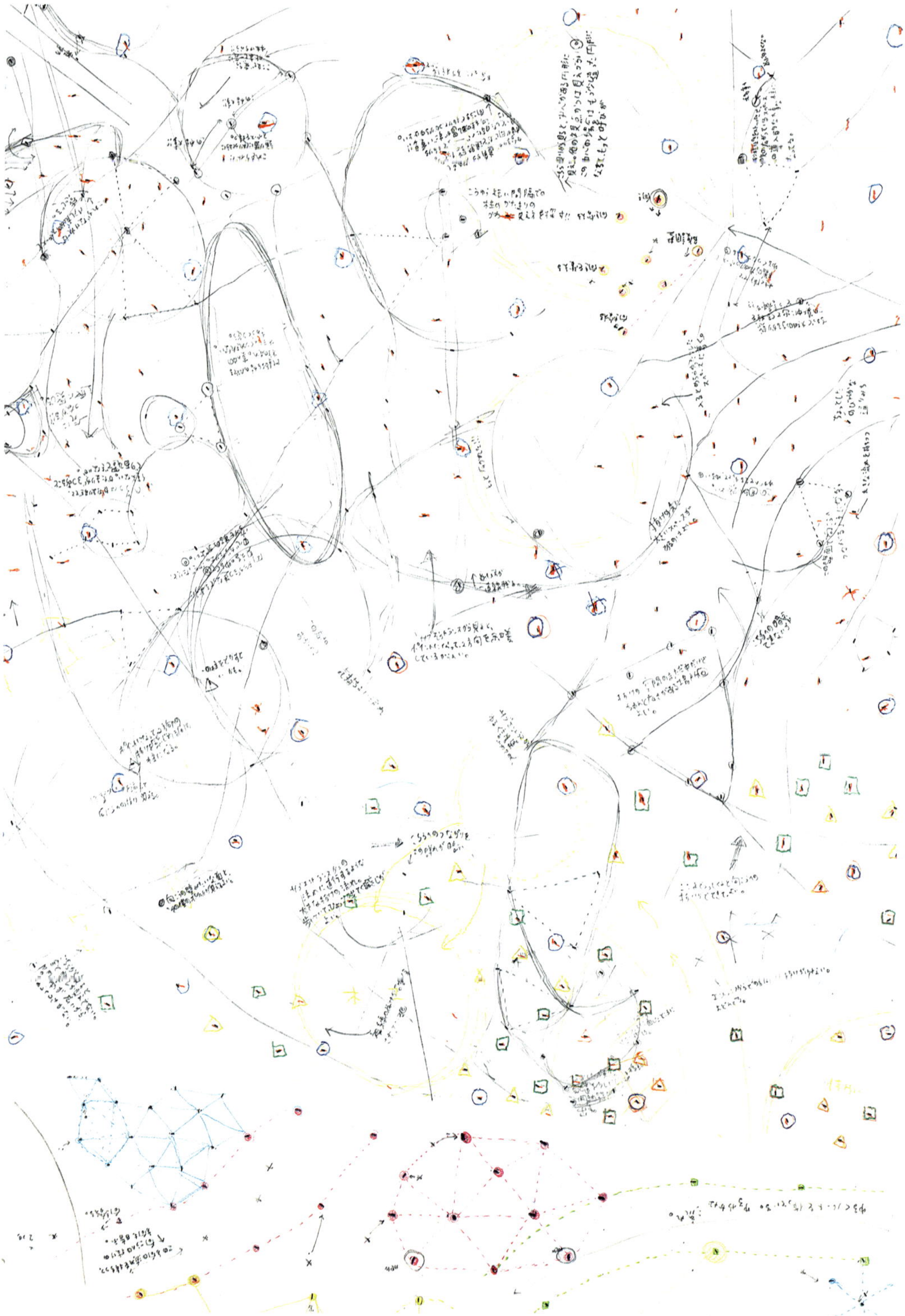

KAIT Workshop at Kanagawa Institute of Technology, sketch

maintained and continues to persist through human beings tending to the space on a daily basis. Rather than architecture being something that is stronger than human beings and exists in absolute terms, I am very interested in the delicate environments that are conceived through means of an intimate relationship between human activity and architecture.

Architecture does not simply exist to protect human beings. A certain balance is created by human beings also actively protecting architecture. I think that the environment that is established through this cyclical and reciprocal balance embodies possibilities for our current times. From a much broader perspective, I feel that this notion leads to our current values in which the belief is for human beings to protect the natural environment in the very same way that the natural environment has always served to protect and nurture human life.

Balloon, exhibition at the Museum of Contemporary Art in Tokyo, 2007

JUNYA ISHIGAMI

Biography

1974 Born in Kanagawa Prefecture
2000 Master of Architecture at Tokyo National University of Fine Arts and Music
Joined Kazuyo Sejima & Associates, Tokyo
2004 Established junya ishigami+associates, Tokyo
2009–11 Lecturer, Tokyo University of Science
2010 Associate Professor, Tohoku University
2014 Visiting Professor, Graduate School of Design, Harvard University
2015 Visiting Professor, School of Architecture, Princeton University

Principal Works

2005 Table at Art Basel, Switzerland
2007 Balloon at Museum of Contemporary Art, Tokyo
2008 Yohji Yamamoto Gansevoort Street Store, New York, United States
Venice Biennale, 11th International Architecture Exhibition, Italy, Japanese Pavilion
Kanagawa Institute of Technology KAIT Workshop, Kanagawa
2010 Venice Biennale, 12th International Architecture Exhibition, Italy, Architecture as air: Study for Château
la Coste (awarded Golden Lion)
2012 House with plants, Tokyo
2014 Cloud Garden, Kanagawa
2015 House and restaurant, Yamaguchi
2016 Pavilion at Park Groot Vijversburg, Tytsjerk, Netherlands (under development)
Russian Polytechnic Museum Reconstruction, Moscow, Russia (under development)
Port of Kinmen Passenger Service Center, Kinmen, Taiwan (under development)

Publications—Selection

2008 *Small images* (Contemporary Architect's Concept Series 2), LIXIL Publishing, Tokyo
2010 *Junya Ishigami* (The Japan Architect 79), Tokyo
Studies for The Scottish National Gallery of Modern Art, Tokyo
Plants and architecture, Tokyo
How small? How vast? How architecture grows, Shiseido Gallery, Tokyo
2011 *Another scale of architecture*, Seigensha, Tokyo
2015 *Christian Kerez—Junya Ishigami* (El Croquis 182), Madrid

GO
HASEGAWA

It is vital to keep on thinking

Mr. Hasegawa, how did your path towards architecture evolve? Why did you decide to study architecture?

My father was a mechanical engineer. He worked for a heavy industries company and planned and drew turbines for big ships. So I was used to seeing drawings, especially at weekends, when he used to draw in the living room. Sometimes he explained the ships to me; probably very specific things that I was not able to understand at the time. But I experienced the concept of scale when I was a child and understood that we can imagine and create huge objects through a scale drawing. The other reason was that I was interested in mathematics at high school, and architecture seemed to be a creative version of mathematics.

When I was at high school, I remember chancing upon a book by Shinohara in the school library and being surprised to see a house designed by an architect. I didn't know that architects designed private houses. Until then I thought that architects only designed public, monumental buildings. I discovered that Shinohara was teaching at the Tokyo Institute of Technology, so I decided to study there, but by the time I began he had already retired and I did not get to meet him.

At Tokyo Tech I met two architects: one was Kazunari Sakamoto, a student of Shinohara's, and the other Yoshiharu Tsukamoto, co-founder of "Atelier Bow-Wow," who started teaching the same year I began studying. Since Tsukamoto was in his early thirties and had no project at that time, he spent a lot of time at school. Now, of course, he is an internationally active architect. Every night after 1 a.m. he would come down to our drawing room and quite often we talked about architecture in general and our project for the design course. As a fourth-year student I chose Tsukamoto's studio and worked with him on some research projects on Tokyo, such as "Made in Tokyo" or "Pet Architecture."

At that time, I was particularly taken with architecture in Holland and in Switzerland. Koolhaas and Herzog & de Meuron were key figures at the time. I learned more about Swiss architecture from Momoyo Kaijima, Tsukamoto's partner at "Atelier Bow-Wow", who had studied with Peter Märkli at the ETH in Zurich in 1996/97. At that time, nobody knew Peter Märkli in Japan. So I took a two-month trip to Switzerland when I was 19, and visited almost every building by Peter Märkli, Herzog & de Meuron, Peter Zumthor, etc. I was interested in and also influenced by Swiss architecture, which is modest, silent and intellectual.

In 2000, during my master's course, I took a trip to France and worked for three months with Lacaton & Vassal in Paris as an intern. At that time, they had just started construction for the Palais de Tokyo, and worked from a small office in the attic space of Palais de Tokyo. They had just come to Paris from Bordeaux and were light, free and enjoyed the pleasures of life. I liked their projects very much.

And what did you do after graduating?
I started to work in Taira Nishizawa's office. He is the elder brother of Ryue Nishizawa and a very good architect. He also graduated from Tokyo Tech, and I stayed at his office for three years, where I worked on two apartments, one gymnasium and some exhibitions.

Why did you choose to work with Taira Nishizawa?
I knew some very good architectural offices in Japan and I wanted to choose the smallest one. Nishizawa's office consisted of just three people: Nishizawa, myself and another colleague. We discussed architecture every night. It was really hard work, but we had numerous beautiful days. I really focused on the projects and it was very formative for my later work.
In 2005, I started my own office when I got a commission for a weekend house from friends of my parents. They knew me because they lived across the street from my parents' house and asked me to design their building. Nishizawa suggested I do it myself, giving me my first project, and that was the "House in a forest."

And then you decided to establish your office in Tokyo, as many Japanese architects have?
I chose Tokyo mostly because I worked and lived there at that time. It could have been any other place, but I like Tokyo very much, because everything is there. I like the variety and atmosphere.

During your time at Tokyo Tech you did research on the "everyday architecture" of Tokyo. How important was this for the development of your own approach to architecture?
Sakamoto and Tsukamoto had both studied the typologies of houses. In Japan we are not used to discussing typologies: architecture is generally understood as a personal creation, as a product of an architect's design skills. I learned about typology from them and began to ask myself "how can we design houses that relate to normal buildings?" How can an architect match the daily life or common qualities of a house? My buildings are generally based on architectural elements, like roofs and balconies, and I think this is because of my interest in architectural typologies.

How much are you inspired by the tradition of Japanese architecture? You use transitional spaces such as the veranda or the *engawa*, but in a unique way.
To be honest, when I started my office, I was not aware of any personal relationship to the tradition of Japanese architecture. When I started teaching in Switzerland and visited cities in Europe, I saw that everything is more fixed and static. Gradually I began to understand that I was used to living in more ambiguous conditions, where public and private and inside and outside are more fluid. It is different in Europe, and that's why Europeans kept on telling me that I had very close ties to Japanese traditions. That helped me understand this.

You spoke about the influence of Sakamoto and his teacher, Kazuo Shinohara. How important are the texts and houses of Shinohara for you?
I never met Shinohara. But what I learned from his projects and his texts was how to see the world. All his works make clear and strong statements—his attitude

House in a forest, Nagano, 2006

towards architecture shows something beyond the existing world of our life. I know of no other architect like him.

My architecture is very simple, as simple as possible, but it's not minimalist. I often ask myself "What is the most important aspect?" and this informs my buildings, making them very simple and clear as a result. I learned a lot from him—every building should have a sharp and clear vision towards the world in itself.

At first glance, your buildings look simple because you often use common elements.

Yes, I always use very normal elements, but the way I use them is different. I transform the proportions, the position or the relationship they have to other elements, in order to emphasize and vitalize their specific potential. For example, in the "House in a forest," I was very interested in recovering the potential of the attic space, which nobody uses any more. I believe architecture is still growing, and that's why I think architectural elements are not fixed yet. They are still in a growing process.

That means that you deal with elements from everyday architecture in your projects—normal elements like roofs or doors—and subject them to a process of transformation? You alter certain elements and take them to a kind of extreme?

The potential and the possibility that architectural elements offer is that they are very familiar to the average person. Everybody knows roofs and balconies. Everybody can understand my buildings—I am not interested in making buildings just for architects. That's a reason why I use common elements, but at the same time I like to shift the banal image of the element as well. I like to combine something very

special and also very normal within one building. I need this creative contradiction in my projects.

One of your strategies is to create a zone that is in-between the façade and the interior of the house. It has a relationship to the inside and to the outside as well.
The idea of "comfort" in a city in Japan or Asia is different to that in Europe. We feel comfortable and can relax when there is continuity of the environment within the house; the house is not just protective in character. There is no strict division between inside and outside because there is just one continuous environment—one world. In Europe, the concept of inside and outside is a defining and fundamental aspect of the space. That's why Westerners are so interested in our ambiguous boundaries, I think. I travel a lot in Asia, and when I visit cities and interesting architecture, I learn directly from vernacular buildings and cities. They show us how we can develop a proper way to live in cities, and I always try to examine how this works. This Asian conception, where one lives in a continuous environment with no strict division between inside and outside and public and private, needs to become one of the strategies for space in the 21st century.

In a special issue of *Japan Architect* "Beyond Metabolism," you published an article that has the title "The Presentness of Renovation." What is your understanding of renovation?
My interest is not just in making something new; I want to deal with things old and new—both aspects. The period in which architects only made something new by rejecting an old idea is over. I think Japanese houses have always been fresh,

Apartments in Nerima, Tokyo, 2010

because of our custom of building detached houses and because architects have always experimented with houses. "New" had a power. But in our generation we have to start thinking how to combine the past and the present, the new and the old. I know that many Europeans are interested in Japanese architecture, because it is always new and also related to our history. But actually we have not discussed history or tradition for a long time, and it was even a taboo—especially after the postmodernism of the 1980s. Now, I think, is the time to think about the continuity of history in Japan again.

As regards renovation, it has become more popular to renovate old housing in Japan. It's a good movement, but many renovation projects simply express the contrast of old and new. I am interested in making situations that go beyond such contrasts. As an architect, I would love to be able to create a time continuum.

What can we expect from you in the future?
I am trying to get a project in Europe. I would like to build there. In Japan, there are just too few chances to get a commission for a public building.

Is Japan built?
We have very few opportunities today and only big companies are powerful enough to get commissions. The process is experience oriented to minimize the risk of a project. That's a very bad situation. I like the European competition system, which is very open—although there are other difficulties of course.

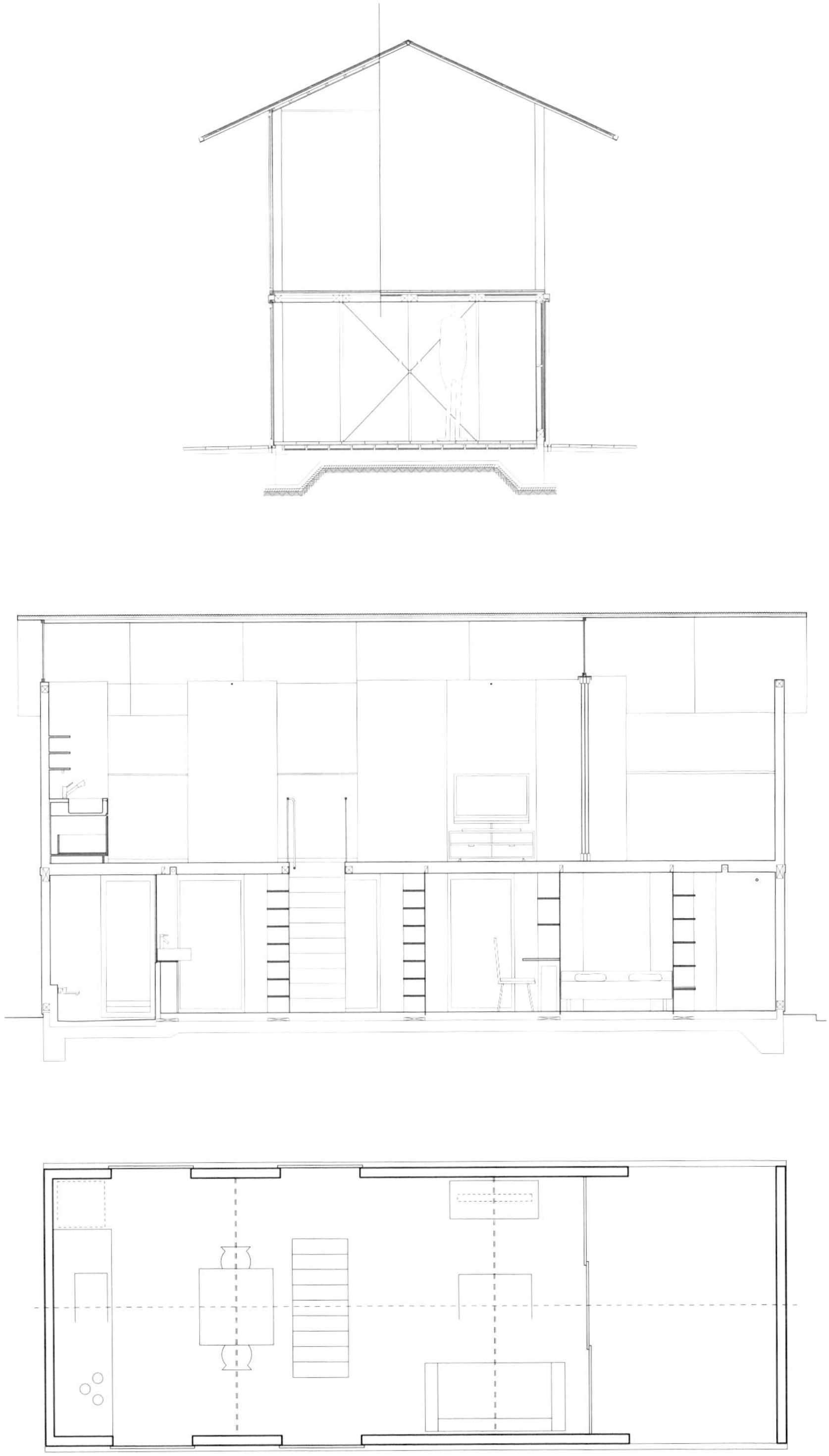

House in Kyodo, Tokyo, 2011, sections and floor plan

House in Kyodo

You taught in Mendrisio in Switzerland for three years. Is international exchange common for architects of your generation?
Things have changed a lot for my generation. Kenzo Tange was invited to Harvard after he was successful outside of Japan. But I was thirty-four when I started in Mendrisio, a young Japanese architect who only had experience of building small houses. Nevertheless, they invited me to Mendrisio. I guess it is because the world is growing much closer together, thanks to cheaper flights and the internet.
We can learn from each other, we are influenced by each other and we have the opportunity to meet each other. That is certainly one of the great possibilities of our generation.

In March 2015 you published a book of interviews with European architects. What was the main idea for this publication?
For more than two years, I had the opportunity to come to Switzerland every two weeks. I met different architects, not only from Switzerland, and I traveled a lot, gave lectures and enjoyed many conversations. I sensed a strong continuity in European history as architects always cared about and were aware of history. Of course there are different positions, but history is an important starting point for many architects. That gave me the idea to make a book of interviews with Álvaro Siza, Valerio Olgiati,

Peter Märkli, Anne Lacaton and Jean-Philippe Vassal, Pascal Flammer as well as Kersten Geers and David van Severen. All the architects I interviewed have different starting points, but they share a special sense of history. I learned a lot from them.

You have finished your doctoral thesis in 2015. What was your topic?
Yes, I have, and my supervisor was Yoshiharu Tsukamoto from Tokyo Tech. It is about the proportions in contemporary architecture. My research is organized in three chapters: one of them focuses on Japanese contemporary architecture and the other two chapters analyze examples from all over the world. In winter 2016 I will publish a new *a+u* monograph which will contain a summary of the thesis.

Can you tell us more about the way you design? Do you design using sketches or models—what comes first? Do you work by hand or use a computer?
Today, I rarely ever draw on the computer. I'll usually make a sketch and my staff then work that up on the computer. But we work a lot with models, discussing and comparing them to each other. This is our approach. I am constantly trying to overcome myself—to avoid perpetuating or rehashing past ideas. I need to change and develop our projects, and that works best with models. A model is a comparatively

objective representation of a project and that is an important distinction. Drawings, by contrast, are very personal for me.

You build a lot of models and at the same time you want to push things further. How do you find the point where you stop designing?

I do not decide on my own. There are many aspects: the situation, the client, the schedule—all kinds of things. Many people ask me this, but I am not consciously aware of saying when to stop. What's important is that we have thought about it from as many aspects as possible. That's more relevant than my decision. And anyhow, a decision is not the culmination of a project; we should always strive to keep on thinking.

Pilotis in a forest, Gunma, 2010

GO HASEGAWA

Biography

1977 Born in Saitama
2002 Master of Architecture, Graduate School of Science and Engineering, Tokyo Institute of Technology
2002–04 Employee at Taira Nishizawa Architects, Tokyo
2005 Established Go Hasegawa and Associates, Tokyo
2009–11 Guest Lecturer, Tokyo Institute of Technology
2012–14 Visiting Professor, Academy of Architecture of Mendrisio, Switzerland
2014 Visiting Professor, Oslo School of Architecture and Design, Norway
2015 Ph.D. in Engineering, Tokyo Institute of Technology
2016 Visiting Professor, University of California, Los Angeles, United States
Visiting Professor, milano international architectural design workshop 2016, Polytechnic University of Milan, Italy

Principal Works

2006 House in a forest, Nagano
House in Sakuradai, Mie
House in Gotanda, Tokyo
2009 House in Komae, Tokyo
2010 Apartments in Nerima, Tokyo
Pilotis in a forest, Gunma
Townhouse in Asakusa, Tokyo
2011 House in Komazawa, Tokyo
House in Kyodo, Tokyo
2012 Belfry in Ishinomaki, Miyagi
2013 House in Shakujiikouen, Tokyo
2014 Row house in Ageo, Saitama
Apartment in Okachimachi, Tokyo
2015 House in Sangenjaya, Tokyo
House in Yokohama, Kanagawa

Publications—Selection

2009 "The Presentness of Renovation", in: *Renovation: Beyond Metabolism* (The Japan Architect 73), Tokyo
2011 *Thinking, Making Architecture, Living*, LIXIL Publishing, Tokyo
2012 *Go Hasegawa: Works*, TOTO Publishers, Tokyo
The Belfry in Ishinomaki, Seibundo Shinkosha, Tokyo
2015 *Conversations with European Architects*, LIXIL Publishing, Tokyo

POSITIONS

Cultural translations: Japanese architecture between East and West

Christian Tagsold

> *"What an Oriental city looks like is, I assume, known to everyone. It is exactly the same as one of our cities, only Oriental."*
> ALFRED KUBIN, *The Other Side*

In his novel, *The Other Side* written in 1909, the Austrian author Alfred Kubin describes a contradictory situation known to many in the West who have studied Japanese architecture: it is familiar but different, similar but exotic.

This is the consequence of a process of many cultural translations. In Japan, exposure to Western architecture since the mid-19th century led on the one hand to the adoption of Western techniques and styles, and on the other precipitated the construction of an own architectural history. It set in motion a process that had already begun in a similar manner several decades earlier in Europe. Architecture and its history was enlisted as means of giving identity to the nation state, and consequently acquired a new function.[1] Old buildings and ensembles were accorded the status of national monuments and woven into a historical narrative of the national style to legitimize the new nation state.

In Japan, however, this process took place in the second half of the 19th century and the first half of the 20th century under quasi-colonial conditions. While Japan managed to avoid colonization by Western powers, it was nevertheless forced to make concessions in the form of unequal treaties.[2] In 1854 and 1858, the first contracts were signed with the United States, who had forced the Japanese shogunate to relinquish its restrictions on contacts with the outside world. Similar treaties with other Western powers followed soon after.

As a reaction to these treaties, a modernization process according to the Western model was rapidly initiated. The young Meiji Emperor issued edicts expounding the value of progress and prepared his people, now citizens of a new unified state, for the times ahead.

In this context, Western architects and cultural scholars such as Josiah Conder from England or Edward Morse from the United States were brought in to prepare students at the new imperial universities for the requirements of the new "modern" age. Conder and Morse were fascinated by the architecture they saw in the country, though they remained convinced of the superiority of Western ways and technology. Unlike Conder, Morse was not an architect but a biologist and archaeologist, but in 1885 he published *Japanese Homes and their Surroundings*, one of the first

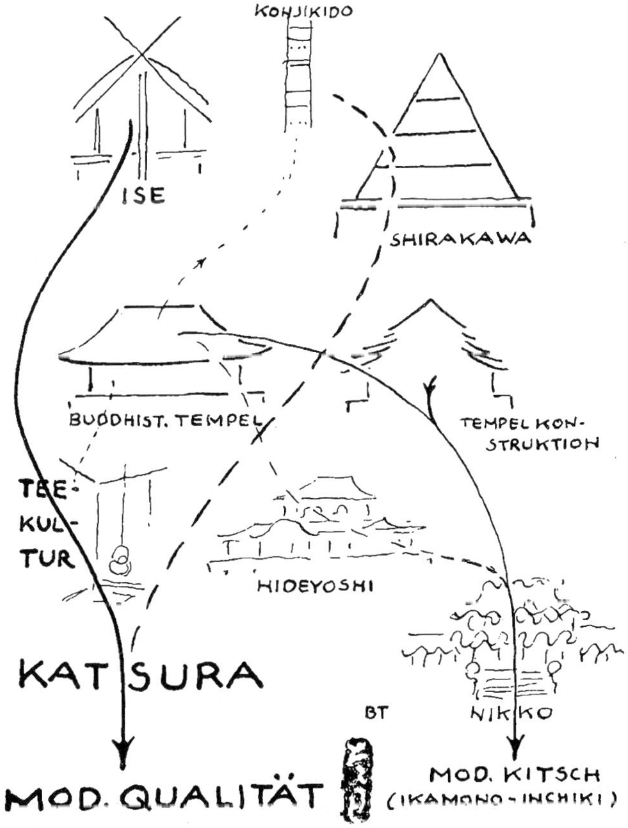

1. The positive line, which begins in the Isé Shrines, was not diverted in consequence of Buddhist influences; but the principle of rational construction as represented in Shirakawa was later destroyed. Buddhism — particularly Zen—contributed in the Tea Ceremony a spiritual aesthetics which for the second time (that is, after Isé) brought Japanese architecture to a zenith in the Palace and garden of Katsura.

The negative line, in which the degeneration of construction into decoration was intensified by the rulers' orders for ornamentation, comes from the Buddhist temple.

Bruno Taut, sketch, Fundamentals of Japanese Architecture, 1936

introductions to Japanese architecture released in the West.[3] Conder, by contrast, focused in his writings on the design of Japanese gardens.[4]

The influence of Western authors was so strong that in the beginning the historical narrative of Japanese architecture resembled that of the European colonies in Asia.[5] In contrast to this, authors such as Morse and Conder were crucial for the early development of historical discourse in Japan, but newly educated Japanese specialists, most notably Okakura Tenshin, were able to reclaim at least some narrative authority from the Western authors.[6] The Japanese state also began early on to play an important role in preserving historical buildings, emphasizing the role that architecture played in the construction of the nation's own narrative.

That marked the beginning of an ongoing discourse in which both Western and Japanese authors compared and contrasted the "self" with the "other" (each from

Shrine, Nikko, early 17th century

their own respective viewpoint), thereby simultaneously contributing to creating and defining each other's culture. This arena of discourse took on more and more shape.

Japanese architecture between Nikko and Katsura

This development can be seen very clearly in the shifting historical reception of the Nikko Shrine and the Katsura Imperial Villa. Until well into the 1920s, the Nikko Shrine was regarded as one of the foremost examples of Japanese architecture. Built in 1617, one year after the death of Tokugawa Ieyasu, the first Shogun of the Edo Period, by his son as a shrine for his father, it is richly decorated with carvings and ornaments. A stopover in Nikko has been a must for Western tourists visiting the country since the beginnings of tourism in the country at the end of the 19th century.[7] In the two decades preceding World War II, however, the shrine became a symbol for the dispute between two generations of Japanese architects[8]: the younger generation of modernist architects saw the Nikko Shrine as a historical parallel to the richly decorated buildings of the establishment of conservative architects of the day. Hideto Kishida, a professor of architecture at the Imperial University of Tokyo, set out the position of the young modernists[9] who argued that the Katsura Imperial Villa better represented the true heart of Japanese cultural heritage. For them, the reductionist qualities of the Katsura Villa made it an expression of what was "modern," and allowed them to legitimize their ideas of building.
In the two pre-war decades, the political and intellectual climate grew increasingly nationalistic.[10] In this context, the fact that the Katsura Villa had imperial status was of particular importance. In the ideology of the right wing, the Shoguns had ruled illegitimately over the Tenno over a period of two and a half centuries. By referring to the Imperial Villa, the young architects could place their aims at the heart of the nationalist discourse, which focused on the Tenno.
Characteristic for this dispute was that the young generation of architects enlisted Western expertise to underline their cause. Bruno Taut, who fled Europe in May 1933 to escape the Nazis, spent several years in Japan and was introduced to the Katsura

Katsura Imperial Villa, Kyoto, early 17th century

Villa by the young architects, among them Tetsuro Yoshida. Taut's confirmation of the aesthetic appraisal of the young architects strengthened their position markedly in the public eye, as even the major daily newspapers reported on Taut's activities and lectures quite intensively.[11] The perceived backing of a Western architect of such caliber helped the young architects gain more recognition, and gradually they were able to realize their conception of contemporary architecture, displacing their older colleagues. Bruno Taut benefited likewise, extending his reputation as an expert on Japanese architecture.[12] He went on to publish four books on Japanese architecture, two of which were translated for readers in Japan. His first book made it onto the list of recommended books for Japanese libraries and was even declared recommended reading by the Japanese Ministry of Culture.[13]

For the young architects of the 1930s and 40s, elements of a modern character became synonymous with the nationalist cause, a position strengthened by the ultra-nationalistic political climate. In some buildings, this connection between (ultra-)nationalist ideology and modern architecture can be seen quite clearly. Shoichi Inoue described a special case[14]: Kenzo Tange's plan from 1949 for the Hiroshima Peace Memorial Park, which became central to his later reputation, was based in part on revised plans for a quite different project. In 1942, Tange had designed a memorial for Japan's declared war objective, the "Greater East Asia Co-Prosperity Sphere," that was to be built at the foot of Mount Fuji but was never realized. Ever since the publication of Inoue's book on Tange's plans and the connection between the two projects, the debate on this link between history and modernism has not subsided, neither in Japan nor in the West.

The example of Tange's design for the Peace Memorial Park shows how the underlying ideas of the young architects persisted long after the self-caused defeat of Japan in World War II. Now, however, the situation was different. Up until 1945, Japanese national and cultural identity had been aggressively propagated as something special. That continued too after the war, albeit in a more passive form. But at the same time, it was also held responsible for the problems of ultra-nationalism. Out of this arose a highly influential discourse called *Nihonjinron*, "theories about the Japanese".[15] Numerous books and articles were published on why being Japanese is different to the rest of the world, which invariably meant the Western world.

Kenzo Tange, Hiroshima Peace Memorial Park, Hiroshima, planning started in 1949

Kenzo Tange, *Daitoa*—Memorial for Japan's declared war objective, the "Greater East Asia Co-Prosperity Sphere," 1942

The theories and topics elaborated in the *Nihonjinron* were published widely and it is no surprise that they recur repeatedly in numerous individual reflections on Japan and its culture, and therefore also in discussions of its architecture. The *Nihonjinron* continued the construction of a Japanese national cultural identity and had an impact on all areas of society.
The controversy surrounding Nikko and Katsura illustrates clearly how the architectural narrative has evolved in a process in which reciprocal cultural translation plays a significant role. Every actual translation was inevitably an interpretation of the other (whether in Japan or in the West) and, as such, every attempt at understanding the other was simultaneously its construction.

A Japanese house in New York

An interesting example of these processes of cultural translation and performance that shows how gradually such processes changed, even long after the end of World War II, is the "Japanese House" in New York, built in 1954. The "Japanese House" (*Shofuso*) was built in the garden of the Museum of Modern Art (MoMA) in Manhattan. In 1949, the MoMA had begun showcasing contemporary houses to present the possibilities of modern architecture. The first of these, designed by Marcel Breuer, was built in 1949, the second by Gregory Ain in 1950. Of the three model houses built, the only one that was decidedly not "modern" was the "Japanese House." The Japanese architect Junzo Yoshimura was commissioned by Arthur Drexler, MoMA's architectural curator at the time, to build a house that should dem-

Junzo Yoshimura, "Japanese House" in the garden of the Museum of Modern Art, Manhattan, New York, 1954

onstrate how modern "traditional" building was in Japan.[16] The house was an immense image gain for the former enemy Japan, and simultaneously excellent advertising for Japanese architecture.[17] However, in an interview[18] Yoshimura declared that he had designed the house especially for the American public and not as an authentic copy of a historical Samurai house.[19] As such, he made clever strategic use of the commission but at the same time bowed to the ideas of his client on the modernity of Japanese traditional architecture.

Architecture in the process of cultural translation

These examples make it clear that architecture in Japan and in the West is subject to processes of cultural translation that go far beyond the realm of architecture itself. Processes of reciprocal cultural translation have also contributed to the underlying construction of the Japanese nation as a whole.[20] Many Western concepts and ideas such as "democracy," the "state" and "citizenship," as well as numerous technical expressions were first introduced, interpreted and assimilated into Japanese culture through such processes. In the West, on the other hand, an interest in the exotic, in other aesthetic expressions arose, as evidenced by the Japonism aesthetic movement at the end of the 19th century.[21] Here Orientalist perceptions of the East, as discussed by Edward Said in his seminal analysis of the Western reception of the East, played a significant role.[22] Nevertheless, Japanese architecture was able to build on this in the post-war period to acquire a status in the West that went beyond such Orientalist attributions.

Overall, it can be said that the idea of a Japanese architectural tradition was constructed through an ongoing interchange between Western and Japanese authors. For a long time, this relationship was heavily skewed towards the West, who laid down the standards. This was apparent, for example, in the education of young architects and architectural historians in Japan who trained at imperial universities in Japan under Western instruction. Little by little, the Japanese side was able to regain a more independent position in the construction of the imperial knowledge system. In the process, the Japanese aesthetic in the 1920s and 30s was ascribed a particular affinity to Western modernism, and through this a Japanese line of tradition was constructed that made it possible to build in the modern style, even during the period of ultra-nationalism leading up to World War II. After the war, the idea of the modernity of Japanese traditional architecture, as seen in the "Japanese House" at the MoMA, gave Japanese architects a chance to establish a reputation in Europe and the United States. The economic upturn in Japan around the same time gave further impetus to the Japanese architectural scene and generated more widespread interest in Japan as a whole. In addition, two international events—the Olympic Games in Tokyo in 1964 and the World Expo in Osaka in 1970—provided Japanese architects with an ideal platform to present their skills to the world. As a result, architecture was able to become the first modern Japanese art form to gain worldwide recognition.

1 Cf. Barry Bergdoll, *European Architecture 1750–1890*, Oxford 2000; Godehard Hoffmann, *Architektur für die Nation? Der Reichstag und die Staatsbauten des Deutschen Kaiserreichs 1871–1918*, Cologne 2000; Michaela Marek, *Kunst und Identitätspolitik: Architektur und Bildkünste im Prozess der tschechischen Nationsbildung*, Cologne 2004; Zeynep Çelik, *The Remaking of Istanbul: Portrait of an Ottoman City in the Nineteenth Century*, Berkeley 1993.

2 For an explanation of the unequal treaties and the implications of the lengthy process of revision for the modernisation of Japan cf. Michael R. Auslin, *Negotiating with Imperialism: The Unequal Treaties and the Culture of Japanese Diplomacy*, Cambridge 2004.

3 Morse's study, with its numerous photographs and detailed drawings, is still used by museums and theme parks for the reconstruction and outfitting of historical "authentic" buildings, and therefore, at a pragmatic level, plays an important role in the historiography of Japanese architecture. Cf. Hyung Il Pai, *Heritage Management in Korea and Japan: The Politics of Antiquity and Identity*, Seattle 2013, p. 54.

4 Josiah Conder, "The Art of Landscape Gardening in Japan," in: *Transactions of the Asiatic Society of Japan* 14(2), 1886, p. 119–175.

5 Cf. Benedict R. Anderson, *Imagined Communities: Reflections on the Origin and Spread of Nationalism* [revised edition], London, New York 2006.

6 Okakura Tenshin (also Kakuzo) was the leading art historian of the Meiji (1868–1912). In 1893 he directed the design of the Japanese Pavilion at the World's Columbian Exposition in Chicago 1893. The Ho-o-den, as the pavilion was called, comprised three sections linked by galleries, each presenting a different stylistic epoch, giving visitors an overview of the history of Japanese architecture. Cf. Judith Snodgrass, *Presenting Japanese Buddhism to the West: Orientalism, Occidentalism, and the Columbian Exposition*, Chapel Hill 2003, p. 29–33.

7 Jonathan M. Reynolds, "Ise Shrine and a Modernist Construction of Japanese Tradition," in: *The Art Bulletin* 83 (2), 2001, p. 316–341.

8 As Shoichi Inoue explains most lucidly in his book on the myth of the Katsura Villa. Cf. Shoichi Inoue, *Tsukurareta Katsura Rikyu shinwa*, Tokyo 1997.

9 The importance of Kishida for the development of Japanese architecture can be seen not least in his students, among them Kenzo Tange, Kunio Maekawa or Ryuichi Hamaguchi.

10 Cf. Gregory James Kasza, *The State and the Mass Media in Japan, 1918–1945*, Berkeley 1988, p. 129–136.

11 The largest liberal daily newspaper *Asahi Shimbun* even reported on Taut's arrival in Tokyo on May 15, 1933. Up to his departure for Turkey on October 1, 1936, more than a dozen articles on Taut were published in *Asahi Shimbun* alone.

12 Bruno Taut, *Fundamentals of Japanese Architecture*, Tokyo 1936; idem, *Houses and People of Japan*, Tokyo 1937; idem, *Nippon mit europäischen Augen gesehen*, Tokyo 1934; idem, *Japans Kunst mit europäischen Augen gesehen*, Tokyo 1936.

13 Inoue, op. cit., p. 71.

14 Inoue, op. cit.

15 Christian Tagsold, *Japan: Ein Länderporträt*, Berlin 2013, p. 18–22.

16 Arthur Drexler, *The Architecture of Japan*, New York 1955.

17 Hiroko Ikegami, "The Japanese Exhibition House in the Museum of Modern Art, New York: Shofuso and the Japan Boom in Postwar America," in: *Kokusai tōhō gakusha kaigikiyō* 52, 2007, p. 56–74.

18 Hisao Koyama, "Yoshimura Junzo ni kiku (Asking Junzo Yoshimura)," in: *Approach*, Spring 1991, p. 4–24.

19 After the end of the exhibition at the Museum of Modern Art, the Japanese House was relocated to Fairmount Park in Philadelphia, where it stands today. There it has an entirely different purpose: in the MoMA, the house served to make the reductionist tendencies of the modern era accessible to the general public, but in Philadelphia it is now a symbol of traditional Japan. Yoshimura himself was awarded the Prize of the Architectural Institute of Japan in 1955 – not for the *Shofuso* house but together with his partners Junzo Sakakura and Kunio Maekawa for the Kokusai Bunka Kaikan International House of Japan in the district of Roppongi in the heart of Tokyo. This building was decidedly modern and utterly different to the Japanese House. Cf. Christian Tagsold, *Spaces of Translation: Japanese Gardens in the West* (Penn Studies in Landscape Architecture), Philadelphia 2017.

20 Shingo Shimada, *Die Erfindung Japans: Kulturelle Wechselwirkung und nationale Identitätskonstruktion*, Frankfurt am Main 2000.

21 A market arose in Europe and North America for Japanese products such as fans, ceramics or bronze sculptures that addressed an increasing interest in the other and the exotic – as also seen in the World Expositions and ethnological expositions. Cf. Stefanie Wolter, *Die Vermarktung des Fremden: Exotismus und die Anfänge des Massenkonsums*, Frankfurt am Main 2005; Timothy Mitchell, "Orientalism and the Exhibitionary Order," in: Nicholas B. Dirks (Ed.), *Colonialism and Culture*, Ann Arbor 1992, p. 289–317; Pai, op. cit.

22 Edward W. Said, *Orientalism*, New York 1978.

The Japanese contribution to modern architecture in Europe

Hyon-Sob Kim

The Japanese contribution to the formation and development of modern architecture in the West seems now to be well acknowledged. Over the last half century, important studies have examined the Japanese role. Of these, Clay Lancaster's pioneering works of the 1940s and 50s were perhaps the most salient and consistent. Published as a series of articles in *The Art Bulletin*[1], they were incorporated in 1963 into one volume, *The Japanese Influence in America*. Other researchers also investigated the relationship between Japanese and American architects, most notably Frank Lloyd Wright.[2] However, these studies are mainly concerned with American modernism and the discussion on the influences on European architecture is generally limited to the *Japonisme*-related Arts-and-Crafts and Art-Nouveau period in the late 19th and early 20th centuries. It is therefore possible that the Japanese impact on European modern architecture was indeed less important than its impact on America. In 1953, Lancaster observed that "although European painting and the minor arts were greatly affected by those of the Far East, the influence on European architecture was not as great as on American."[3] This is plausible because "modern Western architecture was linked with faith in European civilization," with "the romantic faith in speed and the roar of machines," as stated by Chisaburoh F. Yamada based on the standpoint of Nikolaus Pevsner.[4] In 1914, Italian futurists even went as far as to urge modern architects not to crib "photographs of China, Persia and Japan."[5]

Nevertheless, there is still a need to examine how Japan was recognized by European modern architects, in particular before World War II and more specifically between the two world wars. It was in the European continent and during the interwar period that the so-called "Modern Movement" matured and the "International Style" was formed. In fact, many European modernists also referred to Japanese aesthetics in various contexts, and such examples prompt the question of whether Japanese sources were essential to them or were only used in passing. In the first decade of the 21st century, several important studies were published on this topic. Based on an analysis of these studies and other sources, the aim of this essay is to construct an integrated discourse on the role of Japan in European modern architecture.

The Japanese contribution to European modernism: literature review

Yuko Furukawa and Hiroshi Adachi's study *Information on Japanese architecture in the Western World since the late 19th century*, published in 2000, is based on the

Frank Lloyd Wright, Warren Hickox House, Kankakee, United States, 1900

Ho-o-den – Japanese Pavilion, World's Columbian Exposition, Chicago, United States, 1893. Wright's encounter with this building in his mid-20s was significant for his career.

fact that publications were the best vehicle with which to convey information about Japanese architecture to foreign shores and presents a survey of books on Japanese architecture in Western languages published before World War II. While the short descriptions of their chosen books—Edward S. Morse (1886), Franz Baltzer (1903/1907), Ralph Adams Cram (1905), Tetsuro Yoshida (1935), Hideto Kishida (1935), Jiro Harada (1935) and Bruno Taut (1937)—provide good introductions, the published list of 31 books and 17 articles is also of value. Based on this pilot study, the Adachi group in Kobe successively presented a series of analyses on each book. Manfred Speidel's research into "The Presence of Japanese Architecture in German Magazines and Books 1900–50"[6] disclosed further publications not already listed in Furukawa and Adachi's list and can be regarded as a response from a German perspective to the Japanese researchers. The paper asks, "What could a German architect know about Japanese architecture when he, like Bruno Taut in 1933, decided to travel to Japan?" The year 1923 marks "a turning point" for Taut and ultimately for European modernists, because his publication *Die neue Wohnung* from 1923 illustrates the common values of the modern rational and the traditional Japanese in architecture. According to Speidel, however, it was Tetsuro Yoshida's *Das japanische Wohnhaus*[7], published in 1935, that was the most significant watershed for European architects.

While these two studies focus on publications, "A Study on the Influence of Japanese *Tokonoma* on Aalto's Art Display Concept in Villa Mairea, 1937–39"[8] by the author and Anna Basham's *At the crossroads of Modernism and Japonisme: Wells Coates and the British Modern Movement*[9] are case studies that focus on specific architects' treatment of Japanese aesthetics. The flower room in Alvar Aalto's Villa Mairea is known to vividly demonstrate Japanese features.[10] Basham's treatise illustrates Wells Coates' life-long interest in Japan and investigates the Japanese

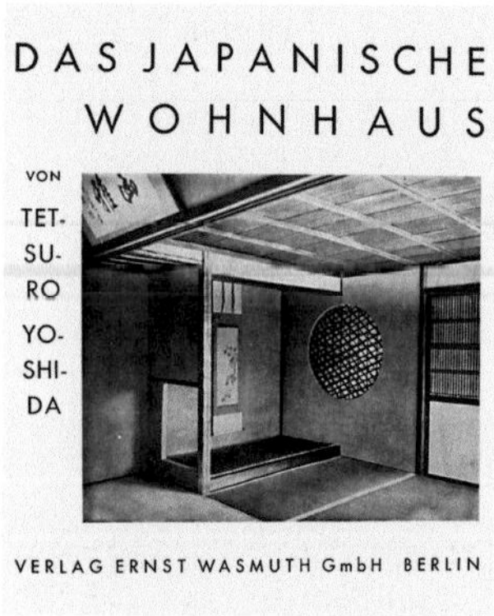

Tetsuro Yoshida, *Das japanische Wohnhaus*, 1935

Katsura Villa, *tokonoma*, Kyoto, early 17th century, from *Das japanische Wohnhaus*

resonance present in his writings and designs from the early 1930s. Coates extracted five points for modern architecture from the traditional Japanese house: frame construction, blurring the boundary between inside and outside, the sliding screen, built-in furniture, and the concept of *tokonoma*, which he later applied in his designs. But Coates, an influential modern architect in Britain, was not the only architect to draw inspiration from Japan. His colleagues Raymond McGrath, Serge Chermayeff and Christopher Tunnard were equally enamored. Basham successfully reveals the largely ignored aspect of the British Modern Movement and its intersection with *Japonisme*.

A further article "Tetsuro Yoshida (1894–1956) and the Architectural Interchange between East and West,"[11] also by the author, takes a different approach, focussing instead on Japanese architects rather than European modernists. By tracing his year-long travels in Europe in 1931/32 and the impacts of the subsequent publication of *Das japanische Wohnhaus*, the study highlights Yoshida's role as "a key mediator of architectural interchange between East and West."[12] As Speidel already pointed out, Yoshida left an interesting testimony in the preface of the book, stating that the publication was initiated during his stay in Europe at the request of Hugo Häring and Ludwig Hilberseimer.

Routes, attractions and applications

Based on the above studies and their accompanying references, we can assemble a collage of the typical Japanese influences on European modern architecture. From this, three aspects are of particular interest:

The routes by which European architects encountered Japanese aesthetics.

Japanese features that attracted European architects.

The application of Japanese aesthetics to modern architecture.

Katsura Villa, *tokonoma*, Kyoto, early 17th century, from *Das japanische Wohnhaus*

The routes by which European architects encountered Japanese aesthetics

European modernists were able to encounter Japan through publications, people and buildings, and also specifically through Frank Lloyd Wright.
Publications must have been the most significant vehicle, as suggested by Furukawa and Adachi's and Speidel's papers. The notable books on Japanese architecture are, to name a few, *Japanese Homes and Their Surroundings* (1886) by Edward S. Morse, *The Book of Tea* (1906) by Kakuzo Okakura, *Das japanische Wohnhaus* (1935) by Tetsuro Yoshida, and *Houses and People of Japan* (1937) by Bruno Taut.
There were also numerous go-betweens—Japanese architects in Europe and European architects in Japan. Teijiro Muramatsu identified about fifteen Japanese architects who studied or worked in Europe between the 1920s and the early 40s, including Kunio Maekawa in Le Corbusier's atelier from 1928 until 30 and Bunzo Yamaguchi in Gropius' office between 1928 and 33.[13] Nevertheless, the degree to which these Japanese architects provided their masters with critical information on Japanese architecture is unknown. As mentioned above, Yoshida's friendship with German architects while travelling was crucial, resulting in his significant publication in 1935.
At the same time, Western architects who spent time in Japan brought back and disseminated first-hand knowledge. Examples include Josiah Conder's series of lectures on Japanese architecture in London in the 1870s and 80s, Taut's lecture in Tokyo in 1935, which was published as *Fundamentals of Japanese Architecture*[14] in 1936, and Richard Neutra's articles on Japanese architecture in *Die Form* in 1931.[15] Of these, Taut is particularly important as a "discoverer" of the Katsura Villa. European architects also had contacts with Japanese people in their own country, such as Aalto's friendship with Japanese diplomats in Finland during the 1930s and 40s.[16] Some European architects encountered Japan through real buildings built in Europe

Zui-Ki-Tei (House of the Promising Light)—Japanese teahouse, Stockholm, Sweden, 1935

Robert van 't Hoff, bungalow, Huis ter Heide, The Netherlands, 1914

such as the pavilions for World Fairs in European countries. Karin Kirsch studied the Japanese pavilions used for these events in *Die Neue Wohnung und das Alte Japan*. Another important building is the Japanese tea house *Zui-Ki-Tei* built in 1935 in Stockholm, which was popular among many architects. Helge Zimdahl published an article on it in 1938 in the Swedish journal *Byggmästaren*.[17] Fred Thompson suggested that Aalto might have visited this building[18], and Richard Weston described its importance to Jørn Utzon and others: "The Zui-Ki-Tei was as important to Danish architects as the Ho-o-den temple and villa at the World's Columbian Exposition in Chicago in 1893 had been for Frank Lloyd Wright."[19]
European architects also explored Japanese motifs indirectly through Frank Lloyd Wright. In the introduction to the famous Wasmuth portfolio *Frank Lloyd Wright: Ausgeführte Bauten* published in 1911, the English architect Charles Robert Ashbee discusses "traces of Japanese influence" in Wright's works.[20] The Dutch architect Hendrik Petrus Berlage, who admired Wright and visited him in America, also recognized Japanese influences on Wright.[21] Allusions to Wright, both in Robert van't Hoff's bungalow in Huis ter Heide, built in 1914, and in Jan Wils' De Dubbele Sleutel in Woerden from 1918 are reminiscent of Japanese architecture, however obscure the connection may be. In a lecture given in 1939 at the Royal Institute of British Architecture, Frank Lloyd Wright declared that "Japanese domestic architecture was truly organic architecture."[22]

Japanese features that attracted European architects

We can identify various attractive features of Japan from the studies of specific European architects. The work of Coates is illuminating in this respect, in particular

Tetsuro Yoshida, Baba Villa, Nasu, 1927. Gunnar Asplund presented this photo for his argument for the Spenglerian "infinite space" in his inaugural lecture at Stockholm's Royal Institute of Technology in 1931.

his five points of architecture derived from the traditional Japanese house. While frame construction is probably not specifically Japanese (the principle had already been refined through the work of Europeans such as Auguste Perret and Le Corbusier), Coates' principles also addressed other major architectural issues such as structure, space and furnishing, which were naturally of interest to other architects. Space, in particular, was emerging as a key element of modern architecture. Gunnar Asplund linked the Spenglerian idea of "infinite space" to "the dissolution of the room" in the Japanese house because the idea of infinite space is made possible by the sliding door that recedes completely. This was surely why many European architects, including Asplund, inquired about this aspect of Japanese architecture when Yoshida visited them in Europe.[23] Related to this spatial idea, flexibility was a further important principle. Sliding doors made it possible not only to blur the boundaries of the Japanese house, but also to flexibly divide and combine interior spaces. Moreover, the Japanese room is multi-functional. To modern architects, this concept of flexible space and function offered a good model for ordinary people's houses with limited space. While many modernists' designs adopted similar flexible principles, it is difficult to distinguish between what is influence and independent development.

Many other characteristics of Japanese architecture, such as simplicity, standardization, tranquility, naturalness and skillful workmanship, were attractive to modern architects in the West. Taut emphasized *"Sauberkeit"* or "purity" as "the quality that Japanese art contributed to humankind but which should also be achieved in all world art."[24] Aalto praised the delicacy of Japanese culture[25], and Charlotte Perriand was impressed by the "harmonious standardization," "juxtaposition of opposites" and "temporality" of Japanese architecture.[26] These architects prob-

Alvar Aalto, Villa Mairea, Noormarkku, Finland, 1939, flower room. The room shows Japanese elements such as sliding door, window lattice and paper lampshade, etc.

Alvar Aalto, Villa Mairea, staircase

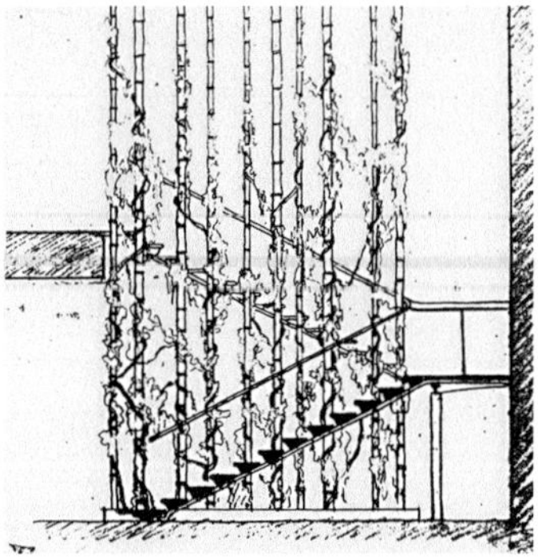

Alvar Aalto, early sketch of bamboo poles for the main staircase of the Villa Mairea, 1939

ably found in Japan "a tradition unspoilt by the academic rules and clichés" of the West.[27] This tradition helped them confirm a universal theory of architecture, though others were merely obsessed with things exotic. Notably, Walter Gropius identified universal values in Japanese aesthetics during his postwar visit to Japan: "Dear Corbu, all that we have been fighting for has its parallel in old Japanese culture. [...] The Japanese house is the best and most modern that I know of and really prefabricated."[28]

The application of Japanese aesthetics to modern architecture

The application of Japanese aesthetics can be recognized in different ways: the direct adoption of elements, the allusion to images, and the extraction of principles, although these categories overlap to a large extent. All three approaches can be seen in one particular case: Alvar Aalto's Villa Mairea

While Aalto referred to Yoshida for many parts of the Mairea design, the flower room best demonstrates his direct adoption of Japanese elements. Not only the sliding door, but also the window lattice, the paper lampshade and a straw mat on part of a wall alluding to *tatami* are elements that are easily related to Japanese design. Also, as Juhani Pallasmaa[29] suggested, the hanging shelf in the room is Aalto's modern translation of the Japanese *tana*. While the bamboo poles in one early sketch for the main staircase were not realized, they can also be interpreted as a direct adoption of a Japanese element.

Wells Coates' interior conversion of "No. 1 Kensington Palace Gardens," undertaken in 1931, is a further particularly good example that shows how a modernist architect wanted to transform a lavish Victorian interior into a simple modest space derived from the Japanese house.[30] His interior design for "34 Gordon Square" also illustrates the adoption of the Japanese sliding door.

Compared with the "direct adoption of elements," the "allusion of images" is more connotative than denotative. Critics identify the allusion to Japanese images based on their own interpretation. Pallasmaa pointed out that the composition of the pool and of the hillock in the Mairea courtyard echoes Yoshida's illustration of a Japanese garden with hills. It is not clear if Aalto really considered this illustration, but it is true that the artificial mound, the pool, and the stepping stones behind them resemble elements of a Japanese garden.

In addition to reproducing formal elements, European architects attempted to extract a number of principles from the built forms of Japanese designs. Asplund's idea of "infinite space," Coates' five points, Taut's *Sauberkeit* and Perriand's "harmonious standardization" are such examples. While some of these principles were new to European architects, others were a confirmation of general theories already held.

Likewise, some of these principles relate to formal elements from the first two categories just as the principle of "infinite space" is related to the sliding door. Aalto consulted Yoshida's book in the design of the large sliding door to the Mairea living room, and the architect and the clients left various "intentional" photographs of the situation when the door was slid out of sight, suggesting that they were fascinated by the effect created by the blurring of the boundary between inside and outside.

Alvar Aalto, Villa Mairea, living room, with removed sliding doors

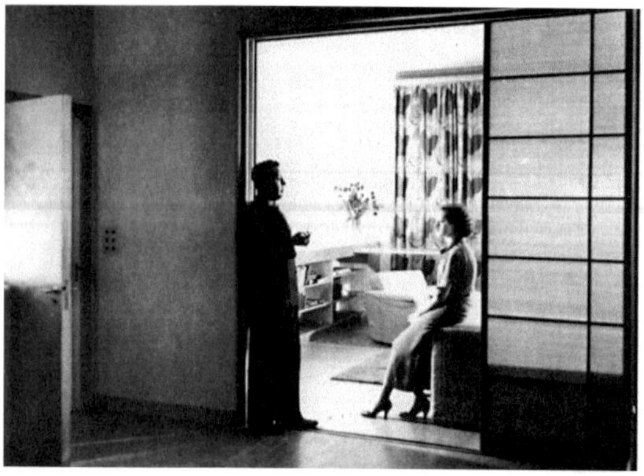

Wells Coates, 34 Gordon Square, London, United Kingdom, 1931

Meaning and critical assessment

The analyses so far offer a view of the Japanese contribution to modern architecture in the West by exploring European modernism as a counterpart to American modernism. It is, however, hard to determine whether the influence was more significant in America or in Europe. It comes down, perhaps, to the diverse ways in which the term "influence" can be interpreted in this context: from mere "allusion," to the rather strong "inspiration," or to the "confirmation" of a universal theory to which the architects already subscribed. Some architects' designs vaguely allude to Japan, while other architects expressed Japanese concepts more actively. For example, Josef Frank's obsession with China and Japan was "his second confession of identity."[31] The main reason for the lack of studies concerning Japanese influences on European modernists, as the author has argued in another essay[32], may be that—in short—Japanese architecture was perhaps not so new to European modernists because the fashion had already swept Europe by 1900. It had been absorbed by European modernism through the Art Nouveau period, and Wright transferred his absorption of Japanese concepts to Europe. At that time, it was therefore hardly possible to distinguish Japanese space from the modern conception of space.

This revisionist history supports the idea of a multi-faceted modern architecture that exceeds the compass of narrow rationalism. The reduced version of modernism, the International Style, which neglected local cultures, has been much criticized by many historians, and the richness and diversity of modernism is being rediscovered. Modern architecture was, in fact, not purely based on the "faith in European civilization" but was also inspired by diverse cultural sources. Therefore, this provides an understanding, particularly for non-Westerners, that the formula "modernization = Westernization" is considerably oversimplified, and that non-Westerners can also

Wells Coates, No. 1 Kensington Palace Gardens, London, United Kingdom, 1931, before and after interior conversion

find the seed of modernity within their own culture. During the modernization period, Japanese intellectuals also did their best to accept Western knowledge and way of living within their spirit, as is apparent in their term *wakon—yosai* or "Japanese spirit, Western techniques." This ideology resonates with Ernest Fenollosa's assertion of a fusion of Western means and Eastern ends.[33] And Japanese culture itself has likewise been formed through multiple interactions with the other East Asian countries.

This aspect links naturally to the idea of "Orientalism" transcending the framework of architecture. Edward Said's *Orientalism* revealed the "Western style for dominating, restructuring, and having authority over the Orient."[34] Despite the prominence of the study, Said did not cover some of the more positive aspects of Westerners' perceptions of the East. This was pointed out by Arthur Versluis, who suggested the term "positive Orientalism," in contrast to Said's more negative perspective: "Orientalism is not a single way of viewing Asia; it is many ways. [...] For convenience, we shall categorize these kinds of Orientalism, distinguishing between negative Orientalism, which disparages Asian religions, cultures and peoples, and positive Orientalism, which regards Asian religions and cultures as valuable, as reflecting perennial truths."[35] This definition of positive Orientalism is applicable to European modern architects' reception of Japanese aesthetics. The European modernists identified key principles and "perennial truths" in the East and applied them to their designs, showing the positive effect of the "cross-fertilization" of culture.

What is still lacking is a more critical understanding of European architects' attitudes towards Japan. What was the fundamental reason for drawing on Japanese ideas? Were there architects who strategically drew on foreign aesthetics to rationalize their design? Or others who may have projected their utopian dream onto a vaguely known wonderland? Did they know Japan at all? Klaus Berger has even argued that

Western painters obsessed with Japanese prints actually "often knew next to nothing about Japan and had no interest in Japanese culture or philosophy."[36] Even so, this does not undermine the basic lesson that cultures evolve in interaction with each other. A culture receives fresh ideas with the power to act as a catalyst through the influence of other cultures. This applies not only to Japan-Europe or East-West exchanges in modern architecture, but also to any cross-cultural exchanges in any period. What is important is to respect the "other" and to try to learn from the differences.

This text originated in the author's former article "Cross-Current Contribution: A Study on East Asian Influence on Modern Architecture in Europe", in: *Architectural Research*, vol. 11 (2), December 2009, p. 9–18.

1 "Oriental Forms in American Architecture 1800–1870", 1947; "Oriental Contributions to Art Nouveau", 1952; and "Japanese Building in the United States before 1900", 1953.

2 Kevin Nute's *Frank Lloyd Wright and Japan,* 2000 and Julia Meech's *Frank Lloyd Wright and the Art of Japan,* 2001, are two well-known examples.

3 Clay Lancaster, "Japanese Building in the United States before 1900: Their Influence upon American Domestic Architecture," in: *The Art Bulletin* 35 (3), 1953, p. 217–224.

4 Chisaburoh F. Yamada (ed.), *Dialogue in Art: Japan and the West,* Tokyo, New York and San Francisco 1976, p. 16.

5 Cited in: Reyner Banham, *Theory and Design in the First Machine Age,* London 1960, p. 129.

6 Paper presented at Japan-Germany architectural exchange symposium, Kobe 2005. Published in: Hiroshi Adachi et al (ed.), *Dreams of the Other,* Kobe 2007.

7 Tetsuro Yoshida, *Das japanische Wohnhaus,* Berlin 1935.

8 Published in: *Geonchuk-yeoksa-yeongu* (Journal of Architectural History) 15 (3), 2013, p. 43–57.

9 Paper presented at the 60th Annual Meeting of SAH, Pittsburgh, PA 2007.

10 See Juhani Pallasmaa (ed.), *Villa Mairea 1938–39,* Helsinki 1998; and *The Aalto House 1935–36,* Helsinki 2003, p. 98–100.

11 Published in: *Architectural Research Quarterly* 12 (1), 2008, p. 43–57.

12 Yoshida was sent to the West by Teishinsho (Ministry of Communications) of the Japanese Government to investigate Western broadcasting facilities, but it seems that he was more interested in surveying the stream of modern architecture in Europe. During the almost one-year-long stay in Europe, he was able to meet a number of leading architects in each country he visited, which became a chance not only to learn from them, but also to inform them of traditional Japanese architecture.

13 Teijiro Muramatsu, "Ventures into Western Architecture", in: Chisaburoh F. Yamada (ed.), op. cit., p. 125–148.

14 Bruno Taut, *Fundamentals of Japanese Architecture,* Tokyo 1936.

15 Richard Joseph Neutra, "Gegenwärtige Bauarbeit in Japan", in: *Die Form* 6 (1), 1931, p. 22–28; "Japanische Wohnung, Ableitung, Schwierigkeiten", in: *Die Form* 6 (3), 1931, p. 92–97; and "Neue Architektur in Japan", *Die Form* 6 (9), 1931, p. 333–340.

16 Göran Schildt, *Alvar Aalto: The Decisive Years,* New York 1986, p. 107 f.

17 Helge Zimdahl, "Zui Ki Tei", in: *Byggmästaren* 8, 1938, p. 82–94.

18 Juhani Pallasmaa (ed.), op. cit., p. 98.

19 Richard Weston, *Jørn Utzon,* Hellerup 2002, p. 20–21.

20 Charles Robert Ashbee, "Frank Lloyd Wright", in: *Frank Lloyd Wright: Ausgeführte Bauten,* Berlin 1911. It was republished in English as *Frank Lloyd Wright: Early Visions,* New York 1995 (1911, 2nd ed.).

21 Hendrik Petrus Berlage, "Frank Lloyd Wright", in: *Wendingen* 4 (11), 1921, p. 79–85; Reprint: Frank Lloyd Wright et al., *Frank Lloyd Wright: The Complete 1925 "Wendingen" Series,* New York 1992, p. 70–86.

22 Frank Lloyd Wright, *An Organic Architecture,* London 1939, p. 3 & 11.

23 Of course, this concept cannot be solely attributed to the Japanese idea. The principle of "blurring the boundary between inside and outside" was becoming increasingly sophisticated in European modernism.

24 Tetsuro Yoshida, "Kenchiku-Yishō-to-Jiyokusei" (Architectural design and *jiyokusei* or self-restraint), in: *Kenchiku-Zasshi* 1129, 1977, p. 61–64 (written in 1942).

25 Alvar Aalto, "Rationalism and Man", 1935, in: Göran Schildt (ed.), *Alvar Aalto: In His Own Words, Otava,* Helsinki 1997, p. 89–93.

26 Irène Vogel Chevroulet, "Japan 1940–41: Imprint and resonance in Charlotte Perriand's designs," paper presented at the session of "East Asian Influence on Modern Architecture in Europe" at the 60th Annual Meeting of SAH, Pittsburgh PA, 2007.

27 Ernst H. Gombrich, *The Story of Art,* Oxford 1989, p. 418.

28 Walter Gropius' postcard to Le Corbusier, sent from Kyoto in June 1954. See Francesco Dal Co, "La princesse est modeste," in: Virginia Ponciroli (ed.), op. cit., p. 386–389.

29 Juhani Pallasmaa (ed.), op. cit.

30 Anna Basham, "At the crossroads of Modernism and Japonisme: Wells Coates and the British Modern Movement," paper presented at the 60th Annual Meeting of SAH, Pittsburgh PA, 2007.

31 Karin Lindegren, "Architektur als Symbol: Theory and Polemic," in: Nina Stritzler-Levine (ed.), *Josef Frank: Architect and Designer,* New Haven 1996, p. 96–101.

32 Hyon-Sob Kim, "Tetsuro Yoshida (1894–1956) and Architectural Interchange between East and West," in: *Architectural Research Quarterly* 12 (1), 2008.

33 Ernest Fenollosa, "The Coming Fusion of East and West," in: *Harper's,* December 1898, cited in: Beongcheon Yu, *The Great Circle: American Writers and the Orient,* Detroit 1983, p. 106.

34 Edward W. Said, *Orientalism,* London 1978, p. 3.

35 Arthur Versluis, *American Transcendentalism and Asian Religions,* Oxford 1993, p. 5.

36 Klaus Berger, *Japonismus in der westlichen Malerei, 1860–1920,* Munich 1980, cited in: Henry Adams, "New Books on Japonisme: Review Article," in: *The Art Bulletin* 65 (3), 1983, p. 495–502.

Between tradition and modernity: The two sides of Japanese pre-war architecture

Benoît Jacquet

The pre-war period in Japan, before WWII, since the Meiji (1868–1912) and Taisho eras (1912–26), is known as a period of intense industrialization and urbanization driven by a strong faith in modernization. However, little is known of the history of Japanese architecture—and its relationship to modernization—during the 1930s and 40s, to the point that it has been largely forgotten. It would seem that the history of Japanese contemporary architecture begins with the period after the war, and even most Japanese historians divide the 20th century into two halves, before and after 1945, as if there were no continuity between them.

Even if the appearance of present-day Japan has little in common with Japan a century ago, it would be wrong to assume that the contemporary architectural discourse started from scratch, suddenly appearing in the 1950s, 60s, or even more recently. The history of modern Japanese architecture extends further back and has evolved over several cycles, growing in spiral fashion and developing different concepts over time.

The two main poles or impulses that inform most of the discourses on architecture in Japan are, firstly, the relationship to modernity, technology and progress at different levels, and secondly, the relationship to traditions inherited from Japanese culture and society. A further additional aspect is the influence of Western architecture and—as we can see in most of the interviews in this book—this is still very present in the discourses of Japanese architects, who often refer to Western architecture and architects when talking about their own works. It is instructive to refer to these relationships between Japanese traditions and Western trends when considering the Japanese pre-war architectural history.

What is architecture?

It wasn't until the end of the 19th century, with the importation of Western techniques and doctrines, that architecture began to be taught in Japanese universities as a new professional discipline in its own right. Leaving aside for a moment the term and its etymology in the Japanese language, what is obvious from the start is that "architecture" was considered to be a Western concept: a theoretical understanding of the world of construction which had previously been the domain of master carpenters and continued to be until well into the Meiji era. As one of the many "foreign

Kingo Tatsuno, Tokyo Central Station, Tokyo, 1914

counselors" employed by the Japanese government, a young British architect, Josiah Conder, was hired to teach Western architecture at the Tokyo Imperial University. Part of the Westernization of Japan was the construction of new buildings to house new activities, and Western architecture became a model for these projects. Conder's teaching was related to decorative arts and ornamentation from Europe, although his personal interests were Japanese art, painting and gardens, on which he published several books.

The first Japanese architects in the Meiji era designed Western buildings according to different historical European styles, and they referred to certain Western concepts of proportions and harmony. Some of these architects, such as Kingo Tatsuno, the architect of Tokyo Central Station, succeeded in creating a particular style that incorporated various foreign elements and materials—for the roofs, windows and walls—with a few Japanese stylistic details. For instance, he designed white horizontal lines on brick walls, echoing the lines marking the precinct walls of Buddhist and imperial properties.

In order to experience Western architecture, it was common for the Japanese elite to tour Europe, and Tatsuno spent four years there. While in London, he worked for William Burges. Burges was Conder's former teacher and was interested in oriental art. He had many questions for his Japanese staff and Tatsuno admitted having difficulties talking about "Japanese things" because his Meiji education had had a completely Western orientation. After returning to Japan, he became a professor at Tokyo Imperial University where one of his first decisions was to hire a master carpenter (*toryo*) and to offer a course on Japanese architecture.

It was therefore only towards the end of the 19th century that Japanese architecture began to be taught at universities. Chuta Ito, who represented the third generation of architect-professors hired by the Tokyo Imperial University, was one of the first architects to be educated with respect to both Western and Japanese architecture. At that time, the optional course on Japanese architecture during the years 1889/91 was run by the master carpenter Kiyoyoshi Kiko. Kiko's family had been in charge of the restoration of the properties of the Imperial Court. At Tokyo Imperial University his course was not predominantly historical: he taught formal and stylistic characteristics as well as the proportion systems of *Shinto* shrines, Buddhist temples and palatial architecture. Although Chuta Ito's generation received an initiation into Japanese architecture, their theoretical background in art history and aesthetics was

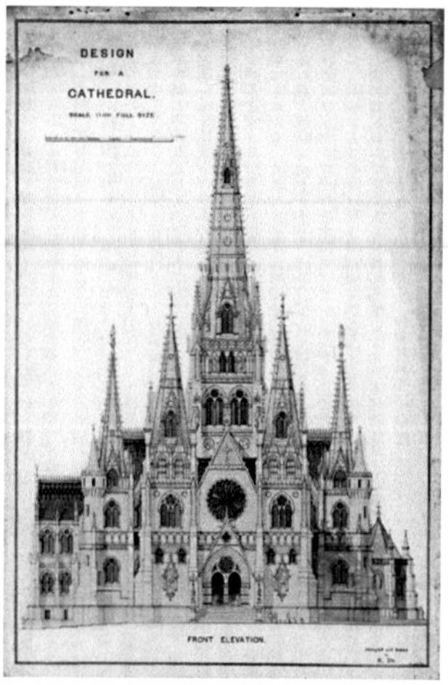

Chuta Ito, graduation design project: design for a cathedral, Tokyo Imperial University, 1882

based on the doctrines of Western scholars. The only book available on architecture in Japan at that time was an illustrated book by Christopher Dresser, *Japan: Its Architecture, Art, and Manufactures,* published in 1882. Like many students during this time, Ito learned German and read books on "world history" by Wilhelm Lübke. He also studied Eugène Véron's *Esthétique* from 1878. Another essential book introduced during the course of architectural history at the Imperial University was James Fergusson's *History of Architecture* published in 1874–75, which has a whole chapter on Asian architecture, dealing especially with Indian architecture.
The influence of this education is evident in Ito's graduate dissertation, entitled *Kenchiku tetsugaku* (Architectural Philosophy), which he submitted in 1892[1], together with his final project "Design for a Cathedral" in the neo-Gothic style of the late 19th century. His dissertation can be considered as the first essay on architectural theory written in Japan. Ito introduced the concept of "artistic architecture" (*bijutsu kenchiku*). His argumentation referred to a vocabulary and to ideas grounded in Western art theories, such as "proportion," "harmony," the "unconscious" and the "spirit." According to the architect and historian Terunobu Fujimori, these terms were borrowed from the British architect and art critic Owen Jones.[2] Ito's intention was obviously to define an understanding of architecture that would transcend its mere "constructive" function. This he called "artistic" or "aesthetic" architecture, meaning architecture motivated by artistic values. According to Ito, construction becomes architecture through an artistic process. While this may seem rather obvious to most architects and designers nowadays, it may not have been so evident in Japan at that time.
In technical literature, the Japanese term now used for "architecture," *kenchiku*, first appeared in 1872 in the *Seiyo kasaku hinagata* (Manual for the construction of West-

ern houses), which is the Japanese translation of Charles Allen's *Cottage building, or, Hints for improving the dwellings of the laboring classes* from 1849–50. *Kenchiku* was also adopted in the first *English and Japanese Dictionary*, edited by James Hepburn in Shanghai in 1867. Nevertheless, the term *kenchiku* was not used to designate the professional association of "architects" established in 1886 under the name *Zoka gakkai*: the "Association of House Construction." It is well known that Chuta Ito held the term *kenchiku* to be more appropriate than *Zoka* and proposed changing the name of this institution, but it was not until 1897 that *Zoka gakkai*[3] was renamed *Kenchiku gakkai.*

Ito's first presentation in front of the "Association of House Construction" was entitled "The Relationship between Architecture and Fine Arts."[4] and aimed to discuss the definition of architecture according to the notion of art (*bijutsu*). Recognizing that the definition of beauty (*bi*) is also a question of taste (*tesuto*), he noted that it is difficult to be totally objective on this matter. Citing that "what an Occidental may find beautiful may not be considered as beautiful by an Oriental," he argued that it should also be necessary to inquire on the "subjective and spiritual feelings of the Orientals, which means the Japanese," and to see what their specific taste[5] is.

"What is 'Japanese taste' (*nihon shumi*)?" is a question that began to be more intensively discussed after Japan began opening up to Western influences at the beginning of the Meiji period, and again at the end of the 19th century when, after the first wave of Westernization, Japan started to refocus on its own tradition. There are several reasons for this first return to tradition. One is the beginning of the colonization of other Asian countries by Japan, starting with Formosa (today Taiwan) in 1895, and the desire to erect architecture on these new territories that was different to neoclassical Western architecture. Apart from the desire to build Japanese monuments in Japan and in Asia, a further reason was the rediscovery of Japan's own architectural heritage.

What is Japanese architecture?

As mentioned before, the generation of Chuta Ito was the first to be introduced to Japanese architecture at university. At the Tokyo Imperial University, Ito worked with the master carpenter Kiko on several restoration projects in Nara, and on the construction of the Heian shrine in Kyoto from 1892 up to the National Industrial Exhibition in 1895—this building being a smaller scale (5:8) reproduction of the Imperial Palace of the first capital Heian-kyo built in 794. At this time, he came into contact with Orientalists, who were working on the inventory of national treasures, such as Okakura Tenshin. Chuta Ito was also on the committee responsible for drawing up the Ancient Temples and Shrines Preservation Law, enacted in 1897. Ito's first statement as an academic was an architectural study of the Horyu-ji[6], which was the first doctoral dissertation to be submitted to the Faculty of Engineering of the Imperial University. The Buddhist monastery of Horyu-ji from the 7th/8th century is the world's oldest existing wooden structure, and Ito considered it to be a prototype of Japanese architecture. His survey is based on the proportions and constructive details of three main buildings: the main hall, the pagoda and the central gate.

Ito believed that the Horyu-ji represented an original and initial style of Japanese architecture, imported from Korea together with the "Greco-Indian" Buddhist civilization. According to Ito, "this architecture is particularly interesting because its forms evidently maintain some dimensions of Chinese style, some traces of Indian style and, on top of that, owe their heritage to the Greek style."[7] This argument concerning the "Hellenistic" origin of Japanese architecture has never been proven but it is not actually Ito's invention, and was widely discussed by art historians at that time.[8] The presence of "entasis" on certain pillars has also been taken as an indication of the influence of Hellenistic architecture—which had come into contact with Indian Buddhism in Gandhara at the time of Alexander the Great. Given the broad origins and realm of influences, Ito concluded that this monument, which for him was the origin of a genuine Japanese style of Buddhist architecture, should be placed in the context of a world history of architecture.

By referring to an external, supposedly objective Western point of view, Chuta Ito's argumentation was also a means of developing new views on Japanese architecture. The "importing" of Western influences in this most original work of Japanese architecture was therefore not only ideological, but also offered a rather attractive argument to foster the study of Japanese architecture—a new and not yet developed field of study at this time—and to promote the restoration and conservation of ancient architecture. It was also a way to open his profession to other fields of study, eventually emancipating a mainly technical practice to more theoretical, artistic and even philosophical levels.

Modernizing Japanese architecture

In Japan, the transmission of knowledge and techniques from master to disciple, as can be observed in all traditional arts, is also common for academic careers, where studies and disciplinary approaches are perpetuated from one generation to another. Of Ito's students, some followed his studies on Japanese and Oriental architecture, such as Hideto Kishida at the University of Tokyo, while others devel-

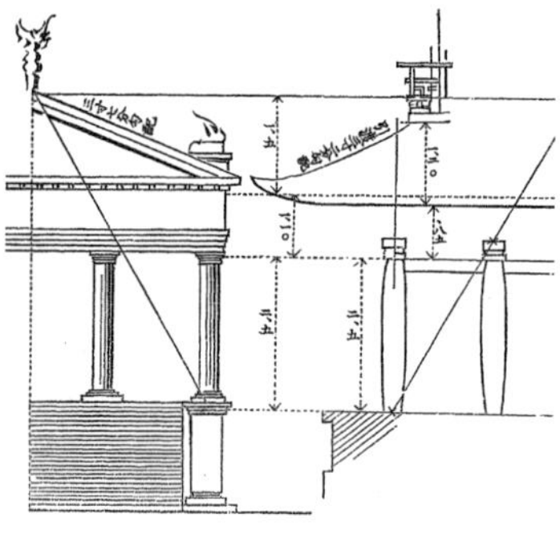

Chuta Ito, comparison between the proportions of an Etruscan temple and the central gate of the Horyu-ji, 1883

Buddhist monastery Horyu-ji, Nara, circa 7th century. Photograph adapted from Chuta Ito, *Horyu-ji*, 1940

Keiichi Morita, *Rakuyu kaikan*, Kyoto University, 1925

oped the field of architectural history, as Keiichi Morita did at Kyoto University. Morita was one of the six members of the Japanese Secession Architectural Association (*Bunriha kenchikukai*) who, in March 1920, decided to present some avant-garde expressionist designs as a manifesto of their desire to revolutionize the "historicist" architecture of their peers. The catalog of their exposition has since become a key reference work in the history of Japanese architecture.

Keiichi Morita started teaching at the Imperial University of Kyoto in 1922 and became known for his studies on classical architecture. He was also the first translator of Vitruvius into Japanese. His first architectural commission, the University clubhouse, the *Rakuyu kaikan*, built in 1925, is representative of a modern Japanese heteroclite style. Other members of the Japanese Secession Architectural Association, such as Sutemi Horiguchi or Mamoru Yamada, went on to form a Japanese Bauhaus group, adopting a so-called International Style that would later become the standard for the modernization of new national institutions such as the building for the Ministry of Communications.

Hideto Kishida was the successor to Chuta Ito but he also belongs to the generation of architects directly influenced by modern architecture. In 1921, as an "expressionist" architect, he designed, together with Yoshikazu Uchida, the Yasuda Auditorium, the Clock Tower building of the University of Tokyo. His doctoral dissertation was on the life and work of Otto Wagner,[9] but he was also in charge of a course on Japanese architecture—which is rather characteristic of the ambivalence of the intellectuals of this period who were concerned with both Japanese traditions and the development of modernity. It was probably this capacity to grasp and understand the principles and aesthetics of ancient architecture with respect to the contemporary developments in architecture that contributed to the success of his publications on Japanese architecture. As Ito had done before him, Kishida also surveyed oriental heritage in Asia and in Japan. His book *Kako no kosei* (Compositions of the past), published in 1929, offered a new, contemporary vision of Japanese architecture that literally "opened the eyes" of the younger generations to their own architectural tradition.

The book *Kako no kosei* is illustrated with 75 photographs of "compositions of the past." Most of these are of Nara's Buddhist temples, but there are also four photographs of the Villa Katsura that were the first to be published in an architectural book. Each page of the book is illustrated with a photograph and a comment that makes

Hideto Kishida, *Kako no kosei* (Compositions of the past), book cover, 1929, edition of 1938

Hideto Kishida, *Katsura-dana* (Katsura shelf), 1929

no reference to the historical context. In the introduction, Kishida underlines the fact that "this book does not pretend, in any case, to be a historical research on Japanese architecture" before going on to state: "My intention is to have a relevant gaze on Japanese plastic arts and to look at past Japanese architecture from the awareness of a man of his time [...] This book is the first to propose a new view on Japanese architecture and I would be glad if it could have any sense and meaning."[10] By this he meant it should be more than of merely historical value: to be meaningful in the present it must have what Alois Riegl called "present-day value" (*Gegenwartswert*), in as far as "*Most monuments are also able to satisfy those sensory and intellectual desires of man that could as well (if not better) be met by modern creations.*"[11] Kishida's comments point to the "modernity" of Japanese architecture. For instance, of the shelves (*tana*) at the Villa Katsura he writes that "when we look at these shelves we experience the same fresh modernism that we feel in front of the Graf Zeppelin [...] We can say that the quintessence of form is condensed in this three *tatami* mat space."[12] Kishida remarks on how the furniture relates to architecture, and how it can define the spatial conception of a room, this conception also being one essential feature of modern architecture.

We also know that Kishida came back from his first trip to Europe from 1926 to 27 with Le Corbusier's publications, and that he asked his student Kunio Maekawa to read them.[13] Maekawa joined Le Corbusier's atelier immediately after graduating and went on to become the leader of the Corbusean group in the 1930s, along with the famous Junzo Sakakura, Antonin Raymond and Kenzo Tange. Each of them, while designing contemporary architecture, also integrated Japanese features into their spatial conceptions. For instance, the Summer House that Raymond built in Karuizawa in 1933 is based on plans designed by Le Corbusier for the Villa Errázuris[14], but as a wooden house with a thatched roof. What is interesting here is that this construction proves that it is possible to build something in wood that was planned as a concrete structure. It shows that the material is thus only a symbol of modernity or tradition—and it is already an example of modern Japanese regional architecture. Another reason why Japanese architects developed a modern wooden architecture at the end of the 1930s was because the use of iron in construction was prohibited due to shortages—and because iron was required for military purposes from 1937 onwards.

The discourse on tradition

Since the first Sino-Japanese War from 1894 to 95, the colonization of Taiwan in 1895, the Russo-Japanese War from 1904 to 05, the annexation of Korea in 1905, the annexation of Manchuria in 1931 and the Second Sino-Japanese War from 1937 until 45, Japanese construction companies and architects were sent to the East Asian colonies to construct and plan new buildings and cities. Most institutional buildings were designed in a new national style—that of the "Imperial Crown"—which was used both in Japan and in its Asian colonies. Apart from the "oriental" roof, these buildings do not represent a convincing, well-founded idea of a contemporary interpretation of Japanese architecture. While most young Japanese architects were willing to follow European modern architectural trends, they were confronted with new, unfamiliar commissions: initially for military buildings that were intended to be purely functional and then with the construction of war monuments. In Japan, the first war monument was the Yasukuni shrine, built in Tokyo in 1869. After that diverse forms of "Memorial Towers for the Fallen Soldiers" were edified in East Asia. These constructions, and also ossuaries, flourished in many places, since some 60,000 Japanese soldiers—and probably as many other Asian soldiers—had already perished on Asian battlefields by July 1939. Most of these monuments were built by artists copying European monuments, but modern Japanese architects, encouraged by Hideto Kishida, started to submit entries to national competitions, and eventually architects began to play a more central role in the construction of a national style after the start of the Pacific War in December 1941.

Antonin Raymond, Summer House, Karuizawa, 1933, reconstruction

In April 1942, at the behest of the government, the Architectural Institute created a committee for the construction of the *Daitoa*-Memorial for the Greater East Asia Co-Prosperity Sphere. Within this committee, Hideto Kishida was in charge of the sub-committee for architectural design and appointed Kenzo Tange as his secretary, and Kunio Maekawa, Junzo Sakakura and two other architects as committee members. Kishida's first initiative was to launch a national competition for the planning of the memorial of the *Daitoa*. He invited all young architects to show their skills and their intentions for the construction of the Memorial of Greater East Asia. This memorial could be placed anywhere in East Asia and the design program was relatively open: one of the few requirements was to design a piece that expressed monumentality and traditionality using contemporary materials and techniques, thus representing the new "Japanese spirit."[15] Kunio Maekawa, who was a member of the jury competition, noted that 63 architects entered the competition[16]—in other words an entire generation of architects.

In July 1942, the members of the Architectural Institute organized a debate on the architectural style of the *Daitoa*. Compared with other cultural disciplines, architecture—a "technical" discipline within the Faculty of Engineering—was not considered a medium of political and cultural propaganda, a point that apparently generated a certain amount of regret among particular architects. Hideto Kishida, who by then was writing a history of German Nazi Architecture[17], enlivened the debate on state architecture by stating that Japan had "reached the level where architecture has to express the volition of the people and the spirit of the Nation," quoting the original German case as an example.[18]

Putting Asia under a Japanese roof—from the expression *Hakko ichiu*, "The whole World under One Roof"[19]—was an explicit goal of the Japanese Empire. In a way, Kenzo Tange had proposed something similar for his winning scheme for the Memorial of the *Daitoa* in 1942. Tange's scheme for a "Holy Sanctuary" on the slopes of Mount Fuji was designed to represent the matrix of all sanctuaries to be built in Asia. Referring to Shintoism, the state religion since Meiji, Tange designed a great shrine—about 75 meters high and 150 meters long. This concrete building was physically and symbolically linked to the Imperial Palace in Tokyo by a road and a railway—both envisaged as routes of pilgrimage. As a connection between the divine Japanese Man—the Emperor and divine Japanese Nature—Mount Fuji, the structure of this sanctuary was planned according to the pattern of ancient imperial tombs, the *kofun* from the 3rd to 7th century.

Kenzo Tange's discourse was constructed under the usual mottos of Occidentalism[20], and Japanese expressions of monumentality presented as a genuine alternative to dominant Western forms. In his explanatory note, he wrote that Western monumentality is characterized by "ascending forms" that have "lost contact with nature and territorial realities." These abstract forms, those of the pyramid or the tower, are the "Lilliputian symbol of the Occident's thirst for domination".[21]

In Tange's scheme for the *Daitoa* Memorial, the unification of man and nature—as one of the accomplishments of *Shinto* worship—is relayed in the construction of an architecture that melts into the environment. This fusion into nature is represented in the rendering of a general bird's-eye-view perspective drawing of the *Daitoa* Memorial. Tange drew a landscape painting where architectural forms disappear into a mystical landscape of mountains and fogs.

Kenzo Tange, Hiroshima Peace Memorial, Hiroshima, 1955. Photo taken by Kenzo Tange, circa 1951

With regard to the development of modern Japanese architecture in the first half of the 20th century, what should be underlined is that the research on traditions—be they historically ancient or recent inventions[22]—has often been confused with political and ideological discourses, which is often the case when dealing with "monumentality." But what is revealing at this stage in history, is that social or political crisis led architects to find architectural responses, spatial ideas and devices.

Tradition or modernity?

Soon after the war, Kenzo Tange participated in the reconstruction of Hiroshima, and subsequently built the Hiroshima Peace Memorial from 1949 until 55, which has become the most visited modern monument in Japan.[23] As a symbol of the reconstruction of Japan, the Peace Center became an example of the creation of modern architecture by referring to Japanese architecture, fueling the discussion on tradition that emerged anew at the beginning of the 1950s after the period of American occupation. In 1953, on the occasion of a symposium entitled "Nationalism vs. Internationalism," which brought together Maekawa, Sakakura, Tange and Yoshida Isoya,[24] these architects debated the relationship of their work to Japanese architecture. Kenzo Tange, who had won the most important war memorial competitions—and later became the first "international Japanese architect"—described this experience as a time of apprenticing traditional architecture. He did not want to apologize for this troubled past or even admit that his research could be seen as having deviated from the thrust of true modernity. He suggested that the originality of his war experience would instead help him to construct a new Japanese modern architecture, and that the post-war period would provide Japanese architects with a valuable opportunity in this regard.[25]

With regard to his reference to Japanese architecture, Tange stated that understanding it in a modern sense, as a mental "image," abstracted from its iconic representations, gave him greater freedom. This type of discourse on tradition became the mainstream for Japanese contemporary architects, and remains so to this day. Paradoxically, by compromising the purity of modernity with national traditions, or by adapting their discourses on tradition in line with other agendas, Japanese contemporary architects seem to have succeeded in overcoming the universal character of modernity. But, looking back in history, we can see that the virtues of Japanese architecture—respectfulness to the values of the environment and regional traditions as well as those of rational and technical modernity—, the virtues that modern Western architects such as Bruno Taut and Walter Gropius praised before and after the war, also correspond to the discursive strategies produced by Japanese architects during the war. This troubled origin of contemporary architecture—that somehow stemmed from discourses on national monumentality—shows us that the construction of modernity is always a compromise with the past.[26] In a certain way, whether consciously or not, contemporary Japanese architects have inherited this immediate past history and, although part of the material culture disappears along with the transformation of Japanese cities, there are still some resilient spaces and spatial conceptions that influence their way of thinking and building.

1 Chuta Ito, *Kenchiku tetsugaku* (Architectural Philosophy), graduate dissertation, Tokyo 1892.

2 See Owen Jones, *Grammar of Ornaments*, London 1856, quoted in Terunobu Fujimori, *Toshi, kenchiku* (City, architecture), *Nihon kindai shisō taikei* (Anthology of modern Japanese thought), vol. 19, Tokyo 1990, p. 343.

3 Chuta Ito, "Akitekuchūru no hongi o ronjite sono yakuji o senteishi waga Zoka gakkai no kaimei o nozomu" (By discussing the fundamental principle and the relevance of the term "architecture," I wish to change the name of the Zoka gakkai), in: *Kenchiku zasshi*, March 1894, p. 80–87. French translation in: Yann Nussaume (ed.), *Anthologie critique de la théorie architecturale japonaise. Le regard du milieu*, Brussels 2004, p. 94–98.

4 Chuta Ito, "Kenchikujutsu to bijutsu to no kankei" (The Relationship between Architecture and Fine Arts), in: *Kenchiku zasshi*, March 1893, p. 80–87.

5 Idem, p. 87.

6 Chuta Ito, "Hōryūji kenchikuron" (An architectural study of the Horyu-ji), in: *Kenchiku zasshi*, November 1893, p. 317–350.

7 Idem, p. 327.

8 See Ernest Fenollosa, *Epochs of Chinese and Japanese Art. An Outline of East Asiatic Design*, vol. 1, Berkeley and Tokyo 2007 (London 1912), p. 127; Claude-Eugène Maitre, *L'art du Yamato*, Paris 1901, p. 24 f; Alfred Foucher, *L'art gréco-bouddhique du Gandhâra. Étude sur les origines de l'influence classique dans l'art bouddhique de l'Inde et de l'Extrême-Orient*, vol. 2, Paris 1922, p. 668.

9 Hideto Kishida, *Ottō Wagunā: kenchikuka toshite no shōgai oyobi shisō* (Otto Wagner: the life and thought of an architect), Tokyo 1927.

10 "Jijo" (Introduction), in: Hideto Kishida, *Kako no kōsei* (Compositions of the past), Tokyo 1929.

11 Alois Riegl, *Der moderne Denkmalkultus*, Vienna and Leipzig 1903. We refer to the English translation, Riegl, Alois, "The Modern Cult of Monuments. Its Essence and its Development", in: Price, Nicholas Stanley; Talley, Mansfield Kirby; Vaccaro, Alessandra Melucco (Eds.) *Historical and Philosophical Issues in the Conservation of Cultural Heritage*, Los Angeles, 1996, p. 78.

12 *Katsura-dana* (Katsura shelf), in: Hideto Kishida, *Kako no kōsei* (Compositions of the past), op. cit., plate 53, chapter 63.

13 Benoît Jacquet, "La villa Katsura et ses jardins: l'invention d'une modernité japonaise dans les années 1930," in: Nicolas Hévé and Benoît Jacquet, *Vers une modernité architecturale et paysagère. Modèles et savoirs partagés entre le Japon et le monde occidental*, Paris 2013, p. 115.

14 Le Corbusier discovers in the *Architectural Record* of July 1934, the house built in Karuizawa by Antonin Raymond based on his unbuilt project for the Villa Errázuriz in Zapallar, Chile, 1930. See Le Corbusier, "Faut pas se gêner…," in: Willy Boesiger (ed.), *Le Corbusier et Pierre Jeanneret. Œuvre complète de 1929–1934*, Zurich 1964, p. 52.

15 Hideto Kishida, "Daitōa kyōeiken kensetsu kinen eizō keikaku no jitsugen o nozomu" (My wishes for the realization of the Memorial Planning of the Construction of the Greater East Asia Co-Prosperity Sphere), in: *Kenchiku zasshi*, August 1942, p. 582 f.

16 Kunio Maekawa, "Daijūroku kenchikukai tenrankai: kyō gi sekkei shinsahyō" (The 16th exhibition of the Institute of Architecture: Judgment report of the architectural design competition), in: *Kenchiku zasshi*, December 1942, p. 960.

17 Hideto Kishida, *Nachisu doitsu no kenchiku* (The architecture of German Nazi), Tokyo 1943.

18 Hideto Kishida, "Daitōa kyōeiken ni okeru kenchiku yō shiki (zaidankai)" (The architectural style of the Daitōa [a debate]), in: *Kenchiku zasshi*, September 1942, p. 718–734, p. 723.

19 This slogan comes from an interpretation of the *Kojiki* (The Records of Ancient Matters), 712.

20 See Ian Buruma and Avishai Margalit, *Occidentalism: The West in the Eyes of its Enemies*, New York 2004, p. 61.

21 Kenzo Tange, "Chūrei shiniki keikaku shushi" (Intentions for the planning of a holy territory in memory of the Fallen Soldiers), in: *Kenchiku zasshi*, December 1942, p. 963.

22 On this cultural process of invention see Eric Hobsbawm and Terence Ranger (eds.), *The Invention of Tradition*, Cambridge 1983; Gérard Lenclud, "Qu'est ce que la tradition?," in: Marcel Detienne (ed.), *Transcrire les mythologies. Tradition, écriture, historicité*, Paris 1999, p. 25–44.

23 Hiroyuki Suzuki, "Seichi sōzō: Tange Kenzō no Hiroshima" (The creation of a holy land: The Hiroshima of Tange Kenzō), in: Hiroyuki Suzuki, *Nihon no "chirei"* (The "genius loci" of Japan), Tokyo 1000, p. 28–48.

24 "Kokusaisei, fūdosei, kokuminsei. Gendai kenchiku no zōkei o megutte" (Internationality, climate, nationality: on the formation of contemporary architecture); "Nationalism vs. Internationalism: symposium by Kunio Maekawa, Junzo Sakakura, Kenzo Tange & Isoya Yoshida," organized by Ikuta Tsutomu, Hamaguchi Ryūichi and Tanabe Kazuto, in: *Kokusai kenchiku 20*, March 1953, p. 2–15.

25 Idem, p. 4 f.

26 Benôit Jacquet presented part of this research at the symposium "Front to Rear: Architecture and Planning during WWII" held at the Institute of Fine Arts, New York University, March 7–8, 2009, under the title "Compromising Modernity: Japanese Monumentality during WWII."

The traumas of modernization: Architecture in Japan after 1945

Jörg H. Gleiter

A fundamental shift is underway in the world of architecture in Japan. For some time now, a new generation of architects has begun to emerge producing self-assured and original work, ending a long phase of disorientation after postmodernism. Many had no longer expected this of the ageing industrial nation. This is not simply another new generation of architects. On the contrary, what makes these young architects different is that they have succeeded in placing Japanese architecture in a new relationship to history. Their work seems liberated from that which has characterized Japanese modernism and the architecture of post-war Japan for so long: the traumas of modernization.

Modern architecture in Japan, like its society, has been heavily influenced by the nation's specific traumatic experiences of modernization. It is only in this context that we can fully understand many of the fascinating and at times bizarre developments in Japanese architecture. The philosopher Ken'ichi Mishima has spoken of the "pains of modernization"[1] – but it is much more than that. These pains, indeed traumas, can be traced to two key events in history. The first was the forced opening of Japan in 1853 after nearly 200 years of self-isolation. To avoid the threat of colonization by the West, Japan saw no alternative but to open itself to trade with the West, and as a result was forced to enter into a process of rapid modernization. This confrontation with the West brought about a collective psychological trauma that Mishima has described as being "between gnawing self-doubt and jubilant self-affirmation, between self-humiliation and arrogance, between a will to adapt and an urge to withdraw, [...] between fascination with the West and an aversion to it."[2]

The second key event relates to 1945, the end of the first war ever lost in the history of Japan, the two atom bomb strikes in Hiroshima and Nagasaki, the surrender of Japan and its subsequent occupation by the United States. The architect Arata Isozaki spoke of how palpable this was at the time: "When Japan surrendered in 1945 [...] I could feel that history was disrupted."[3] The cause for collective trauma was, however, as much a product of the fact that by the end of the war, many cities were largely entirely destroyed, and with them a large part of Japan's historical legacy irretrievably lost. With the exception of a few buildings, Japanese cities, which were mostly made of timber buildings, burned down leaving no traces of ruins. The result was in effect that of a tabula rasa, with little left over on which to base reconstruction efforts. Isozaki's haunting account describes what this meant for architecture: "As a boy of 14, I saw the cities of Japan burnt to the ground before my very eyes. Running through the rapidly collapsing streets like a hunted animal, I escaped the incendiary bombs; but not the complete and utter destruction of everything I knew which ensued in their wake. [...] The effect was psychologically traumatic."[4] This paints a picture of the psychological situation under which Japanese architecture arose in the second half of the 20th century. But the actual beginning of the development of post-war architecture begins not in 1945 but with an earlier high-profile conference "Overcoming Modernity"[5] (*kindai no chokoku*) which took place in 1942 during the military dictatorship, and therefore after Japan had entered into war with the United States. Representatives of countries occupied by the Japanese as well as Japanese politicians and intellectuals took part in the conference. Two years before, the Japanese Foreign Minister Matsuoka Yosuke had announced the creation of the "Greater East Asia Co-Prosperity Sphere" as a means of extending Japan's political, economic and cultural reach to Korea and China and beyond to Southeast Asia and as far as Burma in the West.

The conference was seen as a "historic turning point,"[6] its programmatic title "Overcoming Modernity" directed both against European modernism, and with it European influence as a whole, as well as against *wakon—yosai* (Japanese spirit – Western techniques), the Japanese principle at the core of Japan's process of modernization since the mid-19th century.

The intention of *wakon—yosai* was to restrict Western influence to technological and scientific aspects, thereby detaching it from its specific cultural origins in the Enlightenment of the 18th century. It was a means to neutralize the cultural aspects of the wave of modernization coming into Japan from the West so that this could be recoded with a new symbolic connotation in the context of Japanese culture.

The conference "Overcoming Modernity" marked a change in the aims of *wakon—yosai*. In all areas where modernism was seen as being of European or West-

Tokyo, Sumida Ward, September 1945

Kenzo Tange, Kurashiki City Hall, 1960

ern origin, "Overcoming Modernity" could be regarded as synonymous with "Overcoming the West."[7] The intention was to replace all Western manifestations of modernity with an appropriate Asian model, and to formulate an alternative Japanese concept of modernism.

But in 1945, just three years after the declaration of the program to overcome the West, at a time when the military dictatorship was at the height of its powers, the situation had reversed entirely. Instead of overcoming the West, Japan's surrender had brought Japan into even closer exposure to the West than before. Where the original *wakon–yosai* program had attempted to prevent the loss of cultural sovereignty by colonization, the occupation by the U.S. Armed Forces was tantamount to a colonization of Japan. The ensuing modernization became exactly what it had originally tried to prevent. The modernization program of *wakon–yosai* and the attempt to maintain cultural sovereignty had failed.

National identity

Of particular importance for the construction of identity in post-war Japan was the erection of civic building for institutions such as city halls, concert halls and other places of assembly. Kenzo Tange's City Hall in Kurashiki (1960) is an example of architectural developments in the 1950s that, lacking alternatives, continued to follow the formula of *wakon–yosai* but took it one step further, turning it into a

dialectic process. In contrast to the original program of *wakon—yosai*, Kenzo Tange drew on both architectural traditions, the Western and the Japanese, creating a contradicting play of signs and references.

Tange's building is a subtle interplay of signs, an ambiguous figure that stands between both traditions without favoring one or the other. Made of reinforced concrete, its material composition and typological structure has modern and Western connotations. On a formal level, however, it cites the Japanese log cabin, for example the *Shousou-in* treasure house of the Todai-ji temple (8th century) in Nara, and therefore formally and aesthetically has Japanese connotations. One can see this in the horizontal division of the façade with long beam-like elements that extend beyond the corners of the building in the plane of the façade, recalling the corners of a log cabin. These serve no structural or constructional purpose; they are purely a formal-aesthetic device. This can also be seen in the pairs of beam ends that project at the attica in a manner similar to that of a timber construction. Again they have no structural reason and are merely a formal reference to a fictional timber construction. The same goes for the massive, pylon-like blocks on which the volume of the building rests, like a log-cabin on large stone blocks.

In the interior, this principle is reversed. Here, the references to Western modernism are unmistakable, especially the parallels with Corbusier's Ronchamp Chapel completed in 1954. The splayed, deep window niches, the coarse plaster and rounded walls in the assembly chamber all make reference to Corbusier's architectural language. Here, however, Tange also does all he can to recode these formal

Sachio Otani, Kyoto International Conference Center, 1966

influences. In the window niches as well as the other concrete elements, the imprint of the wooden formwork is clearly visible. This surface texture reawakens the reference to the log cabin.

The third level is that of the urban design. Here too Tange follows the principle of dialectic interleaving. When it was built, the city hall stood on a large plaza-like site reminiscent of the spaces created by the tabula rasa destruction seen in many cities, although Kurashiki itself, a smaller town, was not directly affected. Public urban spaces are not part of the typology of Japanese cities. Large open spaces are only found in Buddhist or Shintoist temple grounds, for example in the complexes of Horyu-ji or Todai-ji in Nara. The large open space in front of the city hall therefore has ambivalent connotations. It can be read as a European-style square, the product of supposed bomb damage, or as a Buddhist temple complex. For the latter, however, it would need to have a large sailing roof. The flat roof therefore undermines the Japanese connotation and favors the Western, modernist reading.

In Kurashiki, Tange confidently plays an intellectual game, transferring, cancelling out and transforming the symbolic codes of the architecture. But his purpose was not just aesthetic but also political. In this he differs from the approach taken by his pupil Sachio Otani, who designed the International Conference Center in Kyoto in 1963–66. The center makes reference to the oldest and supposedly most authentic Japanese architectural tradition, and therefore pursues a clear strategy of symbolic attribution and appealing to national identity. From a formal-aesthetic point of view, he makes reference to Shinto architecture and the pit house, a building type from the Yayoi Period (300 B.C.—300 A.D.). In Japanese architecture, this building is the equivalent of the primordial hut. Although built in reinforced concrete, its formal design—especially the triangular and gable motifs—has strong Japanese symbolic connotations. There is no dialectic play of signs. In terms of creating a new

Japanese national style, Otani sees modernism as a movement with the potential to renew the presumed origins of Japanese architecture, bringing them up to date technologically.

Metabolism

In the same year as the completion of Kurashiki City Hall in 1959, the group of Metabolists[8] formed with the intention of overcoming the notion of *wakon—yosai*. The Metabolists are the first architectural avant-garde movement that Japan has brought forth. The group comprised architects that were so young that they had not taken part in the war and therefore had no political prehistory. Nevertheless, this was not the spontaneous alliance of young rebellious architects that one would expect of an avant-garde movement. The main figure behind the Metabolists was none other than Kenzo Tange, who intended to establish a program of national identity construction for the war-traumatized nation. The founding act of the group was the publishing of its manifesto *Metabolism 1960—The Proposals for a New Urbanism*. Significantly, this took place just at a time when younger generations of architects, among them Team X, had sharply criticized the CIAM (Congrès Internationaux d'Architecture Moderne) and the large-scale urban utopias of the kind propagated by Le Corbusier and Sigfried Giedion no longer served as the dominant urban model.

Metabolism marked a turning point. On the one hand it radicalized the ideas of modern urban design, and on the other it turned the prevailing principle of modernization, *wakon—yosai* on its head. Their buildings and proposals were over-sized and gigantic. Instead of employing dialectic dialog, like in Tange's City Hall in Kurashiki, Metabolism attempted to compensate for the traumas of years past by thinking big. The urban visions of the Metabolists either shot up from the ground into the sky—like Kisho Kurokawa's "Helix City" or Kenji Ekuan's "Dwelling City"—or fled the land entirely and built on water, for example Kiyonori Kikutake's "Marine City" or Tange's project for building on Tokyo Bay. Their architecture was monumental, technical, futuristic, unsettling but also bold and exciting. The decision to build in the sky or on the water was a response to the trauma of the destruction of the cities and the radioactive contamination of the land caused by two atom bombs. Isozaki wrote: "I'm no longer going to consider architecture that is below 30 meters in height. I am leaving everything below 30 meters to others. If they think they can unravel the mess in this city, let them try."[9]

The architecture of the Metabolists should show to the world that Japan could also be a source of bold ideas, and not just an underling of Western occupying forces. Kenzo Tange's project for building on Tokyo Bay was presented as a model example and was even presented in a national television broadcast on New Year's Day in 1961.[10] His project was nothing short of spectacular, a new city on water, extending from the center of Tokyo across the bay in a chain-like manner, taking in the Imperial Palace on the way. Either side of the central axis, which was primarily for rail and car traffic, large axes extended at right angles into the bay along which large building complexes were docked liked ships in a marina. These residential structures were intended for several thousand inhabitants and were shaped like over-sized convex roof forms, although in actual fact they were terraced housing complexes. In his

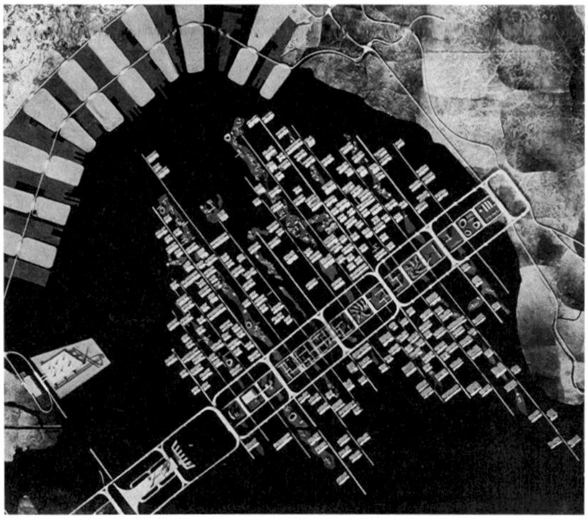

Kenzo Tange, Tokyo Bay Project, 1960

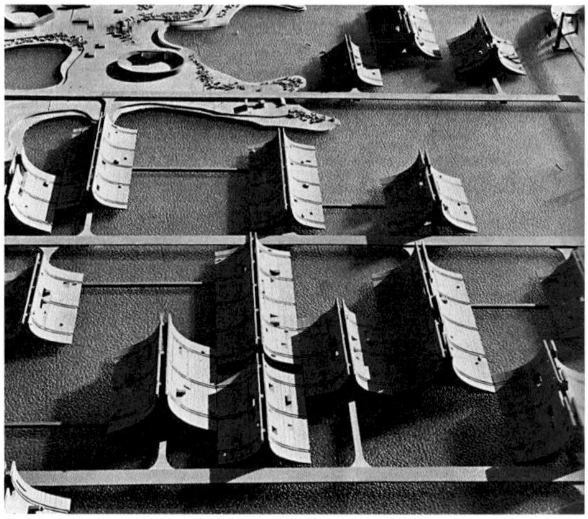

Model

Tsukiji-Plan, the section of the project on the mainland, Tange made reference to the architecture of the European avant-garde, to Russian constructivism, to Le Corbusier's urban utopias from the 1920s and the urban fantasies of the Archigram group. The project was larger than anything Japan had seen before and yet it was not just an abstract, technocratic megaproject. On the one hand, Tange's plan was a radical translation of Le Corbusier's urban visions, but on the other, it employed forms and images that pertained to Japanese national identity. The vast roofs of the residential complexes are reminiscent of the roofs of Japanese temple complexes. Seen in the context of the scale of Tokyo Bay, one can see a likeness to an oversized, water-bound temple complex. The project was therefore not just a bold technical statement but also had symbolic character: the image of a temple embedded in a rural landscape. If one disregards the scale, the clusters of residential complexes bear resemblance to constellations of farmhouses in a village. Indeed, in spring, when the rice fields flood, many Japanese villages are transformed into such water landscapes, the houses appearing to float on a sheet of water that reflects the sky.
Tange's proposal for building on Tokyo Bay therefore has unmistakably Japanese connotations. Kikutake's urban vision for "Marine City" (1963) likewise uses a similar metaphoric image. For his project, Kikutake proposed erecting cylindrical high-rise buildings on artificial round islands that are as high as they are deep. The organic form of the islands is reminiscent of the image of water lilies floating on the lakes and ponds of Japanese gardens, the slender high-rise taking the place of the long stem of the blossom above the water, with the island around them as

Kenzo Tange, Shizuoka Press and Broadcasting Center, Tokyo, 1967

Kenzo Tange, Yamanashi Broadcasting Center, Kofu, 1967

the floating leaves. Kikutake's Metabolist high-tech architecture is invested with natural-philosophical meaning and stands in the tradition of Japanese gardens. While Japanese gardens are typically miniaturizations of objects or landscapes, Kikutake's project took the opposite approach, enlarging natural phenomena to a vast scale.

Ten years after the founding of the Metabolist movement, the Osaka Expo in 1970 marked a new turning point. By then the poetic images of the early projects had given way to entirely technical metaphors. What was intended as the culmination of the Metabolist movement ended in technoid formalism of the kind seen in Kurokawa's "Toshiba IHI Pavilion" or Kikutake's "Expo Tower". This development was already evident in earlier projects such as the "Shizuoka Press and Broadcasting Center" (1967) or the "Yamanashi Broadcasting Center" (1967), both by Tange. The latter in particular was conceived as an extensible system of modules comprised of cylindrical access towers with flexibly-positionable bridges slung between them. Tange's project referred back to his project for building on Tokyo Bay. The model for the building was the timber constructions of the temple complexes, for example the vast substructures of the "Kyomizu-dera Temple" in Kyoto. As such, some of the details of the "Yamanashi Broadcasting Center" make symbolic reference to timber joints, for example the console-like elements for extending the building. But the dialectic interplay of real and imagined materials, of concrete and wood, of Japanese and Western construction had dulled. What was originally a culturally-connotated metaphor had become little more than a throwaway reference, a form of technoid mannerism.

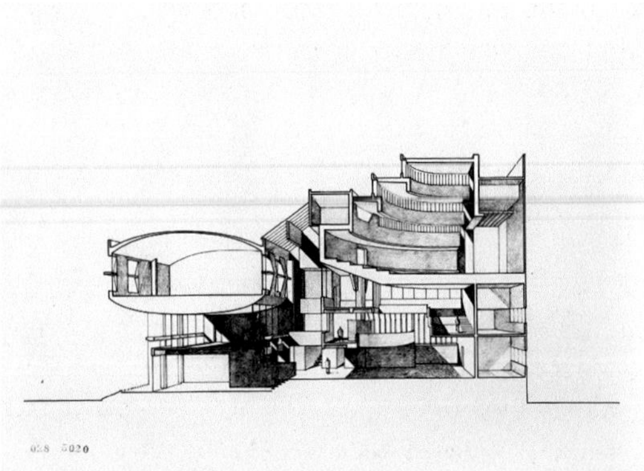

Arata Isozaki, Oita Medical Center, Oita, 1960

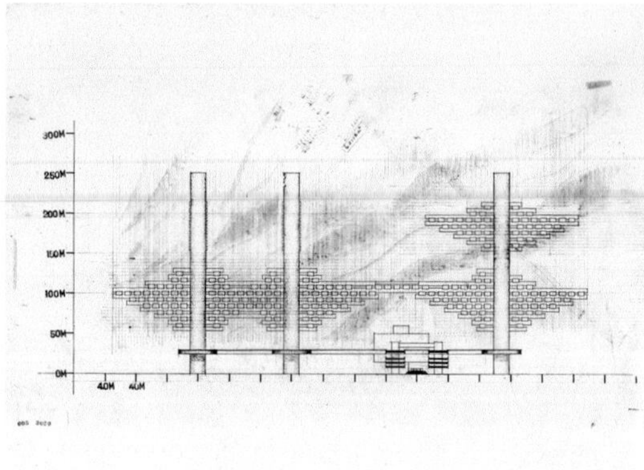

Arata Isozaki, Clusters in the Air (City in the Air, Shibuya project), 1962

Trauma and ruins

To understand the development of architecture in Japan after 1945, it is important to realize the extent of the destruction of Japanese cities after the war. Where cities are made predominantly of wood, nothing remains, just a tabula rasa. There is little substance on which one can build, both physically and conceptually. The material and spatial presence of ruins serve as traces, indexical markings, metonymical evidence of past events—substitute images in the present. Ruins are part of an event that conditions their existence; they are "a present form of past life"[11] and acquire cultural significance through the fact that they serve as a fragment from which one can embark on reconstructing a tradition in the future. Up until then, there had been no cultural concept of a ruin in the predominantly Buddhist and Shintoist Japan. "The first structure that dominated my thinking in my work as an architect," says Isozaki, "was that of the ruin."[12]

The impossibility of representational memorization can be seen in Isozaki's "Oita Medical Center" (1959/60). His broken belief in the ongoing presence of the material world led him to create a bizarre figure of an elongated concrete tube floating above the contaminated earth. The building appears on the one hand to be built to resist possible future destruction, and at the same time its form is autonomous in the absence of images or metaphors that could give it form or historical context. The "Oita Medical Center" is in essence the materialization and formal expression of a trauma. It expresses the futility of attempting to connect with the past but is equally unsure about formulating a vision for the future.

Around the same time, Isozaki also worked on the "Clusters in the Air" project (1960–62). The project arose in close contact with the group of Metabolists, to whom Isozaki chose to keep a distance. In his view, "the Metabolists had no scepticism toward their utopia. I thought they were too optimistic..."[13]. "Clusters in the Air" consists of a series of tree-like megastructures on which detachable modular living capsules are attached like leaves on branches. The natural metaphor was very much in line with ideas of Metabolism, but that was not all. The project also had a cultural connotation, its form echoing the cantilevered consoles of temple architecture where the columns transition into tree-like clusters of beams that support the roof. "Clusters in the Air" is therefore not just a vision of futuristic high-tech architecture, but also makes metaphorical reference to the traditional heritage of Japanese timber architecture.

This project marked the beginning of Isozaki's increasingly confident handling of the pictorial and metaphorical potential of architecture. This can be seen too in the "Future City Incubation Process" project (1962) in which Isozaki takes the modernization formula of *wakon—yosai* a step further, critically reusing his images in a new context. In his collage, he places his megastructure within a field of classical ruins. The massive concrete cylinders appear to rest on the stumps of classical columns and are themselves fragmented. Isozaki's image positions the Metabolists' vision for the future of the city not only in a formal but also a conceptual relationship to European antiquity. Here Isozaki shows the ruins as a common ideal foundation of architecture, although as an architectural principle they are both the beginning and endpoint of the architecture. As Walter Benjamin has described, ruins serve both as a basis from which to construct the future as well as the starting point for reconstructing the past. All architectural practice has its roots in ruins and returns to ruins.

Arata Isozaki, Future City (The City Incubation Process), 1962

From this point on, Isozaki's architecture was subject to the critical reservation that at some point "the future will lie in ruins."[14]

This has led Isozaki to the conviction that it is the signs, images and architectonic metaphors that persist over time and less the actual, material, built architecture. Through their transience, metaphors guarantee the continuity and identity of society, because they persist as something to latch on to in future even when the material legacy is no longer. In the years that followed, we see a move in Isozaki's work towards a free combination of architectural metaphors, in which he collages fragments of reality from the past and present as well as the future. This concept of a dynamically stabilized modernism is what gives his architecture a human face, but also its own particular sense of melancholy.

The waning of an era and a new beginning

The question remains as to whether Metabolism sufficiently prepared the ground for a new, own concept of Japanese architecture to develop. If this was the case, one could speak of Metabolism as a defining epoch, much like other movements such as Expressionism, Functionalism or the New Objectivity. But these movements were broad enough conceptually to encompass a range of architectural practices while at the same time being able to transport a sufficiently evocative image to inspire the development of new paradigms. It is doubtful that this was the case with Metabolism. The Metabolist projects, with their strong technological focus, strive to be culturally hermetic, to be autonomous. They lack the necessary synthetic capacity. Metabolism does not seem to have set in motion an upward arc of development. Rather it helped herald the decline of an era through overcoming the traumas of modernization. To a certain extent, Metabolism arose in negative circumstances: it was at its most potent in 1960, directly after the group was founded and thereafter began to exhaust its potential in fulfilling its function, initially of compensation, then of sublimation and finally of overcoming the traumas of modernization.

Over the last 15 years a new generation of young architects has arisen in Japan who are unencumbered by the external factors of old and who seem to mark the end of the preceding era. Their light, transparent buildings with delicate, wafer-thin outlines do not appear to build on or bear formal similarity to previous models. They do not superficially borrow from traditional Japanese architecture, neither in their form nor materials, and indeed many of them would vehemently reject any such suggestion. In addition, these architects seem neither to feel obliged to embrace Western influences nor to distance themselves from them. Likewise, they seem largely unaffected by current tendencies in digital and parametric design.

The year 1945 is often seen as a starting point in the history of Japanese architecture. In the context of the above, however, it would seem that we should really bring this point forward into the present, at the end of the decline of the preceding era. Only the overcoming of the traumas of modernization in recent years has made it possible for a new generation of architects to reclaim a defining role in shaping Japanese architecture. The new beginning of architecture in Japan and of an own concept of Japanese modernism that is worthy of the name of an epoch was not in 1945; it is now.

1 Ken'ichi Mishima, "Die Schmerzen der Modernisierung als Auslöser kultureller Selbstbehauptung – Zur geistigen Auseinandersetzung Japans mit dem 'Westen'", in: Irmela Hijiya-Kirschnereit, *Überwindung der Moderne. Japan am Ende des zwanzigsten Jahrhunderts*, Frankfurt am Main 1996, p. 86.

2 Ibid, p. 98.

3 Arata Isozaki in an interview with Rem Koolhaas, in: Rem Koolhaas and Hans Ulrich Obrist, *Project Japan. Metabolism talks*, Cologne 2011, p. 37.

4 Cf. Arata Isozaki, "Ruinen" (1988), in: idem, *Welten und Gegenwelten*, Bielefeld 2011, p. 23 f.

5 Irmela Hijiya-Kirschnereit, "Leuchtet Japan? Einführende Gedanken zu einer proklamierten Zeitenwende", in: idem, op. cit., p. 7.

6 Ibid.

7 Cf. Augustin Berque, "Die Zeitlichkeit der japanischen Stadt und die Überwindung der Moderne", in: Hijiya-Kirschnereit, op. cit., p. 194.

8 The group of Metabolists comprised the journalist and architecture historian Noboru Kawazoe (*1926) as well as a group of very young architects, among them Kiyonori Kikutake (1928–2011), Kisho Kurokawa (1934–2007), Fumihiko Maki (*1928) and Masato Otaka (*1923–2010).

9 Arata Isozaki in an interview with Rem Koolhaas, in: Koolhaas/Obrist, op.cit, p. 40.

10 The group formed to coincide with the holding of the *World Design Conference* in Japan in 1960.

11 Georg Simmel, "Die Ruine", in: idem, *Philosophische Kultur: Über das Abenteuer, die Geschlechter und die Krise der Moderne. Gesammelte Essays*, Berlin 1986, p. 124.

12 Arata Isozaki "Ruinen" (1988), in: idem, op. cit., p. 24.

13 Arata Isozaki in an interview with Rem Koolhaas, in: Koolhaas/Obrist, op. cit., p. 25.

14 Cf. Jörg H. Gleiter, "Vorwort", in: Isozaki, op. cit., p. 7 ff.

Japan's architectural system

Jörg Rainer Noennig / Yoco Fukuda-Noennig

Architecture is a relatively new profession in Japan that was not taught at universities of the island nation[1] until the second half of the 19th century. Since then, however, Japanese architecture has established itself with remarkable success at an international level, and is now recognized around the world—and not just by architects. Contemporary architectural production in Japan is multifaceted, sophisticated, and vigorous.

The success of Japanese architecture did not come about by chance, but is the product of a well-functioning system. Japan has developed a special model of the architectural profession that has not only managed to firmly root this new discipline in the country, but has also contributed to it becoming a leading exponent of global architecture today.

It is instructive to consider the particular qualities of Japan's architectural "ecosystem." This essay examines the patterns within this system. The focus here lies not on the work of individual companies and their styles and strategies, but on the systemic mechanisms that create the conditions for a variety of professionals—architecture offices being just one of them—to form synergies through a range of professional and socio-economic processes. This system is characterized by a specific pattern of partnerships, activities, market structures, client relationships, channels, expenditures and revenues.

Partnerships

Which players and roles constitute Japan's architectural system?

Conceptually, the Japanese architectural sphere may be best described as a symbiotic network of creators, producers and promoters. Each has their own specific characteristics and each carries out highly differentiated roles, thereby maintaining a clear division of tasks. Within working partnerships, certain modes of cooperation and commitment have been established over a period of decades, that, in the long run, have given them powerful leverage. One can imagine the Japanese architectural world as an ecosystem akin to Silicon Valley: it is not merely a business environment but a comprehensive work sphere with its specific culture and ethics.[2]

In the Japanese architecture system, one can identify two subsystems, which are intertwined and have direct and obvious crosslinks. The first subsystem is concerned primarily with architectural production and comprises hundreds of small design offices, about a dozen large design and planning corporations (among others, Nikken Sekkei (2,800 employees), Nihon Sekkei (800 employees) and Kume Sekkei (500 employees) and a handful of giant general contractors, the so-called *senekon*

(Japan's five big construction corporations are Shimizu with15,000 employees, Kajima with 15,000 employees, Obayashi with 13,000 employees, Takenaka with 8,000 employees and Taisei with 8,000 employees). In addition, there are a couple of mass-manufacturers of houses—Matsushita (under the name PanaHome), Misawa Home, Mitsui, Sekisui and Sumitomo Forestry—and thousands of well-trained craftsmen and artisans.

The second subsystem concerns propagation, promotion and marketing. This includes a couple of publishing houses and media groups (Shinkenchiku, Toto, Kajima and others), a dozen architecture schools in renowned universities (University of Tokyo, Tokyo Institute of Technology, Keio University, Waseda and others) and several architectural associations.

What's notable about the first "creative subsystem" is the co-existence of large-size corporations and relatively small architectural design studios. While large firms usually employ hundreds of designers and planners in highly specialized departments (for example architectural and structural design, building climatology and project management), the design studios are owner-run offices with between five and 30 employees. Certainly, these small design studios create more identifiable styles and approaches, in contrast to the more impersonal corporations. In the second "promotions subsystem," the universities play a peculiar role in the overall ecosystem, acting on the one hand as a laboratory for academic teaching, and on the other managing the direct placement of graduates with both large corporations and smaller companies.

Office of Jun Aoki

Office of Go Hasegawa

Activities

What processes link the players and institutions within Japan's architecture ecosystem?

There is, without doubt, a complex tissue of interdependences and obligations. One such example is the division of labor between universities and companies in the provision of professional education and learning: the offices serve as an elementary training ground, while the universities instead provide a space of experimentation for students, which also allows professors to identify their specific potential and point them towards appropriate positions in the professional scene. There are no internships in Japanese architectural education. Young candidates acquire the skills and knowledge necessary to practice architecture by working. They learn through accompanying projects in a company, by co-working and co-learning in a shared office. This division of tasks has implications for the work culture. Most architecture offices operate as learning communities with specific roles and rules assigned to each member. There is a hierarchy of age and every member of staff has teaching and learning obligations. Offices are typically open plan to maximize participation and group awareness, and ensure effective knowledge transfer and learning. A lot of training is learned "on the job" in a slow process that builds up tacit understanding and social cohesion.[3] The office is a living community: employees essentially live in the company and the smaller the company, the tighter the social structure. The relationship between senior staff and junior co-workers follows a specific pattern:

Office of Riken Yamamoto

the "masters" are expected to mentor their young colleagues' professional careers. Commissions are sometimes passed on to employees who are about to move on and start their own businesses. In Japan, an employee who leaves is not regarded as a future competitor but as another collaborator in the overall ecosystem.

On another level, there is a division of labor between the small design firms and large corporations. Small studios generally focus on specific design tasks, often private commissions for houses and to a limited extent also public projects. Large corporations carry out design and planning work of greater complexity and financial volume. This can be surprisingly symbiotic: for high-profile projects, small companies often hand over their design to a *senekon* once it has reached a certain level of detail. A trade-off is then achieved between technical reliability and solid construction management on the one hand, and design originality on the other.

Market structures

Although the domestic market in Japan has an extensive public sector segment commissioned by political authorities on national, regional and local levels, public commissions for high-profile projects are rare. Open design competitions are as well rare, and a large part of ordinary public construction is directly commissioned to huge offices. At the same time, due to private wealth, there is a multifaceted market of commissions from individual clients or corporations.

In addition to commercial and corporate architecture, there is an extensive private market for residential design and housing. There is high demand among Japanese clients for well-designed residences and small-size urban dwellings. However, only a part of this market is covered by architects as housing production in Japan is dominated by "off-the-peg" home manufacturers. An industrial manufacturer such as Sekisui House produces about ten thousand prefabricated houses of remarkable quality every year—posing an eminent challenge to architectural designers. Housing commissions for architects are reduced to tasks where the standardized solutions of mass fabrication are not applicable. As a result, architect-designed houses are invariably out of the ordinary due to the conditions under which they arise, as they need to respond to the specifics of locality and site, or include specific desired stylistic features. The much-celebrated mini-houses in the Japanese metropolises are one example of this phenomenon.

At a global scale, Japanese architecture is very highly regarded, although only a comparatively small number of representative architects from the wider Japanese architectural community are responsible for this image. In the past, these were architects such as Kenzo Tange or Kisho Kurokawa; today it is names such as Toyo Ito or SANAA. In the Japanese architecture ecosystem, the future standard bearers are typically identified by magazines and universities, who systematically build up their reputation from an early stage. This was the case with both Toyo Ito and Kazuyo Sejima. As a whole, Japan's architecture market remains a domestic one.

Client relationships

A key condition for the continued success of the architecture sector is good links between creators and customers, i.e. between architects and their clients. In view of the often radical nature of Japanese architecture, it may seem surprising that precisely these works of architecture—with a few exceptions—are often the product of extensive collaboration. This is not limited to collaborations with related professional partners, such as engineers, craftsmen or project managers but also includes collaborations between clients and commissioners. Extensive briefings and presentations strive to involve as many stakeholders as possible.

In the course of these ongoing co-imagination sessions, the architect's task is to outline a project vision that is shared among all contributors. This collective approach also creates generative dynamics: the radical nature of a project is not always necessarily an expression of an individual architect's ambition, but rather the product of group ideation.

Channels and media

Which channels and media are responsible for communicating and propagating Japanese architecture?

First and foremost, there are an astonishing number of architectural magazines in Japan. *a+u* (*Architecture and Urbanism*), for instance, features recent international projects, *Shinkenchiku* (New Architecture) focuses on selected domestic projects, while *GA* (*Global Architecture*) presents high quality documentations of brand

Office of Takenaka Corporation

architecture. The thriving publishing industry testifies not only to the massive level of output of high-quality work in the country, but also to an efficient architecture promotion engine. The publishing houses help to maintain the public recognition not only of large corporations, as is the case with Kajima Corporation, which also owns a leading architectural publication company, but also selected architectural practices. The dominance of architects like Toyo Ito or Kazuyo Sejima, who are well-covered in the media, contrasts with the large pool of talented but largely unknown architectural businesses who constitute the backbone of the architectural ecosystem. The prominent names fulfill a specific role as the public voices of an otherwise cautious architectural production system.

The promotions and propagation engine of journals, universities and associations also serves another important purpose: it successfully stimulates architectural turnover in the domestic market. The media has contributed to a significant re-definition of architectural practice, away from the notion of architecture as a product-based concept towards the idea of continuous servicing.

The promotion of continuous, high-level architectural production and consumption is accompanied by a downgrading of the profession in society (at least from a Western point of view): architects as creators of permanent structures have become service providers, suppliers of creativity and visions. In Japan, architects are not highly regarded professionals in the same way that lawyers or medical doctors are, and there is therefore an astonishing discrepancy between the reputation of architects within the country, which views architects as a secondary profession, and the

Office of Takenaka Corporation

international perspective, which attributes ultimate artistry to prize-winning signature architects like Tadao Ando or SANAA.

Expenditure and revenues

Without doubt, Japan's perfection-driven, craft-intensive and technology-oriented architectural practice is resource-intensive. While average building costs in Japan are not much higher than in other developed countries, its architectural production binds large quantities of resources, and especially human resources. In terms of organization and resource management, neither the small design offices nor the *senekon* can claim to work efficiently. Much effort is invested in communications and coordination.

However, the success of Japan's architecture system rests primarily on a combination of effects of economy-of-scale made possible by the large corporations and synergy gains from symbiotic relationships within the network of diverse institutions and players. Architecture offices and construction companies, in tune with universities, media agencies and associations, have established a professional ecosystem of integrated components for production, marketing, and consumption. This system creates the climate and conditions for multifaceted, sophisticated and vigorous architecture in Japan and also accounts for its remarkable success at an international level.

1 See Benoît Jacquet in this volume and in: Toshio Watanabe, "Japanese Imperial Architecture", in: Ellen P. Conant, *Challenging Past and Present: The Metamorphosis of Nineteenth-Century Japanese Art*, Honolulu 2006.
2 James F. Moore, *The Death of Competition: Leadership & Strategy in the Age of Business Ecosystems*, New York 1996.
3 Ikujiro Nonaka and Hirotaka Takeuchi, *The knowledge creating company: how Japanese companies create the dynamics of innovation*, New York 1995.

References to traditions in contemporary architecture in Japan

Philippe Bonnin

The difficulty of understanding the discourse of contemporary Japanese architects—both in terms of architectural language and oral expression—lies in the fact that they are now to some extent bilingual. Even if they have progressively acquired the language and concepts of modern European, so-called "occidental" architecture and have undertaken study trips to places of inspiration and pilgrimages to see the major works of Le Corbusier, Antoni Gaudí and others, Japanese architects have never completely forgotten their "mother tongue." But, while appearances may look similar and suggest a degree of global uniformity, they stem from entirely different interpretations. The Japanese reading is based on a 1,000-year-old culture, on an architectural history and vision of the world that does not owe much to the West. The following offers an examination of some references to specific Japanese vocabulary concerned with space and architecture that arose during interviews with architects conducted for this publication.

uchi/soto—interior/exterior

European architects will not be surprised to hear that some of the architects interviewed acknowledged great interest in the relationship *uchi/soto* 内 / 外 [1], generally translated as the relationship between interior and exterior. This has long been integral to architectural discourse and is certainly one of the fundamental questions of architecture. The concrete reference, which seeps into one's consciousness in the form of images and spatial arrangements behind the words, behind the seemingly similar expression of dichotomy, is in fact quite different.

Architects' interpretations of *uchi/soto*

The Japanese architects made numerous allusions to the dimensions of interior and exterior: Hiroshi Nakao believes that the associated border between public and private space has become increasingly blurred; Riken Yamamoto attempts to describe the threshold between the exterior and interior as public space; and Ryuji Nakamura notes that traditional Japanese architecture establishes a strong relationship between the exterior and the interior by means of specific intermediary spaces such as the *engawa* 縁側 and the *genkan* 玄関, to which one could add the concepts of the door *mon* 門 or the window *mado* 窓 or indeed the public spaces within the private space *zashiki* 座敷, *roji* 露地, *chashitsu*茶室. Go Hasegawa describes the *engawa* 縁側 as one of the fundamental elements in his architecture and his link to tradition.

Interpretations of *uchi/soto* in the history of Japan

The dichotomous relationship of *uchi/soto* occupies a central place in Japanese culture and concerns not just the architecture[2], but is also profoundly rooted in the basic fabric of society, in language, in ways of thinking, and in a manner more fundamental than metaphoric. In a language that completely dispenses with a system of pronouns like those of Western languages, the designation of people[3] and hence all social relations are achieved by topological specification relative to the current situation. Every social group forms an interior *uchi*—clearly demarcated from the exterior *soto*—in which the individual occupies a place in a fixed hierarchy that establishes his identity and closely ties him to a location: *tono* 殿 (residence) is a polite form for mister, *otaku* お宅 (home) for "you," *uchi* 内 (my house) for myself, *kanai* 家内 (the interior of the house) for the own wife and *okusan* 奥さん (the person out back) also a designation for the wife of another man, etc.

This spatial dichotomy therefore also serves to define basic social space, and rituals exist around this concept that are still highly popular and are regularly carried out. They recall and strengthen the division while investing it with a sacred dimension: on *setsubun* 節分, for example which is New Year's Eve according to the ancient calendar, the household is purified by throwing dried beans *fukumame* 福豆 or

Engawa. Kitamura House, Kawasaki, original location: Horiyamashita, Hadano, 1687

Uchi/soto—interior/exterior. Villa Katsura, teahouse, Kyoto, early 17th century

Interior of a *machiya*. Kanazawa, Edo period

beans of happiness (soyabeans *shiromame*) in four directions and through every opening of the house while shouting *Oni wa soto, fuku wa uchi*! (Devils go out, happiness come in!). When the demons have been chased away, a spell is placed above every opening in order to prevent them from returning.

The relationship of *uchi/soto* in the architecture of Japan

The actual boundary between *uchi* and *soto* is much more fluid and flexible in reality than the dichotomy suggests. The Japanese sense of space is enriched with a variety of transitional areas such as *genkan* or *engawa*, which are necessary for social transactions. This intermediate space not only serves as a connecting element between the interior and the exterior but also as a passageway leading to various rooms, thereby allowing free movement through the house as well as regulating access. It is formed by a long wooden floor protected by eaves that provides access to one or more rooms in a Japanese house. As such, the rooms situated deep in the house, which are the most private areas, are constantly in shadow[4] *in'ei* 陰翳. There one can enjoy the reflections of the gilt decorations on the dividing walls and folding screens. The gold displays a poignant beauty that, it is said, Junichiro Tanizaki (1886–1965) often admired. This decoration illustrates the refined aesthetic sense that is uniquely Japanese, the poetry of understated elegance *wabi* 侘び, and of patina *sabi* 侘び / 寂び. Both concepts originate in the aesthetic defined by the great masters of the tea ceremony in the 16th century.[5]
The *engawa* marks a strict line between the space where shoes are worn, i.e. outside, and the space where one is barefoot, i.e. inside, and it also divides as much as it unites. The ability to freely adjust the positions of the sliding doors makes it possible to modulate the relations mediated by this space. Between the *engawa* and the adjacent rooms, which are normally fitted with *tatami* mats, there are paper-covered sliding doors—*shoji*, with additional *amado* 雨戸 (lit. "rain door", sliding wooden shutters) on the exterior face, which are only closed at night or during heavy rain, and which during the day are stored in a closet called the *tobukuro* 戸袋. The

Oku, Wakasa shrine, Tottori

Meiji age saw the appearance of *garasudo* ガラス戸 (sliding doors with glass panels), which allowed the *engawa* to be closed off during the day while permitting a certain transparency between inside and outside.
Today the *engawa* has become an emblem of Japanese architecture and culture in general. However, it is a relatively recent term and constructive element that arose with the *sukiya-zukuri* architecture at the beginning of the Edo epoch. The word *engawa* appears for the first time around 1690 in the book *Nanboroku* (Memoirs of the Monk Nanbo).

Structure

The fundamental structure of traditional wooden architecture is that of a building core surrounded by one or two peristyles, the so-called *moya/hisashi* structure 母屋 / 庇.[6] Highly stereotypical, despite a range of stylistic, historic or regional variants, this follows the *Koho* 構法[7] system of construction and the *Kiwari* 木割り[8], stereotomy, a system of traditional measurements and proportions created by the carpenters *daiku* 大工. This envelopment of the building's "heart" *moya* (the character 母 is the same as that for mother) by one or two enveloping *hisashi* (areas surrounding the core of a building) has given rise to the concept of depth *oku* 奥.[9]
Fumihiko Maki has theorized at length about *oku*. Jun Aoki achieves this by superimposing layers to generate the desired level of depth. In his case the superimposed filters hint at a space behind, while making it more distant. In a discussion, Junya Ishigami describes the paradoxical effect of the *shoji*, which divides space but still lets us hear the noises from the next room through the transparent, paper-covered sliding doors.

Materiality

Architects lavish much attention on building materials, preserving their historical value, infusing them with semiotic value, turning them into atmospheres. First and foremost, wood or *ki* 木 [10] as the dominant material used in the structure of traditional architecture, then *ishi* 石 stone [11], *mizu* 水 water, *tsuchi* 土 earth, and *washi* 和紙 Japanese paper.
The attention paid to materials is made clear by Ryoji Suzuki in his reflections on the ageing of materials as well as by Jun Aoki, who even describes concrete as an "ornament," much like the white paint of modern architecture. Hiroshi Nakao goes as far as to say that space is directly connected to material, and Suzuki too, whose works are entitled "Experience in Material," thereby making reference to material and space.

Space, Architecture and Tradition

From the above, it is evident that translating the sense of space—of how space is structured—from one culture to another is more difficult than at first appears. It is, however, by no means impossible, as was once famously proclaimed at the exhibition on the *ma* 間 [12] in the Musée des Arts Décoratifs in 1978. Although some would rather portray the two spatial systems as being entirely and definitively incompatible, with careful study—not unlike that of the work of ethnologists who give us insight into cultures we have not had contact with before—the task is certainly not impossible.
Behind this assertion of the impossibility of comprehension lies an irrational fear that still persists today, namely that one's own culture and identity risk being displaced or subsumed by a culture believed to be dominant.[13] This alien culture is simultaneously admired and rejected, coveted, desired, envied, wished for, imitated, then learned and spun forward.
The suppression of Japan's native culture during the first few decades of the Meiji era led unavoidably to an upsurge of nationalism, as described by Benoît Jacquet. The tension between these two cultures has never subsided, and surfaces in several statements in the interviews in this publication.
The majority of architects clearly affirm the compelling strength of Japan's spatial culture. At the same time they see a necessity to learn and re-read the buildings of Japan's past—and not just the elaborate architecture of the temples, sanctuaries and palaces *tera/miya* 寺/宮, as well as the modest vernacular architecture of rural houses *noka* 農家, houses (townhouses) *machiya* 町家, and general dwellings ("houses of the people") *minka* 民家—in order to interpret these from a contemporary standpoint and give them renewed consideration. Nonetheless, the architects express diverse interpretations of space and architecture.
Some architects argue that there is a specifically Japanese way of thinking about space. But what might this be?
Ryoji Suzuki recalls the fact that the modern designation of space as *kūkan* 空間 [14] reached Japan rather late from Europe as a means of translating Western concepts (as did the term for architecture: *kenchiku* 建築). Consequently, he is reluctant to use this term as it denotes a fixed space, a concept he questions. For Suzuki, space

is an experience, a process, better expressed by the Japanese term *ma*, which is strongly anchored in his culture. He sees space as having no boundaries, as never stopping, continuing into the depths across partitions more mobile than fixed, always preferring ambiguity rather than the clear definition of open or closed, near or far, allowed or forbidden.
Junya Ishigami adds an interesting proposition to this, namely a Japanese culture of mixed space, which is simultaneously an abstraction and something physical.
Go Hasegawa, after teaching in Switzerland and visiting cities of Europe, remarked on how "everything there is more fixed and more precise." This led him to a clearer understanding that the Japanese habit of living with greater ambiguity could constitute the main difference between a city in Japan and those of Europe.
Ryuji Nakamura remarked that he had previously at university thought of architecture as something hard, solid and heavy. Later he went in search of something softer, an architecture that uses more subtle materials, oriented towards an image of vernacular architecture.
Hiroaki Kimura talked about a project for a tea pavilion *chashitsu* 茶室. He admitted to not having known a great deal about the tea ceremony and its architecture before embarking on the project. But he was quickly surprised by the radical change in atmosphere in the pavilion during the ceremony: "When you drink the tea, the window is closed, and you do not talk. After drinking, the window is opened and you talk and laugh and relax." He freely admits, however, to lacking experience in the use of the best-known elements of traditional Japanese architecture: the *shoji* and wooden construction. Instead, he is more interested in the specific relationship between the interior and the exterior (*uchi/soto*), and the skillful articulation of the boundary by means of the *engawa*. These he expresses through a formal modern language, which he says originates in the Occidental manner but is a subtle blend of influences. A process of hybridization is underway.
Sou Fujimoto himself admits that as a student he had little interest in organized study trips to see the roots of traditional Japanese architecture in Kyoto and Nara. His curiosity grew later after leaving university, which today means that he respects history while extending it in novel ways.

Ki—wood

Ishi—stone

Washi—paper

Noka, Shinakawa-go, Gifu

Tera, Guzei-ji temple, Higashiomi, Shiga

Fumihiko Maki would seem to exemplify the recent history of Japanese architecture. Referring to his time in the United States and his involvement in the Metabolism movement, he likes to underline his hybrid background in modern Western as well as Japanese architecture.

He has also studied the way in which the vernacular architecture of traditional housing in Japan, what Bernard Rudofsky called *architecture without architects*, composes traditional urban spaces, a subject also investigated by Arata Isozaki and Teiji Ito.

Turning away from the dominant trend towards modernity, Maki came back to the main concepts of architectural space in Japan: *oku* and *ma*. In a famous article, he outlines his particular ideas about *oku*. He used this principle in his design for a crematorium in the form of a long pathway that reveals itself in an unfolding process. Here the end is unknown at the beginning, allowing every moment and every element of ritual to unfold in its own time, culminating in the final phase, the most important of all. With this approach he effectively invokes a profound and ancient dimension of the Japanese spatial culture, which gives just a vague glimpse of the space in the following stage rather than revealing it in broad daylight, perfectly clear and visible to all. He combines an architecture that is resolutely modern in its materials and apparent form, with a notion of space anchored in the depths of tradition, one that is not immediately accessible. Instead we have to learn to feel, to experience and to acknowledge it.

Machiya, Kyoto

1 "*uchi/soto* 内 / 外 indoors/outdoors", in: Philippe Bonnin, Nishida Masatsugu and Inaga Shigemi (ed.), *Vocabulaire de la spatialité japonaise*, Paris 2014, p. 517 f. In the following use is made of notes taken from this essay and the authors are only mentioned in the footnotes insofar as these are not one of the editors.

2 "*Ie* 家 the house", in: Bonnin/Masatsugu/Shigemi, op. cit., p. 179–181. Riken Yamamoto, for example, insists that in Japan the family house holds a very important place.

3 Philippe Bonnin, "Nommer/Habiter: Langue japonaise et désignation spatiale de la personne", in: *Communications* 73, September 2002, p. 245–265.

4 Bernard Jeannel, "*In'ei* 陰翳 half-light", in: Bonnin/Masatsugu/Shigemi, op. cit., p. 184–186.

5 Augustin Berque, "*Wabi/sabi* 侘び / 寂び simplicity/patina", in: Bonnin/Masatsugu/Shigemi, op. cit., p. 523 f.

6 Nishida Masatsugu and Philippe Bonnin, "*Moya hisashi* 母屋/庇 the heart/peristyle", in: Bonnin/Masatsugu/Shigemi, op. cit., p. 353–355.

7 Kazumasa Watanabe and Philippe Bonnin, "*Koho* 構法 the system of construction", in: Bonnin/Masatsugu/Shigemi, op. cit., p. 272–274.

8 Nishida Masatsugu and Philippe Bonnin, "*Kiwari* the stereotomy of wood", in: Bonnin/Masatsugu/Shigemi, op. cit., p. 257 f.

9 Augustin Berque, "*Oku* 奥 the background", in: Bonnin/Masatsugu/Shigemi, op. cit., p. 372–374.

10 Mechtild Mertz, "*Ki* 木 wood", in: Bonnin/Masatsugu/Shigemi, op. cit., p. 251–255, with specific remarks by Hiroshi Nakao.

11 Bernard Jeannel, "*Ishi* 石 stone", in: Bonnin/Masatsugu/Shigemi, op. cit., p. 188–190.

12 Augustin Berque, "*Ma* 間 space", in: Bonnin/Masatsugu/Shigemi, op. cit., p. 294–296.

13 Marc Bourdier, "*Teikan shiki* 帝冠式 the imperial hairstyle", in: Bonnin/Masatsugu/Shigemi, op. cit., p. 484–485, relating to this period during which the official architectural style was "Western" while dominated by a roof "in Japanese style".

14 Philippe Bonnin, "*Kūkan* 空間 space", in: Bonnin/Masatsugu/Shigemi, op. cit., p. 281–283.

Editors

Hubertus Adam studied art history, philosophy and archaeology. From 1996 to 1997, he was editor of *Bauwelt* magazine in Berlin, from 1998 to 2012 editor of the architectural journal *archithese* in Zurich. In the years 2010 to 2015 he was director of the S AM Swiss Architecture Museum in Basel. He is a freelance architecture critic, curator, author of numerous books, texts for publications, catalog essays and magazine articles on 20th century architecture and has lectured widely at different institutes, universities and architecture symposia. He lives and works in Zurich.

Daniel Hubert studied architecture at Cologne University of Applied Sciences and earned his diploma in 2009. From 2010 to 2012 he was editor of *der architekt*, the magazine of the Association of German Architects (BDA) He ran project work at the Chair of Spatial Design at RWTH Aachen University. He was a research assistant and lecturer at the Institute for Architecture, Construction and Theory at the Faculty of Architecture of Cologne University of Applied Sciences (now the TH Köln). He works as an architect and freelance author and lives in Cologne.

Susanne Kohte studied architecture and urban planning at the Technical University of Karlsruhe (now KIT Karlsruhe Institute of Technology) and the Swiss Federal Institute of Technology in Lausanne. She has worked with Shigeru Ban in Tokyo, Balkrishna Doshi in Ahmedabad as well as in architecture offices in the Czech Republic, Germany and Switzerland. In 2001, she founded her own architecture office SUKO. She has taught at the Department of Fundamentals of Architecture at Karlsruhe University and from 2002 until 2006 at the Chair of Urban Design at the Technical University of Hamburg Harburg (now HafenCity University). From 2008 to 2015, she taught at School of Engineering and Architecture at Lucerne University of Applied Sciences and Arts and in 2013 became Stand-in Professor at the TH Köln (formerly Cologne University of Applied Sciences). Her academic work, publications and work as an exhibition curator is concerned with modern architecture and urban development with particular focus on India and Japan.

Authors

Philippe Bonnin is an architect and anthropologist. He studied architecture at the National School of Fine Arts from 1967 to 1972 in Toulouse and Paris. Since 1979 he works at the French National Center for Scientific Research (CNRS). Since 2002 he is "directeur de recherches" at the CNRS, "directeur du laboratoire" at the AUS (Architecture, Urbanisme et Société) and "fondateur du réseau JAPARCHI" in the French Society of Japanese Studies. Philippe Bonnin is author of several publications and articles on architecture, housing and space in Japan as well as in France. For his publication *Vocabulaire de la spatialité japonaise*, CNRS Editions, he received the "prix du livre de l'Académie d'Architecture 2014."

Yoco Fukuda-Noenning is architect. She studied architecture at the Japan Women's University in Tokyo and did her master course at the Waseda University in Tokyo. In 2014, she completed her Ph.D. at the Japan Women's University in Tokyo on Manor houses in Great Britain. She moved to Germany in 2005 and is a correspondent for *a+u (Architecture and Urbanism)* since 2006.

Jörg H. Gleiter studied at the University of Tübingen, the Technical University of Berlin, the Architectural Institute Venice (IUAV) and Columbia University in New York. He worked in the office of Eisenman Architects in New York and various architecture offices in Italy and Germany. He completed his Ph.D. at the Bauhaus-University Weimar. From 2003 to 2005, he was Visiting Professor of Philosophy of Architecture at Waseda University in Tokyo, from 2005 to 2007 Stand-in Professor of Design and Architectural Theory at Bauhaus-University Weimar and from 2005 to 2012 Professor of Aesthetics at the Free University of Bozen-Bolzano in Italy. In 2007, he completed his habilitation thesis at the Bauhaus-University Weimar. In 2012, Jörg H. Gleiter became head of the Chair of Architectural Theory at the Institute of Architecture of the Technical University of Berlin, of which he is also managing director. He is founding editor of the book series *ArchitekturDenken* (Transcript Verlag Bielefeld) and co-editor of the internet magazine on architectural theory *Cloud-Cuckoo-Land.*

Benoît Jacquet is an architect and historian. He studied architecture at the Nancy School of Architecture, the Polytechnic University of Catalonia, Barcelona School of Architecture (ETSAB) and the Paris-La Villette School of Architecture as well as landscape architecture at the DEA "Jardins, Paysages et Territoires" School for Advanced Studies in the Social Sciences (EHESS) in Paris. He holds a Ph.D. in Engineering from

Kyoto University (2006) and a Ph.D. in Architecture from the University of Paris (2007). Since 2008, he is Associate Professor at the French School of Asian Studies in Kyoto and Invited Professor at Kyoto University. He co-edited *From the Things Themselves: Architecture and Phenomenology* (2012), *Vers une modernité architecturale et paysagère. Modèles et savoirs partagés entre le Japon et le monde occidental* (2013) and *Dispositifs et notions de la spatialité japonaise* (2014). He also carries out construction and renovation works in Kyoto and received a "Holcim Awards 2014 Asia Pacific" prize with the architectural firm Mikan for the project "High-Tech Low-Tech: Sustainable research center featuring traditional woodworking methods."

Hyon-Sob Kim is Associate Professor at the Department of Architecture, Korea University. He studied architecture at Korea University as an undergraduate, and completed his doctoral thesis on Alvar Aalto and modern architecture at the University of Sheffield, United Kingdom, in 2005, funded by the Korean Government Overseas Scholarship. A research grant from the AHRC (Arts and Humanities Research Council, United Kingdom) enabled him to proceed to the subsequent project "East Asian Influence on Modern Architecture in Europe, 1918–1938" at the same institution for the following two years. Since 2008, he has been teaching architectural history at the Korea University, and has extended his research interests to include modern architecture in Korea and contemporary architectural theories. As well as working as a visiting researcher in Japan (Building Research Institute, 2001) and in Finland (Alvar Aalto Academy & University of Helsinki, 2005–06), he has recently stayed in the United States for his sabbatical year on the 2014–15 Visiting Scholarship of the Harvard-Yenching Institute. His numerous writings have been published nationally and internationally.

Jörg Rainer Noenning studied architecture in Weimar, Krakow and Tokyo. From 1998 to 2001, he worked in various architecture offices and as a freelance architect in Tokyo and was a research associate at Waseda University in Tokyo from 1999 to 2001. From 2001 to 2009, he was a member of staff at Dresden University of Technology, completing his Ph.D. in 2007 at the Bauhaus-University Weimar. From 2009 to 2015, he was Junior Professor for Knowledge Architecture at the Dresden University of Technology, before becoming director of the Knowledge Architecture Laboratory and Stand-in Professor for Industrial and Commercial Architecture at the Dresden University of Technology. He has also held visiting professorships at the Higher Institute for Electronics and Digital Training in Toulon and the University of L'Aquila.

Christian Tagsold studied recent and modern history, sociology and Japanese studies at Friedrich-Alexander University of Erlangen Nuremburg (FAU) and Mie University in Japan. In 2000, he completed his Ph.D. in sociology on "The Construction of Cultural Identity in Japan—the 1964 Olympic Games in Tokyo" at Friedrich-Alexander University. From 2006 to 2013, he was a member of staff at the Department of Modern Japanese Studies at Heinrich Heine University in Dusseldorf, and in 2012, his habilitation thesis on "Spaces of Translation: Japanese Gardens in the West" was awarded the "JaDe Prize" of the German Foundation for the Promotion of Japanese-German Culture and Science Relations. In 2013, he became Professor at the Department of Modern Japanese Studies at Heinrich Heine University in Dusseldorf.

Index of names

Illustration credits

All plans and drawings of projects are copyright of the respective architecture offices.

Adam, Hubertus 8–16, 33, 57 right, 59 bottom, 61, 75, 89, 105, 119, 124–125, 147, 175, 189, 196, 198, 218 right, 233, 242, 245 right, 264
Alvar Aalto Foundation 220 right
Ano, Daici 120, 126, 128, 130–132, 151, 156
Anzai, Shigeo 62, 65
Arata Isozaki & Associates 246–247
Baan, Iwan 148, 153, 155, 159, 197, 200–201
Bennetts, Peter 145
Bernoulli, Markus 220 left and center, 221
Bonnin, Philippe 259 left, 261, 263 right, 265
Cohn, Matthew and Susie 222–223
Frank Lloyd Wright Trust / VG Bild-Kunst, Bonn 2016 215 left
Fujitsuka, Mitsumasa 88
George Braziller Inc. 241
Hara Laboratory, Institute of Industrial Science, University of Tokyo 80–82
Hasegawa, Go 194–195, 202, 252
Henschel Verlag 240
Hiroaki Kimura + Ks Architects 90, 93, 95–96, 98–100, 102–104
Hiroshima Peace Memorial Museum 210 left
Hubert, Daniel 49, 133, 161, 203, 251, 260, 263 center
Jacquet, Benoît 231
Jun Aoki & Associates 123
junya ishigami+associates 176, 182, 184, 188
Kim, Hyon-Sob 218 left
Kitajima, Toshiharu 29 bottom, 30–31
Louis Vuitton / Daici Ano 129
Maki and Associates 20, 24–25, 27–28, 29 top, 32
Maki and Associates with Masato Otaka 26
Makoto Sei Watanabe / Architects' Office 106, 110, 113–114, 116, 118
Miyagi Prefecture Sightseeing Section 45
Nakamura, Kai 41–43
Nakasa, Takeshi / Nacása & Partners Inc. 47, 134, 137–140, 142–143, 146
Riken Yamamoto & Field Shop 83, 86–87, 253
Rougier, Michael / Getty Images 211
Ryoji Suzuki Architect & Partners 66–67, 69, 71–73
Ryuji Nakamura & Associates 162, 165–173
Sakano, Takaya 190
Sammlung Tagsold 208
Satake, Koichi 84–85
Schroeer-Heiermann, Christopher 187, 245 left, 263 left
Schütte, Nicole 259 right
Sou Fujimoto Architects 160
Studio GAYA 50, 55–56, 57 left, 59 top
Takenaka Corporation 255–256

Taki, Koji 39
Tange Associates 210 right, 235, 244
Toyo Ito Associates Architects 34, 37, 48
US Army, Center of Tokyo Raids and War damages 239
Wasmuth Verlag 209, 216–217, 219

We have taken the utmost care in researching image rights. However, should a copyright holder inadvertently not be named, please contact the publisher with the correct information.

Acknowledgments

This publication is based on the lecture series "Positions of Japanese Architecture," organized by Daniel Hubert and Susanne Kohte from 2013 to 2014 at the Faculty of Architecture at Technische Hochschule Köln. The interviews were conducted between August 2015 and March 2016.

We would like to thank everyone who has contributed to this publication.

We want to thank our dialog partners and their assistants and employees Chiyuki Arita, Naoko Esaki, Kyoko Kawahata, Julia Li, Nikki Minemura, Yasuko Okuyama, Yuma Ota, Kengo Sato, Haruka Shoji, Eiko Tomura, Minako Ueda and Makiko Wakaki.

We also want to thank Nao Nomura, Chris Schroeer-Heiermann, Tokiko Kiyota, Maren Heuser and Constantin von Richter for their dedication.

This publication would not have been realized without the Faculty of Architecture at Technische Hochschule Köln, we are grateful for making it possible.

Finally, we would like to thank the Japan Foundation, Japanisches Kulturinstitut Köln and the JaDe-Foundation for supporting this publication.

Technology
Arts Sciences
TH Köln

JAPANFOUNDATION
JAPANISCHES
KULTURINSTITUT

Editors
Susanne Kohte, Cologne
Hubertus Adam, Zurich
Daniel Hubert, Cologne

Project management Birkhäuser
Henriette Mueller-Stahl, Berlin

Copy editing
Julian Reisenberger, Weimar

Translation
ARCHITEXT, Derek Henderson, Dresden
(essay by Philippe Bonnin)
Julian Reisenberger, Weimar
(introduction and essay by Jörg H. Gleiter)

Layout, cover design and typesetting
Silke Nalbach, Mannheim

Production
Katja Jaeger, Berlin

Paper
135 g/m² LuxoArt Samt 1.1

Printing
Grafisches Centrum Cuno GmbH & Co. KG,
Calbe

Printed with the support of the Stiftung zur Förderung Japanisch-Deutscher Wissenschafts- und Kulturbeziehungen (JaDe-Stiftung; Foundation for the support of Japanese-German academic and cultural relations).

Library of Congress Cataloging-in-Publication data
A CIP catalog record for this book has been applied for at the Library of Congress.

Bibliographic information published by the German National Library
The German National Library lists this publication in the Deutsche Nationalbibliografie; detailed bibliographic data are available on the Internet at http://dnb.dnb.de.

This publication is also available as an e-book (ISBN PDF 978-3-0356-0715-4; ISBN EPUB 978-3-0356-0717-8) and in a German language edition (978-3-0356-0845-8).

P.O. Box 44, 4009 Basel, Switzerland
Part of Walter de Gruyter GmbH, Berlin/Boston

Printed on acid-free paper produced from chlorine-free pulp. TCF

Printed in Germany

ISBN 978-3-0356-0846-5

9 8 7 6 5 4 3 2 1
www.birkhauser.com